tability and Change in an
English County Town

Stability and Change in an English County Town

A social study of York 1801–51

ALAN ARMSTRONG

Senior Lecturer in Economic and Social History
University of Kent at Canterbury

CAMBRIDGE UNIVERSITY PRESS

CAMBRIDGE UNIVERSITY PRESS
Cambridge, New York, Melbourne, Madrid, Cape Town, Singapore, São Paulo

Cambridge University Press
The Edinburgh Building, Cambridge CB2 2RU, UK

Published in the United States of America by Cambridge University Press, New York

www.cambridge.org
Information on this title: www.cambridge.org/9780521204231

© Cambridge University Press 1974

First published 1974
This digitally printed first paperback version 2005

A catalogue record for this publication is available from the British Library

Library of Congress Catalogue Card Number: 73–92785

ISBN-13 978-0-521-20423-1 hardback
ISBN-10 0-521-20423-2 hardback

ISBN-13 978-0-521-01987-3 paperback
ISBN-10 0-521-01987-7 paperback

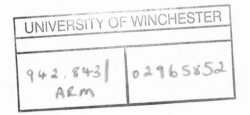

To my Father and Mother

Contents

Figures

Tables

Tables

xii

List of Abbreviations

The following abbreviations have been used, mainly in the bibliography and notes but occasionally also in tables.

Ann. Rept.	Annual Report
BTCA	British Transport Commission Archives
Ec.H.R.	*Economic History Review*
E.R.	East Riding of Yorkshire
JSS, JRSS	*Journal of the (Royal) Statistical Society*
M.B.	Municipal Borough
mfr.	manufacture
N.R.	North Riding of Yorkshire
P.B.	Parliamentary Borough
PP	*Parliamentary Papers*
Pop. Stud.	*Population Studies*
PRO	Public Record Office
R.D.	Registration District
R.G.	Registrar-General
V.C.H.	*Victoria County History*: History of Yorkshire: the City of York
W.R.	West Riding of Yorkshire
YC	*York Courant*
YCR	York Corporation Records
YG	*Yorkshire Gazette*
YH	*York Herald*
YNMR	York and North Midland Railway

Preface

The objectives of this book are discussed in my introductory chapter; here it is only necessary to say that I hope students of social and urban history will find it useful, and that general readers mainly interested in the historical development of York will find its emphasis on quantification novel and interesting. Like many other first books, this one originated as a doctoral thesis. It was entitled 'The Social Structure of York, 1841–51' and was presented to Birmingham University in 1967. From the thesis, as it stood, I have deleted a certain amount of 'traditional' social history, especially on education, religious life and poor law policy; and in keeping with the socio-demographic emphasis of the remainder, have developed some themes rather more fully and added a few new ones. In particular I have carried out elementary analyses of the course of fertility and mortality rates in York during the decades down to 1840. These are based on the published *Parish Register Abstracts*, and although I have gone somewhat further than previous historians of York, my findings are provisional and should be viewed primarily as a starting point for future research. For the quality of the source is the subject of a continuing debate. Most recently P. Razzell (1972), in a paper entitled 'The evaluation of baptism as a form of birth registration through cross-matching census and parish register data', has suggested that on the basis of the average experience of forty-five parishes, omission of births from the baptismal registers was roughly constant at one-third, perhaps even from the 1730s, through to about 1801, after which there was a slight improvement. Correspondingly, taking account of known rates of national population growth after 1801, death–burial registration was also much worse than has generally been assumed, though again, improving. Average omission rates of 34, 39, 28 and 16 per cent are suggested for the decades 1801–10 to 1831–40.

Preface

Critics of Razzell's cross-matching technique have pointed out that place of birth and place of baptism may differ, and both be correct; also that the names originally recorded in the baptismal register for illegitimate children may subsequently have changed if their parents eventually married. Also, it is clear that the experience of individual parishes varied widely. Here, I merely wish to point out that even if registration in York was defective to the extent mentioned above, the implications for my tentative argument would be that the calculated birth and death rates presented in chapters 5 and 6 are distinct underestimates, but that the trends they show remain valid. Using Razzell's omission rates for baptisms (in effect a multiplier of about 1.33 as against 1.15 actually used) in table 6.2 would have the effect of raising York birth rates throughout the years 1799–1823; but unless York registration was even worse than this, the unfavourable comparison I made with national fertility levels would stand. Moreover, the modest trend to improving registration suggested by Razzell would enlarge the very slight decline in fertility in the table. On mortality, if York omissions were of the order of one-third down to *c.* 1820 and improving markedly after that date, the death rates put forward in table 5.1 are certainly too low, but the long-term trend, more certainly than ever, would be to improvement, as I have suggested. Nor would the death rate for 1820–2 (24.8 on the assumption of 28 per cent omission calculated by Razzell for the 1820s) be inconsistent with my view that subsequently, the favourable trend was halted (see pp. 115–7).

Whether or not omission rates in York were this bad, or worse, is for future researchers to determine, using an adaptation of Razzell's methodology. I have suggested on p. 111 and in chapter 6, note 2, that the problem of under-registration may have been less acute in York than elsewhere: and although Razzell maintains what has long been suspected, that omission was greater in more populous places, the multiplicity of small parishes in York may have tended to offset this, since on his own evidence, the quality of registration was distinctly better in small parishes. Moreover, it is interesting to note that one of the best examples he gives is the parish of Acomb, adjacent to York.

Razzell commends the quality of the 1851 census data, which was 'of a very high order of accuracy indeed'. And after this digression, I ought perhaps to say that the focus of this book, like the original thesis, remains the 1840s, reflecting the better data available in the civil registration and census returns of that period.

Since the inception of the thesis some years ago many individuals have helped by easing my work in various practical ways, by discussion and simply through warm encouragement. To begin with, I should like to acknowledge the helpfulness of the staffs of the British Museum, Public Record Office, Borthwick Institute of Historical Research, British Transport Archives (York), Somerset House Library, university libraries at Birmingham, Nottingham and Kent and especially the reference and archival sections of York Public Library. At different times, I have welcomed the friendly advice of Professors A. W. Coats and T. C. Barker and the late W. H. B. Court and J. D. Chambers. Dr E. A. Wrigley examined the original thesis and made various helpful comments, whilst I have profited in numerous ways from discussions over the years with several colleagues interested in this kind of approach to social history, notably Professor H. J. Dyos, Dr M. Anderson and Dr P. M. Tillott. Professor D. E. C. Eversley conceived the original idea of sampling from the census enumerators' books and supervised the thesis on which this book is based. It was a privilege to study under his guidance, and my debt to him is incalculable.

Last but by no means least, I must acknowledge the cheerful and capable co-operation of the secretarial staff of this college, my publishers for their care in handling a difficult manuscript, and my wife, Heather, for encouragement and support over a long period during the course of this research.

Eliot College,   Alan Armstrong
University of Kent at Canterbury
November 1973

1 *Introduction*

Until recently, neither social history nor urban history was
held in high esteem by the vast majority of professional historians. Social history, emphasizing homely themes (how the
people ate, dressed and 'lived') was thought to be less rigorous
and demanding, a soft option in the university context and
suitable primarily for C and D streams in schools. It was widely
regarded as 'economic history with the hard bits left out',[1] and
the net result of generations of neglect was that even in the
early 1960s, social history could still be validly described as the
'Cinderella of English historical studies', in Perkin's phrase.[2]
The analogy may prove to be particularly apt; everyone will
recall Cinderella's triumphant emergence from backstairs
obscurity and many historians would now agree that social
history bids fair to follow suit. Thus Eversley speaks of the
emergence of a 'new kind of social history', less concerned with
the domestic manners of the various classes or their sports and
pastimes than with tracing the development of social structure
and popular culture;[3] and Perkin's perceptive essay sets out
some of the goals for a subject which has undoubtedly lacked,
in the past, a central unifying theme. He urges that social
history is nothing more and nothing less than the history of
society, and aims to understand the life of men in the past, in
its setting of society and institutions. The pursuit of this objective
should lead the historian to address himself to five inter-related
aspects of social life – ecology (the physical environment),
social structure, the functioning of the body politic and pathol-
ogy (social problems), the last being solved or evaded in
the light of the fifth aspect, 'the society's psychology, the
way it reacts upon itself' (its aims, moral criteria and public
opinion).[4]

It may be anticipated that the social sciences will have a
good deal to do with shaping the new social history. Ashton

once wrote that economic historians (we can now add social historians), are concerned primarily with groups; 'their subject is not Adam, a gardener, but the cultivators of the soil as a class; not Tubal-cain, a skilled artificer in brass and iron, but metal workers or industrialists in general. They deal less with the individual than with the type.'[5] In the same vein, Wilson has contrasted with the political and individualist pre-conceptions of the historians of Acton's generation, 'the sociologized history of our own day which is less concerned with individuals and more with men as members of social groups'.[6] This does not mean that the new social history will be dull, for there is all the excitement of pioneering to look forward to. Nor does it suggest that the social historian is on the point of losing his identity. For ultimately, the aims of the social historian differ from those of the social scientist, however freely each draws on the expertise, conceptions, insights and evidence of the other. As Perkin points out, social historians do not seek practical knowledge, descriptive laws, governing principles or predictive generalizations; they are concerned with concrete events and processes fixed in time and space, with 'particular societies at particular times in particular places'.[7]

The neglect of social history by past generations of historians has been matched by an equal disregard for urban history, even in this country, the first to undergo thorough-going industrialization and urbanization. Certainly the Victorian years saw the publication of many grim treatises on the pathological conditions to which these developments had given rise, well epitomized by Dr John Kay's *Moral and Physical Condition of the working classes employed in the cotton manufacture in Manchester* (1832). And with the increasing emergence of civic pride, and a felt need for a sense of identity and style, local histories as such began to appear. Some of these, such as the works of Langford on Birmingham (1871, 1873), Picton on Liverpool (1873) and Hardwick on Preston (1857), are still of value to modern historians, at least as a starting point; but for many metropolitan and provincial boroughs all that comes down from that period is 'a vast sorry assortment of relics and annals' which for many places 'still keep a dreary and ludicrous vigil'.[8]

The defects of this species of local history are well known. It was generally written from an exclusively parochial point of view, and was highly antiquarian in character. Not until the twentieth century did professional historians make any serious attempt to grapple with urban history. Even when a degree of interest was aroused, as would be expected from the immaturity of social history, urban history was first approached from the perspectives of the better-established disciplines. Among the more distinguished contributions giving pre-eminence to political themes, there come to mind Redford and Russell's *History of Local Government in Manchester* (1939–40), and Gill and Briggs' *History of Birmingham* (1952); whilst among histories emphasizing industrial and commercial affairs, Hoskins' *Industry, Trade and People in Exeter* (1935), Chaloner's *Social and Economic History of Crewe* (1950), Prest's *Industrial Revolution in Coventry* (1960) and Church's *Economic and Social change in a Midland Town: Victorian Nottingham 1815–1900* (1966) figure prominently. Particularly successful in its blend of economic, social and political factors was Barker and Harris's *A Merseyside town in the Industrial Revolution: St. Helens, 1750–1900* (1959); and almost unique in its emphasis on social conditions, Pollard's *A History of Labour in Sheffield* (1959).

These and others were the professional pioneers, unconcerned (I believe rightly) by the agonized heart-searching now current among British and American scholars on the issue of whether urban history is, ever can be, or should be, an independent discipline; or whether it can only be the *locale*, the scene of activity rather than the activity itself, a derivative rather than a substantive study, as Dyos has put it.[9]

Such profound questions are certainly worth posing; but the typical historian is an empiricist by instinct, and a failure to settle abstract questions of this sort is unlikely to deter him. He may take heart from Checkland's advice to start with monographic themes, and while he may not go very far in establishing new frames of reference, he may well put others in a position to do so. In any case, much of the methodological thinking is apt to be done, not by the metaphysicians of the subject, but by the doers. 'The definition of urban history that we require should not be that of the grammarian, who seeks a precision that is permanent, but should rather be an operational one, with all the adaptability that this implies.'[10]

This study of York during the first half of the nineteenth century may be regarded as an example, albeit imperfect, of both the new social history and urban history. It is not a comprehensive history of either *genre*. I have eschewed descriptions of the provincial 'season', sporting and cultural activities, colourful and quaint illustrations of customs, manners and social events, etc. The spheres of local politics and ideology, important though they are, have been left to others;[11] and instead there is a heavy emphasis on social structure and demographic trends.

Habakkuk has remarked that population may well be treated as a central theme in economic history.[12] Not all economic historians would agree, but it would at least be conceded that demographic change is a key branch of their subject. It is also apparent that demographic and social structural analysis will in the future come to form the backbone of social history. Perkin remarks that 'the study of population is central to the social historian's purpose', and from the urban historian's point of view, is likely to be at the very least, a common point of departure, serving to frame further questions.[13] It is peculiarly well-suited to the comparative approach, given that the data upon which it is based are amenable to quantification, and were originally collected in a more or less uniform manner; which is not, of course, usually the case with other classes of historical records, which generally throw a more fitful light on the matters with which they deal. In the remainder of this introduction, I shall describe the key sources which have been employed, and the methods of analysis applied to them.

SOURCES IN GENERAL

Briggs has pointed out that the Victorians themselves approached this growth of their cities first and foremost in terms of numbers, and used such statistical techniques as were available at the time to illuminate 'the problems of the system as much as its achievements'.[14] Thanks to their endeavours many quantitative sources exist for the period, which often have yet to be properly appraised by historians. For instance, although the original certificates of births, deaths and marriages relating to the period after the introduction of civil registration in 1837 are regrettably unavailable to historians, little systematic use has been made even of the published abstracts made from them; that is, the Registrar-General's 'Annual Reports', which give totals of vital events and much other useful information (for example on literacy), year by year, for each registration district. Parliamentary papers in general deserve much more careful scrutiny than they usually receive; certainly historians single out unique reports on questions which appear to be of special interest, but what is contained in routine returns of this or that is all-too-frequently overlooked.[15] Even sources well known to local historians are apt to be under-utilized; no historian of York has apparently taken serious notice of Dr Laycock's 'Sanatory table' (reproduced as figure 4), although several have made extensive use of the literary or descriptive material which his report contains. There is a vast amount of documentation relating to the operations of the Poor Law in the Public Record Office series M.H., as well as another set of annual reports, although in this instance, York at least has been better served, Sigsworth having scrutinized the material.[16] The contents of the *Parish Register Abstracts* of 1801–41 have been passed over perhaps too readily by historians warned against their value as a source for the study of national demographic trends. Except for analysis at the national level, the contents of the unique Religious and Educational censuses of 1851 have tended to be ignored.

5

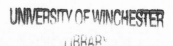

Material from these and from other sources will be drawn on at appropriate places in this study, but the principal source used has been the census enumerators' books of the 1841 and 1851 censuses, which afford the basic framework for the study of social structure.

THE CENSUS ENUMERATORS' BOOKS OF 1841 AND 1851

(*i*) *Basic methodology*

The censuses of 1841 and 1851 were the first to be conducted on modern lines, that is, by distributing householders' schedules and collating the information so derived by stages. The original schedules have not survived, but the books into which the enumerators had to transcribe all particulars, are open to historians at the Public Record Office once they become a hundred years old.

The enumeration books of 1841 thus record: address of premises; whether a house was inhabited, uninhabited or building; the name, sex and age (to the lowest term of five years only, in the case of those aged 15 and over) of each person who lived there on census night; the profession, trade or employment of each person and finally, whether that individual was born in the same county, or whether in Scotland, Ireland, or Foreign Parts (see figure 1). In general the same information was required in 1851, but ages and birth-places were to be given precisely, and above all, the introduction of a new column headed 'Relationship to head of family' was a major advance; it means that the historian can now identify (rather than infer) sons, daughters, other relatives, lodgers, etc., in relation to the head of household. Thus, this is the first census which can be used for the precise study of family and household structure (see figure 2).

In 1851, especially, the census authorities pronounced themselves much gratified by the results. 'The information was cheerfully furnished, and, on the whole, we believe, with a nearer approach to accuracy than has before been attained,

{ *Example of Enumeration Schedule,*
{ *shewing how Entries may be made.*

PLACE.	HOUSES		NAMES of each Person who abode therein the preceding Night.	AGE and SEX.		PROFESSION, TRADE, EMPLOYMENT, or of INDEPENDENT MEANS.	Where Born	
	Uninhabited or Building.	Inhabited.		Males.	Females.		Whether Born In same County.	Whether Born in Scotland, Ireland, or Foreign Parts.
George Street		1	James Johnson	40		Chemist	Y.	
			Jane do.		35		N.	
			William do.	15		Shoem. Ap.	Y.	
			Anne do.		13		Y.	
			Edward Smith	30		Chemist's Sh.	N.	
			Sarah Peakins		45	F. S.		I.
do.	96	1	John Cox	60		Publican	N.	
do.	1 B		Mary do.		45		Y.	
do.	1 B		Ellen do.		20		N.	
			James Macpherson	25		M. S.		I.
			Henry Wilson	35		Army	N.	
			n. k.	above 20				
Extra Parochial Place, named The Close.		1	William Jones	50		Farmer	Y.	
			Elizabeth do.		40		Y.	
			William do.	15		Navy	Y.	
			Charlotte do.		8		Y.	
			n. k. do.		5 months		Y.	
			Richard Clark	20		Ag. Lab.	N.	
do.	96	1	Robert Hall	45		Tailor	Y.	
			Martha do.		30		Y.	
			John Muller	25		Tailor J.		F.
			Ann Williams		20	F. S.	N.	
Chapel Row.		1	Edward Jackson	35		Ind.	N.	
			Charles do.	30		Cl.	N.	
			James Lowry	20		M. S.		I.
TOTAL in Page	96 2 B	5		15	10			

B b

Fig. 1 Printed specimen page: 1841 census enumerators' books

[Example of the manner in which Entries should be made in the Schedule Book.]

vii

Parish or Township of Oxford	Ecclesiastical District of St. James	City or Borough of	Town of	Village of Binford				
Name of Street, Place, or Road, and Name or No. of House	Name and Surname of each Person who abode in the house, on the Night of the 30th March, 1851	Relation to Head of Family	Condition	Age of Males	Age of Females	Rank, Profession, or Occupation	Where Born	Whether Blind, or Deaf-and-Dumb
31 Mayfield Lane	William Johnson	Head	Mar.	61		Bricklayer's Labourer	Bucks; Aylesbury	
	Sarah Do.	Wife	Mar.		55		Surrey; Walton	
	Eliza J. Do.	Daur.	U.		9		Do. ; Do.	
	William T. Do.	Son		10		Scholar	Do. ; Do.	
	Caroline Do.	Daur.			8	Do.	Do. ; Do.	
One House building								
32 Mayfield Lane	John P. Day	Head	Mar.	25		Agricultural Labourer	Surrey; Dorking	
	Mary Do.	Wife	Mar.		25		Do. ; Walton	
	Mary Do.	Daur.			3 m.		Do. ; Do.	
33	George Newman	Head	Mar.	54		Basket Maker	Kent; Chislehurst	
	Susannah Do.	Wife	Mar.		47		Surrey; Mitcham	
	John G. Do.	Son	U.	23		Basket Maker	Surrey; Walton	
	Frances Do.	Daur.	U.		19		Do. ; Do.	
	End of the Ecclesiastical District of St. James; and also of the Village of Binford							
Total of Houses... I 2; U —; B 4.			Total of Males and Females...	5	7			

Fig. 2. Printed specimen page: 1851 census enumerators' books

here or elsewhere. The working classes often took much trouble to get their schedules filled up, and to facilitate the enquiry.' Not once, in ensuring the completion of over 4 million schedules, had the penalties of the law been enforced.[17] Such comments may not tell the whole story; there is local evidence that the co-operation of the Irish in the Bedern district of York was not procured without some difficulty.[18] On the national level, it is suspected that there may have been an omission of some $4\frac{1}{2}$ per cent of the 0–4 age-group.[19] In the matter of the exactness of age-statements the quality of the data was what would today be regarded as 'rough'; the calculation of Whipple's coefficient on the basis of the stated ages of adults in York yields 120·4 for men, and 129·0 for women,[20] whilst Tillott has compared the ages of 353 persons in the villages of Hathersage and Braithwell in successive censuses (1851, 1861), to show that the correspondence is far from perfect.[21] Similarly, for Preston, Anderson has shown that 14 per cent of 475 persons traced in two successive censuses (1851, 1861), gave different, though not necessarily seriously discrepant birthplaces.[22] So far as the occupational returns are concerned, throughout the nineteenth century the census authorities were wont to complain of inadequate and inaccurate statements, and a 'foolish but very common desire of persons to magnify the importance of their occupational condition'.[23]

No doubt, therefore, *like any other historical source*, the enumerators' books give only an imperfect record; yet by contrast with most other historical source material, they possess several important attributes. As Dyos has observed, they contain reasonably accurate and comprehensive information, in a standardized format capable of being treated in a uniform manner, across various communities in 1851, and ultimately, right through the second half of the nineteenth century.[24]

At the time of the inception of this study, very little use had been made of the material in the census books. A few urban historians had used it to provide useful, but carefully selected illustrative evidence, and only one scholar, Lawton, had attempted anything resembling a systematic analysis. His pioneering study was based on samples (the basis of the sampling method was not stated), and threw interesting light on occupational groups, birthplaces and age–sex structure in Liverpool in 1851; but for the most part, the reader was left to form his own impressions about the relationships *between* variables, which remained unmeasured.[25]

It was with a view to examining the relationships between Lawton's variables (as well as others which he did not consider, such as household and family size, distribution of lodgers, relatives and domestic servants), that this study was undertaken. In a sense, the object was to squeeze more evidence from the information collected by the Victorians than they themselves had derived and published in the printed census volumes; or than later historians had tried to do. As a community for the study York seemed a suitable choice. That it was not one of the boom towns of the nineteenth century, nor apparently much affected by technological and economic change during the first half of the century seemed a positive recommendation. After all, despite all the mysteries which remain, we know far more about society in the manufacturing towns and very large cities in this period; most of the information gathered by government agencies and by private individuals related to what contemporaries thought of as 'problem' cities, as Ashton and others have recognized.[26] Not appearing to present obvious pathological characteristics, country towns, both large and small, tended to be ignored. Yet in fact, they were still the norm, so far as urbanization in the mid-nineteenth century was concerned. Looking at the country as a whole, only about 8 per cent of the population aged 10 and over was employed in the classical industrial revolution industries of cotton, wool, iron, railways, machine-making and coal and iron ore mining. Our country was still, in 1851, one where 11 per cent of all females of 10 and over were domestic servants, where over 20 per cent of the male population of 10 and upwards still worked on the land, and where, as Clapham has pointed out, more were employed about horses than on the railways, and there were more handicraft blacksmiths than men in the great iron works.[27]

In addition, York's population of 30,000–40,000 seemed neither too big to make the task of drawing of samples excessive, nor so small as to unduly limit the value of the results. Historians at least, will also appreciate that a long-standing personal familiarity and affection for the place was another, though less critical factor in the choice.

Ten per cent samples were drawn from the census enumerators' books on a systematic basis, recording the details in notebooks and later transferring the data, after some coding, to standard eight-column punched cards to facilitate rapid analysis. The details have been described fully elsewhere,[28] and there is no need to repeat them. But it is only fair to point out to the reader that the procedures used may be criticized from two points of view:

(i) Floud and Schofield have asserted that my sampling procedure was apt to yield a biased sample.[29] It entailed taking every tenth household, but where that household turned out to be institutional or quasi-institutional, dropping it and taking the next normally acceptable household; the next household taken was the ninth, thus preserving the original sequence. My critics suggest that certain households thereby had a double chance of selection ('one might, for instance, have an overweighting of schoolmasters living next to their schools'), and further, there would be an over-representation of normal households in those districts of the community where institutions or quasi-institutions were thick on the ground. In principle, these authors are of course correct, although their arguments are hypothetical in character; on the other hand, it is clear that only overall community results could be biased in the manner suggested (these are in any case the least interesting being only averages), and moreover, the replacement procedure to which they object was used only 11 times in drawing a sample of 781 households in 1851.[30] Thus there is unlikely to be any significant bias in these particular samples, and any reader requiring further assurance on this point is invited to consult the series of tests on the samples given in Appendix I. No historian, and no social scientist other than the most pedantic purist would be likely to deny their representativeness. Nevertheless, future researchers should keep this point in mind.

(*ii*) If this exercise were to be repeated, I should adopt slightly different conventions for the determination of 'households' in the enumerators' books. In 1851, enumerators were instructed to supply one schedule to each 'occupier' (i.e. the resident owner or any person paying rent for the whole of a house), or (as a lodger) for any distinct floor or apartment. In transcribing schedules into his enumeration book, the enumerator should,

under the last name in any house (i.e. a separate and distinct building and not a mere storey or flat) draw a line across the page as far as the fifth column. Where there is more than one occupier in the same house, he should draw a similar line under the last name of the family of each occupier, making the line . . . commence a little on the left-hand side of the third column.[31]

The specimen page for 1851 (figure 2) illustrates this, and that for 1841 (figure 1) an analogous method of single stroke and double stroke, with apparently the same object in view.

Thus, in the samples used here, each fully ruled off enumeration schedule was regarded as a household, but where two schedules or more were used (with the intermediate shorter line), all the inhabitants were regarded as members of one household and those on the second schedule denoted as 'lodgers'. In effect, in a small minority of cases, there is some confusion between the household and what might be called a '*houseful*', and a definite overcount of lodgers. Future researchers in this field would be well advised to follow in preference the conventions adumbrated by Anderson, which recommend that the word 'head' be taken to initiate a new household, and the introduction of the next 'head' as the cut-off point.[32] As a rule, the effect of these departures from what has become established best practice since these York samples were drawn in 1961–2 is fairly minimal, but readers will be reminded where there is any danger of important distortion.

(ii) *Classification of occupations*

Few of the difficulties facing the local, regional or urban historian are as critical as those stemming from the need to classify census occupational data. From one point of view, the reduction of occupations into broad categories is bound to occasion some loss of detail, whilst on the other hand, historians simply cannot work without some degree of classification.

In this study, census occupational data has been arranged according to two principles – the industrial, which throws light on the economic contours of the society under consideration; and secondly, by social ranking or class. On the first, there is little which needs to be said here. The basis of the scheme of allocation used to arrange *printed* census data on a broadly industrial principle is to be found in an article written by Charles Booth, and elaborated by myself elsewhere.[33] In this study it has been used only in connection with a few tables in chapter 2, but, I hope, to useful effect. Since the development of this method of analysis followed my work on the material in the census enumerators' books, it was not applied to that data, although there is no reason, in principle, why it should not be.

All households in the census samples were however, given a social classification, which will be referred to frequently, especially in chapter 7. This rested on the Registrar-General's scheme, which refers to five classes, 'homogeneous in relation to the basic criterion of the general standing within the community of the occupations concerned', viz.,

> Class I   Professional, etc., occupations
> Class II   Intermediate occupations
> Class III Skilled occupations
> Class IV   Partly skilled occupations
> Class V   Unskilled occupations.

The 1951 attribution lists published by the Registrar-General were used to give a classification for each household head, with the following modifications in 1851:

1. All employers of 25 or more were raised to Class I, whatever their classification in the Registrar-General's lists.
2. All 'dealers', 'merchants' (except those distinctly described as brokers or agents (class II) or hawkers (class V)), and all persons engaged in retail board, lodging and catering were initially classed as III, despite the fact that the Registrar-General's lists place them variously.
3. From class III (or in a few cases IV), *upon consideration of individual cases*, those who employed at least one person (other than members of their own families), were then raised to class II. In boarding, catering, etc., the employment of one or more servants was taken to count for this purpose, and the general effect was to raise into class II all those whose undertakings were at all substantial; for, at a minimum, the employment even of an apprentice is an obvious indication of self-employed status.
4. House and land proprietors, whose 'living off interest' or 'of independent means', annuitants and paupers were placed in classes I, I, I, I, II and V respectively. A few very uninformative entries ('Husband away', 'spinster', etc.) were placed in a residual class X. Retired persons were classified on the basis of previous occupations.

For the 1841 sample, it was necessary to proceed on a somewhat different basis, since individuals were not asked to state whether or not they were employers, nor the number of their employees. Accordingly the maintenance of servants was brought into play as a criterion of class at various points, and the social classification scheme, again using the 1951 attributions as the point of departure, was as follows:

Class I. Professional, etc. (as in 1851), less the handful of large entrepreneurs, not identifiable.
Class II. Individuals who would have been classed as II or III on the 1851 procedure, provided they employed at least one servant.
Class III. The same, where no servants were employed.
Classes IV and V. According to the initial attribution lists.

I have set out the details more fully elsewhere, and discussed some of the principal objections that can be brought forward against these procedures, such as the inherent tendency in the

Registrar-General's scheme to produce a swollen class III.[34] The most trenchant criticism commonly made is that it is anachronistic to classify mid-nineteenth century occupational data on a 1951 basis, since changes in the class structure have occurred on a vast scale: it has been suggested that the first attempt by the Registrar-General to order occupations on this basis (in 1911), would be preferable. However, it is not difficult to show that little difference would be made by using the earlier attribution lists, and whilst it is obvious that major changes in social class composition have occurred over the years, I believe that they have been largely structural; that is, change has been for the most part a question of relative increases or decreases in the proportion of the labour force employed in various occupations, rather than shifts in the socially accepted hierarchy of individual occupations.

I am not, of course, claiming that merely to assemble the occupied population under a limited number of headings is the same thing as divining the essence of 'class'. Yet it has been wisely said that whilst 'occupation may be only one variable in a comprehensive theory of class . . . it is the variable which includes more, which sets more limits on the other variables than any other criterion of status';[35] to which I should add that the social classification scheme used here does not pretend to be more than an attempt merely to render order into empirical data in such a way as to further understanding and facilitate fruitful analysis.[36] I should prefer it to be judged from the point of view of its success in achieving these limited aims, rather than as a theoretical construct pretending to any kind of absolute validity.

Chapters 2–7 will examine the social characteristics of York through the application of the methods described here, and I shall return to general issues in chapter 8.

2   *The economic characteristics of York during the first half of the nineteenth century*

> York may be said to belong to a class of cities existing in England; antique, yet manifesting no signs of decay, with a stationary population, but full of quietness and interest. Such cities are Durham, Oxford, Cambridge, Salisbury, Winchester, Chester, and a few others. York, however, is the queen of them all.
>
> J. G. Kohl, *England, Wales, and Scotland*, 1844

ECONOMIC STRUCTURE TO 1841

In Roman and medieval times, York was acknowledged to be the second city of the kingdom. It was noted as an administrative and commercial centre, a port, and cloth-manufacturing town in the Middle Ages, but evidently began to lose some of its economic importance as early as the fifteenth century. The city retained considerable political significance, mainly as the seat of the Council of the North, until its surrender after the battle of Marston Moor in 1644; but since that time its history has become more local in character. Paying due respect to its ancient dignity, the compiler of a mid-nineteenth-century geographical dictionary remarked that York was 'at present the second city of England in respect of rank, though not of importance'.[1]

During the first half of the nineteenth century, the city nevertheless remained a regional communications centre and market town of some note; both features may be ascribed to its geographical situation. The Vale of York is crossed by a terminal moraine which runs approximately from Stamford Bridge to Tadcaster, which has always been a good means of road communication between Eastern Yorkshire and the Pennines. York is situated at the point where the Ouse breaks through the ridge, being therefore at a crossing of north to south routes (by moraine) and east to west routes (by river).

In Roman times York lay at the tidal head and bridging point of the Ouse. The city has direct communication with the sea, although the river is inclined to silt-up and has many bends, making the distance to Spurn Head nearly 100 miles, almost twice the distance between the two places in a straight line. It was perhaps natural that York would decline relatively to Hull as a port of international importance with the decay of its native cloth-making industry in medieval times, but there were other factors accelerating the trend, notably the increased size of ships in modern times. Nevertheless a brisk road and river traffic continued to exist in the early nineteenth century, favoured by the proximity of growing centres of manufacture and mining in the West Riding. This gave rise to a steady flow of coal and manufactured goods in one direction, and of agricultural produce in the other. Statistics of the 1830s suggested that '110,000 sheep and 53,000 cattle are driven from York to Leeds annually ... [and] ... the agricultural produce sent by carts from York to Leeds annually is 3,950 tons', whilst along the Ouse Navigation and Aire and Calder canal, 98,000 tons of coal were conveyed annually from the West Riding to York, and 30,000 tons of grain, flour, etc., passed in the reverse direction, with much smaller quantities of other merchandise.[2]

On account of its geographical situation, York was very well-placed to provide marketing facilities and supplies for a very extensive farming area indeed. While no doubt most West Riding agriculturists (generally specializing in livestock husbandry and believed to practise only indifferent tillage), tended to look directly to Leeds and other industrial towns for markets, there is the rest of the county of York to consider. The North Riding had an envied reputation for breeding and rearing cattle, sheep and horses, many of which found their way to the markets of York. So did much of the produce of the East Riding, an area for which the most lyrical comments of agronomists tended to be reserved. Here, James Caird identified three distinctive divisions; the Plain of Holderness, strong land, occasionally indifferently drained but generally well-suited to grain cultivation and 'altogether dependent on the price of corn'; the chalk Wolds, light and easy to work, set out in large farms ('the farmers are probably the wealthiest men of their class in the county'), where 'large and numerous corn ricks give an air of warmth and plenty, whilst the turnip fields, crowded with sheep, make up a cheerful and animated picture'; and lastly, Howdenshire and the Vale of York, an area embracing 'a wide variety of soil, from the rich warp lands along the Ouse to stiff cold clays and thin moorish sand', the cold infertile clays around Howden being thought least desirable.[3]

Thus, by nature York was, in modern times, well adapted to further development as a market town and distributing centre for its rural hinterland; it was also a route centre of traditional importance and, as we shall see, continuing potential. But to the regret of many contemporaries, it showed no signs of developing as a great industrial town: 'We have no manufactures, we have no complicated machinery in operation; we have no weavers, no dyers, no shipbuilders, no mines', complained a newspaper correspondent when the subject of the provision of a Mechanics' Institute was broached in 1827.[4] Baines, compiling his directory a few years before, had stated that the manufactures of York were neither numerous nor on a large scale.[5] A manufactory existed in the twenties which made 'flint glass vessels and common phials', and was described as an 'extensive' undertaking in 1840. A manufactory of white and red lead was also noted in 1818, which actually used a steam engine but a directory of 1838 remarked that it had been closed 'within the last few years'. Several linen factories, described as being 'on rather a large scale', were established during the twenties. Two successful iron-foundries were also in operation at this time, a number that had increased to five by 1838. The drug trade seems to have passed into an important phase, along with comb making, during the 1830s.[6]

Such were some of the developments which impressed the compilers of directories between 1818 and 1841. It is unnecessary and probably impossible to chronicle the development of each of these industries, but perhaps worth attempting to estimate their scale in 1841. In table 2.1 the numbers of persons employed in each of the activities mentioned above are listed. Alongside them has been set the numbers of firms, according to a convenient directory.

TABLE 2.1   *The major manufacturing industries of York, 1841–3**

Occupation	No. of persons employed	No. of firms	Average size of firm
Glass manufacture	54	3	18
Flax and linen manufacture	118	8	15
Iron manufacture	25	6	4
Chemists and druggists	76	38	2
Comb manufacture	107	9	12

* 1841 Census. Occupation Abstract; Williams (1843).

In addition to the industries listed in the table, all other manufacturing activities employing more than 50 persons can be examined in the same manner. The average size of coach-making firms was 18·5; leather-processing and manufacture 4; engineering 11; printing 7; whitesmiths 3; and cabinet makers and upholsterers 5.

Clearly, York had signally failed to attract modern, large-scale, progressive industry; in a word, the direct effects of the Industrial Revolution had passed it by. The following statistics, again based upon the occupational returns of 1841, are eloquent:

	York		England and Wales	
	Males	Females	Males	Females
Proportion of occupied labour force in major manufacturing and extractive industries (Textile mfr. and dyeing; metal mfr. and fabrication; coal and ore mining)*	8.9	2.2	17.4	16.6

* Derived from table 2.2 below. *N.B.*, the national statistics include rural areas.

These introductory generalizations on the economy of York during the early decades of the nineteenth century suggest two interesting lines of further enquiry. Firstly, I shall examine the factors said to account for industrial 'retardation', and secondly, the characteristics of the existing, ostensibly 'pre-industrial' economy, which merits much closer analysis than it has hitherto received.

THE CAUSES OF INDUSTRIAL BACKWARDNESS

If York was industrially backward in the first half of the nine-teenth century, there must obviously have been certain factors acting as a drag upon the city's economic development; or so it has always been thought. We may first consider an institutional explanation.

It has often been argued that one of the reasons why the new manufacturing towns grew so rapidly was that they were not hindered by ossified trading privileges and achaic regulations.[7] If this was generally so, then York, as an ancient corporate city, might be expected to have suffered accordingly. Indeed, the eighteenth-century historian, Drake, wrote that the grants and charters given to the city had almost proved its ruin.

Our magistrates have been too tenacious of their privileges, and have . . . by virtue of their charters . . . locked themselves up from the world, and wholly prevented any foreigner from settling any manufacture among them . . . the paying of a large sum of money for their freedoms with the troublesome and changeable offices they must often undertake, would deter any person of enterprise from coming to reside at York.[8]

A newspaper correspondent of 1790 further remarked, 'If the inhabitants of this city would rouse themselves to some spirited exertions . . . and the Corporation open the gates to all trades-men and manufacturers inclinable to settle among us, York might once again lift up its head and recover its ancient consequence.'[9]

It was the rule that, to set up a business in York, one had

to be a freeman, who alone could trade, vote and rule. This could be accomplished by servitude (i.e. seven years' apprenticeship to a freeman); by patrimony (the sons of freemen were entitled to freedom as their birthright); and by redemption (by order of the Mayor and Aldermen, on payment of a £25 fee).[10] Would the fee of £25 in fact act as a deterrent to a young entrepreneur who could not become a freeman by other means? And how far was this restriction still active in the first half of the nineteenth century?

That the restriction was active is suggested by the fact that there were about 2,400 York freemen in 1833, and approximately 1,800 businesses listed in a directory about the same time.[11] Without doubt most freemen acquired their status as a birthright; but the Corporation was evidently accustomed to sell, on the average, about thirty freedoms a year in the twenties.[12] Thus a few felt it worth while to buy their way into York; but it must remain an open question how many ambitious young men without much capital were deterred from settling there. After all, the expenses of a freeman did not end with the payment of £25. A freeman had certain obligations, both social and civic. While the social obligations may have depended on the individual, on the side of civic responsibilities, a freeman had to pay for exoneration from offices, which apparently was commonly done.[13] Contemporaries had no doubt that this factor was important. Before the Municipal Commissioners, the Town Clerk stated, 'this does amount to a restriction of trade within the city ... it is to obtain this privilege [of trading] that freedoms are purchased ... those who carry on trade without it are likely to be prosecuted'. Alderman Oldfield, a prominent wine and spirit merchant, agreed, remarking that he would like to see the town opened. 'I have not lived to this period without seeing the injurious effects of the present system ... it would not have been so bad as this if the bar had not existed.'[14] The Corporation's power to make traders take up their freedom passed away with the coming into operation of the Municipal Corporations Act of 1835, but by this time, no doubt, the booming *parvenu* towns of the north had still further attractions to offer to the ambitious young man.

Another restriction surviving into the nineteenth century was the alleged rights of the Company of Merchant Adventurers. This medieval society had obtained a new charter in 1580 which restricted to its members the right to sell all wares brought from beyond the sea, excepting salt and fish. Apparently the charter had produced no significant increase in the city's foreign trade, for in the words of a modern historian, 'regulation was its only watchword, precedent its only ideal. Adjustment and experiment were ruthlessly suppressed'. In 1827 an important court case was heard, brought by the Company of Merchant Adventurers against a druggist, who had been selling foreign wares without being a member of the Company or having a licence from them to do so. Judgement was given against the plaintiffs, the judge ruling that the language of the charter was 'utterly inconsistent with the custom claimed' which was perhaps not surprising in view of the changing sentiments of economists and legislators in the period.[15] At all events, the Company, thus non-suited, made no attempt to bring an action on other grounds, and in the absence of evidence to the contrary, it would seem that their power to regulate the sale of foreign goods disappeared with the decision of 1827.

Whilst it may be that the survival of outmoded restrictions had some marginal effect in deterring young men to set up in York, it clearly does not account for the failure of existing freemen to expand or diversify their businesses significantly in the first forty years of the new century. The lack of modern manufacturing industry was also widely attributed by contemporaries to the high cost of coal. Sheriff Meek claimed that when a railway should eventually bring coals to York at the same price for which they could be delivered at Leeds, 'there could be no obstacles to the establishment of manufactures in this city, the same as at Leeds'. He calculated that £16 or 16 guineas was charged on a vessel carrying about fifty-eight tons of coal, this sum being made up of dues paid out on the

Barnsley canal, the Aire and Calder canal, and at Naburn Lock, along with the charge for the vessel. Thus 5–6s. a ton would be added to the pit-head price of coal, and coal costing about 5–6s. at Leeds would cost around 11s. a ton at York.[16] At first sight this would appear to have been an enormous handicap to the development of manufactures in York, but, as Sigsworth has made clear, this could only have been the case with regard to heavy industry. He has argued that the cost of coal was not a high proportion of the production costs in linen manufacture or of iron-processing after the initial smelting stage, to take two industries which were already established in York.[17] This suggests that the high cost of coal was not the only factor in explaining York's retarded industrial growth, and further support for this thesis may perhaps be found in the history of the industrial development of the town in later years. The advent of the railways sharply reduced coal prices, but no industry the rise of which could be attributed to the availability of cheap coal has ever appeared in York.

The most recent interpretation of the 'retarded' industrialization of York is a variant of the institutional type of explanation. Sigsworth suggests that we ought to look to the general nature of the city's government if we are to find reasons for the 'apparent apathy'.[18] York was governed in accordance with a charter granted to the city by Henry VIII in 1518. The Corporation consisted of a Lord Mayor, Recorder, 2 Sheriffs, 12 aldermen, '24' ex-sheriffs, (who in 1835 numbered 32), 6 chamberlains, and 72 common councilmen. The functions of the Corporation were to administer its own property, the markets, bridges, prisons, city walls and certain charities; and, after 1727, to maintain the condition of the River Ouse. Membership of the Corporation was restricted to Anglicans until 1828, which was the case in all boroughs until the repeal of the Test and Corporation Acts in that year.[19]

A useful indication of the Corporation's sense of civic responsibility is said to be provided by the history of its management of the affairs of the Ouse Navigation. During the eighteenth century various attempts were made to improve the navigation by dredging, by the provision of new locks at Naburn in 1757, and Linton in 1771. Staithes and cranes were maintained at York. But towards the end of the eighteenth century, and at the beginning of the nineteenth, the position seems to have worsened with regard to river maintenance.[20] In 1832 an engineer, Rhodes, was engaged to survey the Ouse from Linton (ten miles north of York) to Selby. His report showed the neglect of recent years. Evidently the only extensive work done during the first three decades of the century to the Ouse had been the building of a new lock-house at Naburn. Its dimensions were 61 ft × 18 ft, and it could accommodate ninety people. This building drew the strongest criticisms of the Municipal Commissioners, who were able to establish that it was primarily used for dinners and social occasions, while no worth-while improvements had been carried out 'for the last thirty years'. Even the Tory *Yorkshire Gazette*, which had regretted the whole enquiry, admitted that the Trustees had slumbered, and that the expenditure on the Naburn Lock-House was 'indefensible'.[21]

This was a good instance, writes Sigsworth, of the Corporation's 'inattention to the needs of a growing city'. He points out that the Corporation lived in an atmosphere of financial embarrassment. The Corporation's income came from rents of various properties, market tolls, and a rate levied from time to time for the repair of the city walls, bridges, and staithes. Added to this was income derived from payments for freedoms and exonerations from office. Rents received could only be increased as the leases came up for renewal, and income from the other sources was subject to wide fluctuations. There had been no significant increase in the revenues since the eighteenth century, and the general rise in prices which took place during the Napoleonic Wars worsened matters. It was found that the cost of maintaining and paving the roads and streets rose from £279 to £653 (1808–12), and that the cost of repairing Corporation property was increasing. A Committee of Inquiry into the State of the Corporation's finances sat in 1812, and found that the Corporation owed £10,000, including £3,700 in tradesmen's bills. During the years that followed, the Lord Mayor's salary was reduced, some Corporation property was sold, and resort was had continually to the device of annuities. By these means income was made to exceed expenditure in all but two of the years 1813–32. Capital expenditure had to be met by borrowing however, and the dying Corporation left a debt of £21,000 as a legacy to the new City Council, £11,000 evidently incurred in the years 1833–5.[22] No doubt then, in so far as the York Corporation was guilty of lethargy, financial embarrassment rather than corruption was the root cause.

Yet the attitude of the Corporation to its responsibilities was not wholly neglectful. The cattle market was moved by joint action of the Corporation and City Commissioners in 1826 to a situation outside the walls. Because an initial provision of 616 pens for cattle and 6,750 for sheep were found to be inadequate, a further 4,000 temporary pens were erected. The Ouse Bridge was rebuilt at a cost of £80,000 in 1810–20. Street improvements were carried out intermittently, though not on the scale of the eighteenth century.[23] It seems likely that if there had been no strong body of public opinion against such a course, the Corporation would, in the early years of the century, have carried out a wholesale destruction of the city walls. However much to be deplored on aesthetic grounds, it may be argued that such a policy would have been an active and symbolic move in the direction of 'progress' on the part of the Corporation.

Moreover, defective local government was by no means peculiar to York. The Municipal Corporations Commission (1835) remarked of the 246 borough towns in general that 'the Corporations look upon themselves, and are considered by the inhabitants, as separate and exclusive bodies . . . in most places all identity of interest between the corporation and the inhabitants had disappeared'. Furthermore, revenues that ought to have been applied for the public advantage were frequently diverted from their legitimate use.[24] The existence of disreputable corporations at Bristol, Ipswich and Leicester did not

prevent these cities from growing faster than York in the
period. Bristol's population, for example, rose by 103 per cent
between 1801 and 1841, despite the existence of 'a financially
embarrassed corporation characterized by a supine neglect
of public interests'. Ipswich, where the corporation displayed
political partisanship and 'mean corruption' increased by 127
per cent; and Leicester, despite a refusal on the part of the
oligarchical Tory corporation to spend on improvements of
any kind, attained 214 per cent.[25] On the other hand the
existence of effective and workman-like corporations at Pen-
zance, Sandwich and Southwold[26] did not lead to significant
growth there. Some of the fastest growing cities of England
were virtually without government of any description.[27] In
fact it is difficult to put forward a convincing argument along
these lines unless careful comparisons are made between cities
which had similar potentialities for growth in other respects.
The case against the civic leadership cannot be regarded as
proven, and even if it were it is unlikely to have been the sole
reason for York's failure to industrialize.

Perhaps the question has been wrongly phrased, and we
ought not to search for factors inhibiting industrial growth
that would otherwise have taken place as a matter of course –
for that appears to be the assumption underlying the thought
of contemporaries and recent historians on this point. The
staple industries on which the rapidly expanding settlements
of the nineteenth century based their prosperity were iron-
smelting, coal-mining, cotton and wool textile manufactures,
and ship-building. Surely York had no outstanding *positive*
advantages to offer any of these industries? As an inland town
it was not suited to ship-building; there was no coal to be
mined, and York was too distant from coal to make iron-
smelting feasible. The iron-processing works which existed
were more likely to be, and were in fact, specialist rather than
large-output producers.[28] With regard to textiles, York had
no fast-running streams to provide the water power which
seems to have given an early impetus to the location of mills
on the Pennines.[29] Furthermore, in the case of cotton, the

eastern climate was unlikely to be suitable, quite apart from the city's distance from the point of entry of raw cotton, at Liverpool. This is to say nothing of the economies of inter-related specialization which must have been most advanta-geous to the established manufacturing districts, even by the 1830s.[30]

THE CHARACTERISTICS OF THE EXISTING ECONOMY

In reviewing the supposed reasons for the lack of development of modern industry in York, emphasis has been lain on the side of stagnation. It is true that between 1801 and 1841, the population grew by only 71 per cent, as against 416 per cent for Bradford, 187 per cent for Leeds, 257 per cent for Hudders-field, and 123 per cent for Hull, etc. Yet growth of 71 per cent in forty years may well have been more rapid than at any other time in the history of the city. Expansion along existing lines was therefore such as to merit further appraisal.

Once again, the occupational data of 1841 afford a useful starting point. These have been sorted into the various cate-gories first employed by Charles Booth in 1886,[31] and in turn, combined into appropriate permutations for analysing the occupational structure and economy of York to best advantage (see table 2.2).

In addition, 1,297 individuals (316 males, 981 females) were described as persons of independent means. This is in the ratio of 1:22 of the population, as against 1:36 nationally.

I have already discussed the absence of modern industry from the economy, and the low proportion indicated in table 2.2 for agriculture is natural to any town. Among males, the comparatively high proportion described as general labourers may be noticed, although it is certain that the nineteenth century census abstracts consistently understated the propor-tion of unskilled workers both at the local and national levels. Nevertheless, the proportion of male labourers appears to have been higher in York than in neighbouring industrial towns of the West Riding (Leeds 7·4, Bradford 4·3, Sheffield

TABLE 2.2   *Occupational structure of York compared with England and Wales, 1841**

		York		England and Wales
		Absolute no.	(%)	(%)
(I)	*Males*			
(1)	Modern manufacturing and extractive industries (Textiles and dyeing; metal manufacture and fabrication; coal and ore mining)	696	8.9	17.4
(2)	Agriculture, etc.	433	5.6	28.8
(3)	Building	965	12.4	8.1
(4)	Transport	306	3.9	3.4
(5)	General (unspecified) labour	787	10.1	7.1
(6)	Domestic service	457	5.9	5.4
(7)	Public service and professional; banking, insurance, etc.	668	8.6	5.5
(8)	Other manufacture (i.e. handicrafts); dealing, wholesale and retail, etc.	3,462	44.5	24.4
		7,774	99.9	100.1
(II)	*Females*			
(1)	Modern manufacture and extractive industries	71	2.2	16.6
(2)	Agriculture	2	0.1	3.9
(3)	Building	6	0.2	0.1
(4)	Transport	6	0.2	0.2
(5)	General labour	2	0.1	0.8
(6)	Domestic service	2,321	71.7	55.7
(7)	Public service, professional, etc.	105	3.2	3.1
(8)	Other manufacture (handicraft); dealing, etc.	722	22.3	19.6
		3,235	100.0	100.0

* 1841 census. Occupation Abstract.

5·0), which might be expected to follow from the absence of modern industry, since entry into local skilled trades continued to be through formal apprenticeship channels.

Building occupied a larger role in York than in the nation at large; but a much more striking characteristic of the male labour force is the vast proportion engaged in the miscellaneous handicraft and dealing operations summed into category 8. Here are included the bakers, booksellers, butchers, innkeepers, grocers, tailors, jewellers, pipe-makers, saddlers, drapers, wine merchants, brush makers, clock makers, etc., who abounded in York. No less than 44 per cent of this group (males), and 75 per cent (females) were engaged in the prepparation of articles of dress and apparel, and in the retailing of food and drink.[32]

The line between handicraft manufacture and retailing cannot be drawn with any accuracy for an economy of this nature of course, but we are fortunate in being able to draw on the results of a recent pioneering study of retailing during the period which includes York as one of a number of case studies. Alexander has shown on the basis of an examination of Pigot's directories, that in 1822 York's ratio of 1 shop to 55 population was higher than in any of the other communities he studied (Merthyr Tydfil, Liverpool, Bolton, Leeds, Manchester, Norwich, Leicester and Nottingham). Down to 1848 the overall percentage increase in shops was lowest in York, but still, in 1848, with 1 shop to 36 population, it stood second only to Nottingham. At both dates, Alexander observes, York shops were 'numerous and highly specialized'.[33]

Lastly, table 2.2 indicates an above average proportion of male employment in public and professional services, together with banking, insurance, etc., and an astonishingly high proportion of female domestic servants, a service activity which accounted for nearly three-quarters of all female employment in the city. These findings, taken in conjunction with the comparatively large number of persons of independent means, have a certain consistency, and contrast vividly with the situation in neighbouring industrial towns (table 2.3).

TABLE 2.3   *Selected social indicators for four Yorkshire cities, 1841**

	York	Leeds	Bradford	Sheffield
Persons of independent means per 1,000 population	45	21	15	20
Select professions (armed services, law, church, medicine, education, banking and accounting), per 1,000 occupied (less domestic servants)	44	21	15	21
Domestic servants, per 1,000 population	88	37	27	39

* 1841 census. Occupation Abstract.

Such statistics add substance to the contemporary suggestion that 'society' in York was 'superior to that of most provincial towns',[34] and table 2.4 lends further support.

TABLE 2.4   *Assessed taxes in various towns, 1845–7, with incidence of taxation per head**

| | Assessed taxes, Year ending 5th April | | | Mean: | Popula- tion in | Assessed taxes per |
	1845 £	1846 £	1847 £	1845–7 £	1841	head £
York	7,969	7,996	8,247	8,071	30,152	0.27
Cheltenham	17,545	17,631	17,977	17,718	31,207	0.57
Bath	30,646	31,027	30,878	30,850	52,346	0.59
Liverpool	30,479	30,299	30,662	30,480	282,656	0.11
Manchester	12,506	11,714	11,761	11,994	240,367	0.05
Leeds	6,738	6,641	6,664	6,681	151,063	0.04
Birmingham	20,621	26,294	26,075	24,330	181,116	0.13
Halifax	3,016	2,986	3,018	3,007	26,694	0.11

* Based on *PP* 1847–8 xxxix 233, and 1841 census.

The assessed taxes of the period should not be confused with an income tax, nor with a property tax as such. They were levied on items of luxurious consumption (carriages, man-servants, racehorses, etc.) and also included window duty on houses with more than seven windows; hence, they fell only upon the well-off sections of the community. The table shows that whilst York was not in the same class as the spa towns of Bath and Cheltenham as a centre of conspicuous consumption, the level of assessed taxation per head was over twice that indicated for the series of industrial towns chosen for comparison.

The retailers and associated handicraft producers of York, along with those engaged in professional and commercial activities, and probably to some extent the builders, had one thing in common; namely, a high degree of dependence on outside demand. It was widely recognised that trade was highly dependent on local markets, among the citizens of York itself and its rural hinterland. 'The principal trade, however, engaged, is retail, which is generally pretty brisk, supported by the many genteel and opulent families in York and its respectable vicinage', commented a directory in 1829. An earlier directory had listed 33 peers, 34 baronets, and 819 'seats of the gentry' in Yorkshire.[35] It seems likely that York's status as a social centre for the aristocracy was on the wane, and had perhaps been declining ever since the advent of fast coach services to London in the late eighteenth century.[36] Among those whose livelihood would have been sustained best by distinctively upper-class demand, there were frequent complaints of decline. Alderman Oldfield, a prominent wine and spirit merchant declared with some feeling that 'Everything is going away from us and nothing is coming . . . notwithstanding the increase in population, I don't know that trade has increased at all with it.'[37]

However, by far the most substantial share of demand for York's goods and services must have come from the non-gentle farming population of the surrounding area. Whilst no doubt most West Riding agriculturists would have looked to the markets and fairs of Leeds and other large towns for buying and selling, there were nevertheless 14,000 farmers and graziers in the North and East Ridings alone, including the Ainsty.[38] Although there were busy little markets at Howden, Malton, Helmsley, Pickering, Beverley and elsewhere, it is noteworthy that, apart from York, there was only one centre of population with more than 10,000 inhabitants in the whole of the area, that is Hull. Thus if farmers were doing well, one could expect York with its many markets, fairs and services to prosper. In the event of agrarian difficulties, the town would be likely to stagnate. What evidence I have been able to recover on the periodicity of economic development in the city is best interpreted in this way. Unfortunately, much of it comes from census sources (1801, 1811, 1821, 1831), which for obvious reasons does not lend itself readily to a detailed annotation of this view.

In 1795 the price of wheat in the United Kingdom, which had averaged 48s. per quarter in 1781–94, suddenly leapt to 75s. 2d., under the impact of an especially bad harvest in 1795. Throughout the years 1795–1820, the average stood at 82s. 11d., and never fell below 51s. 10d. Generally speaking, the case is similar with respect to other cereals, whilst meat prices followed suit, standing at an 1813 peak of over 100 per cent above pre-war levels.[39] These high-price levels, coupled with fantastic annual fluctuations, are attributed by agricultural historians primarily to the effects of adverse seasons and to the inflationary consequences of government war finance and the over-issue of notes by the country banks; whatever the causes, it is probable that the highly prosperous conditions enjoyed by local farmers and landlords were conducive to the growth and prosperity of York. The population of the Municipal Borough increased by 12.8 per cent and 13.7 per cent in 1801–11 and 1811–21, and the number of houses by 10 and 26 per cent. The annual number of marriages, which had averaged 172 in 1781–94, shot up (significantly, in 1796) to 233, and then averaged 275 down to 1810, and 198 from 1810–20.[40] Net gains by immigration on the other hand, were less impressive; it is possible that this reflects inherent deficiencies in my methods of calculation (see ch. 4, pp. 78–9), but it could also be explained by a shortage of prospective immigrants due to wartime demands on the rural labour force, or to the existence of more attractive opportunities in other towns.

Agricultural prices fell sharply in 1821–3, giving rise to cries of 'depression' from the landed interest and pleas for help from the legislature; that is, for help additional to that already provided by the notorious Corn Law of 1815. Landlords and farmers were now in the position of having to accept the fact that future price levels would probably stabilize at levels very little higher than those of the pre-war period, and had to adjust themselves accordingly. Yet it would clearly be wrong to conclude that the 1820s as a whole were a time of uniform agrarian depression; there is evidence of rent and wage reductions serving to reduce the farmers' costs, and price-relatives for agricultural produce in general (as against industrial goods), demonstrate that farmers were by no means at a marked comparative disadvantage. As against an index of 126 for agricultural prices (1821–30) that of principal industrial products stood at 109 (an average of 1865 and 1885 prices = 100).[41]

On the local level there are clear indications of the continuing prosperity of the fairs and markets in these years; when the cattle market was placed outside the walls on an enlarged site in 1825, the move was attributed to 'the very great augmentation which of late years has taken place in the business of our fairs and markets'.[42] During the decade 1821–31, the population of York grew by no less than 20.5 per cent, marriages were buoyant (averaging 247 for 1821–30), and there was a net gain by immigration of some 2,000 persons (see chapter 4). Between 1822 and 1834 the number of retail shops expanded at 5.2 per cent per annum,[43] and there is evidence of considerable activity in building. The number of houses rose by no less than 1,541 (45 per cent), between the two census dates, and the calendar of public building, starting in the previous decade but continuing with vigour through the 1820s, includes the following: rebuilding of the Ouse Bridge and approaches (1810–20), Friends' Meeting House (1818), Lendal Chapel (1815), Albion Chapel (1816), St George's Chapel (1826), Lady Peckitt's Yard Chapel (1830): repair of the Minster after the fire of 1829; construction of substantial buildings for the Yorkshire Philosophical Society (1827–30), York Savings Bank (1819), and the Dispensary (1828); new buildings for St Peter's School (1830), the canons residentiary (1824), Anne Middleton's Hospital (1828), and a new deanery (1831); construction of a gas-works (1823), and new prison buildings (1814 and 1826). In addition, there were extensive street improvements in the 1820s.[44]

The indications are, however, that the buoyancy of the 1820s was not maintained in the subsequent decade. On the whole, agriculture was less prosperous and the prices obtained for corn, were, if anything, somewhat tighter, certainly for part of that decade. The Gazette price of wheat in 1832–7 averaged 50s. 3d., as against 63s. 4d. for 1824–31, and when 1838–41 saw a series of bad harvests, prices did not rise so high as they would formerly have done, owing to the 1828 modification of the Corn Laws, which had introduced a sliding scale.[45]

There is independent witness to difficulties in the East Riding deriving from the evidence of Charles Howard, an influential large-scale farmer living at Melbourne (ten miles south-east of York), to the *Select Committee on the State of Agriculture* (1836), and to a Lord's Committee on the same subject sitting the following year. He allowed that sheep-farmers on the Yorkshire Wolds, who had fortuitously escaped the 'dreadful rot that took place in the three wet years terminating in 1831', were realizing good prices, and had little to complain of; but on the 'productive, strong' arable soils of Holderness and the 'poor, strong' land of Howdenshire in the south of the county, the farmers were declared to be 'insolvent, taken as a body'. A number of Howdenshire farms were 'utterly unlet and uncultivated, lying completely waste', whilst landlords, if anything, were in still worse straits than their tenants, rents having fallen by about 40 per cent since 1816, 'and occasionally 50 per cent on strong cold lands', whilst in Yorkshire generally, at that moment, estates were 'almost unsaleable'.

His comments on the implications of these conditions for the affairs of York tradespeople are worth quoting extensively, and incidentally illustrate their heightened perception of the facts of local economic life:

Q. 5450   What is the state of the tradesmen in your neighbourhood?

I reside not very far from York and I am most acquainted with the tradesmen in York; they complain very heavily. On inquiry as to an agricultural petition which was recently sent up from the Yorkshire Associations to the House of Commons, I found that the shopkeepers in York were much more anxious to sign that petition than the farmers were. They have learnt that they are entirely dependent upon the landed interest, and that if the landlords have not money, and if the tenants have not money, they can sell no goods.

Q. 5451   Is that not rather a change in the opinions of the tradesmen?

Decidedly so.

Q. 5452   Since when have they changed their opinions?

I recollect that corn was extremely high in 1812, and about that period the shopkeepers used to complain heavily of it, and fancied that it was very much to their detriment; they are now convinced that without corn can be sold at a remunerating price, they cannot carry on business to advantage.[46]

A reflection of this flat state of affairs may be seen in the slow disposal of Earl de Grey's Clifton property in the mid-1830s.[47] The *Yorkshire Gazette* had anticipated that the sale would 'have the effect of encouraging the erection of many villas and suburban residences, possessing the pleasantness and salubrity of the country, along with the convenience of contiguity to a city where there are a cheap and abundant market, excellent shops and every facility for the education of a family'. Yet, in February 1836, only forty out of 216 lots were actually sold. Hutton observes that 'an error of judgement seems to have been made in putting it on the market at that particular time', and notes that over the next few years most of the remaining lots were sold privately. Seth Agar, a prominent York grocer, bought eight lots all fronting the main street or the green, no doubt with a view to speculation; yet during the next few years he built only four new dwellings involving the destruction of three old ones. Possibly the explanation of the unexpectedly slow development of Clifton lies, Hutton suggests, in the competing demands for capital on the part of the York and North Midland Railway (£300,000) and Great North of England Railway (£1 million) – but general business conditions and a lack of impetus in the local economy may explain just as much, if not more.

In such an unpropitious economic climate, it is not surprising that the consequences for York were reduced population growth (9·8 per cent for the Municipal Borough), a check to previous gains from immigration (see chapter 4), and, apparently, a much slacker period for the building industry. It is true the addition to the total housing stock was 1,003 (a 20 per cent increase during the decade), but it is clear that with the exception of the redevelopment of the modern Parliament Street area in 1834–6, much less public building was being carried out, and probably safe to assume that the requirements of local landed proprietors would have been sharply curtailed. In England and Wales as a whole, many fewer houses appear to have been built in 1831–41 than in the previous decade, which must have made it difficult for York's building operatives to migrate; at all events, as we have seen, the proportion claiming to be engaged in that industry remained comparatively high in 1841 – although of course the census tells us nothing about casual or under-employment.

An examination of the major occupational groupings of 1841 has revealed something of the nature of the economy as it existed during the first forty years of the nineteenth century. We have seen that York showed no signs of developing as a modern industrial town, and the reasons for this have been discussed. Variations in the rate of development along existing lines (retailing, handicraft production, services, building), have been shown to have been largely dependent on the state of agriculture. The next decade was to see a marked change in the springs of growth.

ECONOMIC DEVELOPMENT, 1841–51

In the years 1837–51 York was becoming an important railway centre. Despite the existence of what were, for that time, extensive transport facilities by road and river, conveyance remained slow and expensive. The average coach fares to Leeds were 9s. (inside) and 6s. (outside). A journey to Leeds generally took three hours, to London twenty-four. To transport goods as far as Leeds evidently cost from 13s. 4d. to £2 per ton by wagon. Goods traffic passed beween Leeds and York via the Ouse Navigation at an average cost of 7s. per ton, but occupied from four to ten days in transit.[48]

Pamphlets advocating a railway connection had appeared as early as 1826.[49] It was not, however, until 1833 that after a meeting of prominent citizens had been addressed by Meek on the advantages of cheaper fuel, steps were taken to set up a Provisional Railway Committee. It was intended either to construct a line directly to Leeds, or to build a link to the Leeds–Selby line, at South Milford. During the following months, alternative schemes, including direct lines to London, were considered. It seems that the greatest spur to immediate action came from outside, when in the September of 1835 the North Midland Company was formed to put into operation George Stephenson's plans for building a railway from Leeds to Derby. Coupled with schemes that were in the air to connect Leeds and Darlington, this seemed a threat to York. The citizens seem to have been in a state of some agitation – 'If our city be inactive now, the line from London to Edinburgh will be by Leeds, leaving York completely out . . . the future of the city of York is most seriously involved.' George Hudson, Treasurer of the York Railway Committee, evidently went to Stephenson and begged him to make the terminus of his North Midland line York, not Leeds, but Stephenson would not be drawn. All schemes of a direct connection with London were now regarded as utopian, and a shorter line linking York with Stephenson's North Midland line was regarded as common sense, for it

37

would achieve the double object of linking York with Leeds and establishing a communication with London.

At an 'enthusiastic' meeting of citizens on 13 October 1835, it was resolved that a company be formed to build a railway from York to link up with the North Midland line. A capital of £200,000 should be raised in £50 shares, and subscribers to an earlier York and Leeds scheme should have their shares merged into the new company. An optimistic prospectus ('a dividend of 13½ per cent may ... be fairly reckoned upon'), was issued in January 1836.[50] The first York and North Midland Bill enjoyed an easy passage through Parliament, and in August 1836 the new company held its first formal meeting.

On 29 May 1839 the first stretch of the line, as far as South Milford on the Leeds and Selby line, was opened with great festivities. Meek made a speech expressing the hope that when the railway system was completed, London would be the head, Edinburgh the feet, and York the heart. From the opening of the railway onwards the York and North Midland shares stood at a 20 per cent premium of £10 apiece.[51] By 1840 this stretch of line had been extended a few miles, and now linked directly with the North Midland Railway at Altofts. York had gained railway access to Leeds and the West Riding, and to the Midlands and London.

The really decisive issue for York's future development as a railway centre, however, was the question of the connection with towns farther north. Within a few weeks of the formation of the York and North Midland Company in 1835, a group of promoters inspired by the Quaker capitalists of the Stockton and Darlington Railway met in Newcastle to discuss the building of a railway southward into Yorkshire. The great question to be thrashed out was whether the new railway should run from Darlington to York, or to Leeds. An engineer, Thomas Storey, was engaged to survey the proposed routes, reporting in 1836 in favour of the line to York. Such a line would pass over 'even terrain', and would cost considerably less than a line to Leeds; (£1 million as against £1,750,000). A line to Leeds would have necessitated expensive excavations, embankments, tunnels and bridges. A connection with the north-east was finally established by March 1841, that is, the Great North of England Railway. There ensued a pause in railway-building, but in the years following 1844, important branch lines to Scarborough (1845) Market Weighton (1847) and Knaresborough (1848) were completed.

Other writers have traced the history of these railways in considerable detail, and there is no need to echo their findings; my concern is with their economic effects on the district. The impact on other forms of transport is clear. Obviously the long-distance coach and wagon services were doomed. The time needed for a journey to London fell from twenty hours to ten, and to Leeds from three hours to less than an hour. Fares fell rapidly too. Coach fares had stood at 3d.–4d. a mile, but the York and North Midland charged 1.323 pence to 2.227 pence per mile, according to class.[52] Local coaches continued to ply for some years until they too were driven out with the building of further lines.

Precisely the same advantages (cheaper and faster services) were offered by the railways for the conveyance of goods over large distances. The road-wagon agents promptly restyled themselves as 'carriers by railway'. It is worth distinguishing between local village carriers and long-distance road-wagon operators. The former were not driven out of business, but went from strength to strength. While the railway carried a growing amount of traffic, it clearly could not serve all the villages, and the local carriers benefited from this. While in 1843, 67 carriers operated from 26 inns to serve 73 villages and townships, in 1855, 107 carriers operated from 29 inns in York to some 91 different villages.[53] Many of these carriers no doubt lived in the villages, but within York itself the numbers of people described in the censuses as 'carriers' rose from 33 (1831) to 93 (1861).

Concern had been felt by some citizens at the probable effect of the introduction of railways on the Ouse Navigation. The Navigation took its first steps to meet railway competition in 1836, when it raised its tolls, hoping to pay off some small part of its large debt and also to be able to lower them once again after railway competition had been started.[54] This was done, but various sources attest to the damage done to the Navigation by railway competition in the forties. The directories list the various river services, and indicate a general run-down in the amount of shipping involved. The receipts of the Ouse Navigation averaged £3,968 per annum in the period 1836–41 but only £1,817 per annum in 1842–50. That these figures were not merely reflections of lowered toll-rates is suggested by the fact that the number of loaded coal vessels arriving in York also fell markedly, from an annual average of 863 (1830–9) to 437 (1840–9).[55] The subsequent history of the Navigation was generally such that it did not see prosperity again until the end of the century, when an important flour-milling industry had arisen in the city.

These were, however, little more than interesting side-effects. What was the broader impact of the railways upon economy and society in York? Contemporaries thought it considerable; several guide-books dwelling on the antiquities and shopping facilities of the city were published in the 1840s, and as early as 1841 the *York Herald* commented that 'since the various railroads have been brought into operation, everyone must have observed the influx of visitors they have brought here, which must be a considerable benefit, in various ways, to its tradesmen and commerce'.[56] McCulloch's *Geographical Dictionary* (1852 edn.) observed that 'a decided increase of trade has been experienced since the completion of the railways',[57] and Baines, writing some thirty years later, remarked that 'the introduction of the railway system into this part of England gave fresh occupation to the capital and enterprise of the more wealthy and enterprising inhabitants of this ancient city ... [having the effect of] rendering the city of York a connecting point on a large scale between the north and the south, and the east and the west'.[58]

It so happened that the 'railway decade' saw the most rapid intercensal population increase of the century, 26 per cent for the Municipal Borough. Through the whole of the nineteenth century, this decade saw the most favourable net balance of immigration (see chapter 4). The number of houses in the Municipal Borough rose by 1,119 (a 19 per cent increase), to which one can add 293 more for St Olave Marygate, Heworth, Clifton and Fulford; these suburbs were growing much more rapidly than hitherto. The number of shops rose by 5.5 per cent per annum between 1841 and 1848, as against 2.7 per cent per annum between 1834 and 1841.[59] How far, and in what ways, were these manifestations of growth connected?

Other than the railway, the only other likely factor of growth would have been an upswing in the demand of farmers for non-agricultural goods and services, having the kind of effect I have suggested for the twenties. On the whole, however, the years 1841–51 were not good for cereal farmers. Prices were high in 1841, but steadily declined to 1846; as a result of the sadly deficient harvest of that year, there was a very strong upward movement in prices in 1847, before the new harvest was reaped. From that time onward, to the end of the period, prices were again in rapid decline. Wheat imports were high in 1841–2, thus preventing the farmer from enjoying the full benefit of relatively good prices; whilst after 1846 and the Repeal of the Corn Laws, grain importations soared, leading to loud lamentations of distress.[60] We are obliged to conclude that York's unprecedented growth in this decade owed little to the prosperity of agriculture.

Apart from increasing the numbers of tourists and visitors, the coming of the railways could have stimulated the economy in three ways:

(a) in acting as a cost-reducing agency, enabling other industries to develop on the basis of cheaper transport facilities;

(b) in the construction process, acting through the multiplier;

(c) in the provision of new jobs.

The first of these appears to have been comparatively unimportant. As contemporaries had forecast, the price of coal immediately fell sharply, and by 1844 stood at 6–9 shillings per ton.[61] But their further anticipations as a result of this were not realized. No industry owing its rise to cheap coal has ever appeared in York, and moreover, no industry has ever arisen on the strength of the cheap distributive facilities that the railway afforded. Sigsworth has pointed out that the famous York cocoa and confectionery firms did not grow to significant size until the last decades of the century. Their rise, he correctly asserts, owed far more to the rise of real wages that characterized the 'Great Depression' than to the existence of railway connections which after all, had then been in existence for some forty years.[62]

Doubtless, even in the 1837–41 period, the actual construction of the York and North Midland and Great North of England lines helped to relieve the general torpor of the region to some extent. From 1844 onwards the network thickened as plans for further lines passed into execution in the area. Moreover, even where the basic connections had been made, there was a fair amount of ancillary building to be done. In York the original temporary station was replaced in 1841 and added to in 1846. Works were built in 1842 for the repair of railway engines, and in 1849 for the repair and painting of carriages. A commodious railway hotel was constructed in 1852.[63]

Without a full study of the subject in its own right, it would be difficult to say just how far such necessary works benefited York firms, brought about induced investment and stimulated employment in and around the city. But it is known that at least one York builder made a great deal of money out of railway work, that is, C. T. Andrews, who rose to be Sheriff of York. Lambert writes that in the early days, 'whenever possible, spoils in the form of contracts were reserved for York firms' in the building of Hudson's lines; and evidence of continuing support from railway orders is recorded for William Bellerby, who, over the years, enjoyed contracts to build stations and wagon works for the Scarborough, Whitby and Saltburn line, for the North Eastern Railway at York, Shildon, Darlington and Harrogate, and for joiners' work at the North Eastern Railway General Offices.[64]

When we turn to the direct employment given by the railways, we are on somewhat surer ground. The census returns of 1841 list only 20 York residents as employed in railway service. The figure seems remarkably small, and it is probable that some railway employees were subsumed under other headings. The records of the York and North Midland Railway show that it had 115 workers to start with (inside and outside York), but the number had risen to between 800 and 900 as early as 1846.[65] By 1851 the census suggests that at least 500 York residents were directly employed by the railways. This figure is made up of railway engine drivers, stokers (91), others engaged in railway traffic (233), and railway labourers (99). In addition it is probable that some of the engineers, engine-makers, etc., whose numbers rose from fifty-six in 1841 to 156 (1851), were connected with the railway industry; it is also likely that the small increase in the numbers engaged in coach and carriage building (111 to 122), concealed a degree of shift from making horse-drawn conveyances to railway vehicles; while a large proportion of the porters (whose numbers rose from forty-three to 196) were almost certainly railway employees.

It is true that the 500 (or so) railway workers represented only about 3 per cent of the total occupied population in 1851. But three-quarters of them were immigrants, who would not otherwise have been living, working and spending in York, along with their dependants.[66] Had it not been for railway developments and the need to house newcomers, it is unlikely that the already swollen building industry would have grown; that is, there would have been some 300–400 less building workers (69 per cent immigrants[67]), again with dependants, living, working and spending in York. Without railwaymen and more building workers, in all probability the numbers of retailers would not have expanded, especially in view of the stagnant demand of the agricultural interest. To some extent the very nature of the expansion in retailing reflects the increased importance of 'working-class' demand, in that 66 per cent of the 1841–8 expansion in retailing can be accounted

c

for by the boot and shoe trade, butchers, and 'general shop-keepers', while the number of pawnbrokers increased from three to five. By contrast, a series of trades likely to cater primarily for higher-class demand (booksellers, drapers, lace dealers, hosiers, hatters, grocers and tea dealers, and silversmiths) showed no net expansion whatsoever, taken as a whole.[68]

Although it is impossible to trace the operation of the multiplier in a fully satisfactory manner, it appears that there would have been very little growth in the 1840s, had it not been for the introduction of the railways. Yet, when one examines the occupational structure indicated by the 1851 census, another perspective has to be put on the matter. The 500 railwaymen take on reduced significance, representing only a tiny minority of the occupied population. It is salutary to compare the occupational structure of 1851 with that of 1841, using comparable conventions. (See table 2.5).

In addition, the ratio of those styling themselves as 'independent' (184 males, 702 females) had fallen back to 1 in 41 of the population. This was still well above the national proportion (1 in 85), but the decline in both the local and national figures suggests that it was becoming increasingly the fashion to state an occupation of some kind. Very probably, the sharp drop indicated for domestic service reflects greater precision in the occupational returns generally, since on a national level the male proportion fell from 5.4 to 2.6 per cent of the occupied male population, and from 55.7 to 40.4 per cent for females, between the two dates.

Some of the other features in table 2.5 reflect well-documented changes in York. For example, large numbers of Irish immigrants swelled the numbers of those recorded as agricultural labourers, and a significant increase occurred in the proportion of males under transport. The increased proportion of females included in the professional category is doubtless connected with the expansion of educational provision during the 1840s, which naturally produced more teachers (72 per cent of the group).

'Modern manufacture' was still sparsely represented, but

TABLE 2.5 *Occupational structure of York in 1851, compared with 1841**

		1841 Percentage (See table 2.2)	1851	
			Absolute no.	Percentage
(I)	*Males*			
(1)	Modern manufacturing and extractive industries	8.9	999	8.9
(2)	Agriculture, etc.	5.6	1,116	9.9
(3)	Building	12.4	1,336	11.9
(4)	Transport	3.9	858	7.6
(5)	General (unspecified) labour	10.1	684	6.1
(6)	Domestic service	5.9	389	3.5
(7)	Public service and professional; banking, insurance, etc.	8.6	1,056	9.4
(8)	Other manufacture (handicrafts); dealing, wholesale and retail, etc.	44.5	4,787	42.7
		99.9	11,225	100.0
(II)	*Females*			
(1)	Modern manufacturing and extractive industries	2.2	56	1.1
(2)	Agriculture, etc.	0.1	109	2.1
(3)	Building	0.2	5	0.1
(4)	Transport	0.2	25	0.5
(5)	General (unspecified) labour	0.1	83	1.6
(6)	Domestic service	71.7	3,021	58.9
(7)	Public service and professional; banking, insurance, etc.	3.2	296	5.8
(8)	Other manufacture (handicrafts); dealing, wholesale and retail, etc.	22.3	1,534	29.9
		100.0	5,129	100.0

* 1841 and 1851 censuses. Occupation Abstracts.

the size of category 8, representing the miscellany of small-scale handicraft producers and dealers, remains impressive. From this point of view, there had been little change; the general characteristics of the city's occupational structure stood largely unaltered. Directories of 1851 and 1855 reiterated that York was 'not signalized by numerous or eminently important manufactures', and that 'the trade of York principally arises from the supply of the inhabitants and the numerous and opulent families in the neighbourhood'.[69] York products going forward to the Great Exhibition of 1851 characteristically included a patent razor, various wood-carved exhibits, a side-saddle covered in Berlin-wool, specimens of ivory and tortoise-shell combs, a 'carved marble slab', a model of the North and East Riding County Pauper Lunatic Asylum, 'a peculiar ... meteorological instrument of new construction ... in artificial marble', and a series of objects contributed by the Museum Curator, 'to illustrate new processes of preserving zoological specimens'.[70]

3 Some social characteristics of early Victorian York

Many of the outstanding social features of York during the period follow quite naturally from the fact that, as established in the last chapter, its economy remained primarily pre-industrial. A review of some of these characteristics is a necessary part of the contextual treatment necessary to preface the socio-demographic material covered in chapters 4–6, and the emphasis is on matters which are in principle amenable to measurement.

POVERTY

Passing visitors did not notice much obvious poverty; J. G. Kohl remarked 'Everything has a quiet, pleasing and becoming air ... there is nothing about the place to indicate poverty or decay ... there were fewer beggars than in London, Manchester Glasgow or Newcastle. The people, like the city itself, seemed all to have a decent and orderly look'.[1] But it is clear from this author's own account that he was primarily interested in the antiquities of York, and he stayed with his Quaker friends; so that like many thousands of visitors to the city, well-acquainted with the Minster, walls and gates, he probably saw nothing of the less agreeable enclaves of Walmgate and elsewhere.[2]

In fact York was destined to be the setting of one of the two most influential enquiries into poverty at the end of the nineteenth century, which revealed a far higher incidence among the working-class population than would have been anticipated by most Victorians. In what B. S. Rowntree described as a fairly representative provincial town, 7,230 persons, (or 9·9 per cent of the total population), were found to be existing below a stringently defined and carefully costed 'poverty line'; that is, they lived in families where total incomes were below those necessary to obtain the minimum necessities for the maintenance of 'merely physical efficiency'. These were deemed to be in 'primary poverty' and in addition, another 13,072 persons, or 17·9 per cent of the population, were in 'secondary' poverty; their incomes appeared to be such as to carry them over the poverty line, but mis-spending on items not comprised in the minimal budget (especially betting and drink) caused them to fall below it.[3]

Ideally, one would wish to make comparisons with the position in the 1840s, on exactly the same basis, but whilst it would not be difficult in principle to draw up the necessary local cost of living series to bridge the intervening years, the non-industrial nature of the city means that wage-material for the early period is both sparse and unsystematic.[4] In addition, the incomes and profits derived from self-employment (which may have been more common in York than in many English towns), would tend to be irregular, and in any case, are unknown. Some tentative comparative comments may nevertheless be made. To begin with, the 'demographic' potential for poverty, as indicated by the study of age structure and dependency ratios, may be compared with that of the nation as a whole, and with York in later years (table 3.1).

TABLE 3.1   *Age-structure of the population of York and England and Wales; various dates**

Proportion aged	York 1841	York 1851	England and Wales 1851	York 1891	York 1961	England and Wales 1961
0–14	31.6	32.0	35.4	33.8	22.8	23.3
15–59	60.5	60.4	57.2	58.9	59.7	59.7
60 and over	7.9	7.6	7.3	7.3	17.9	17.1

* Census age abstracts at given dates.

The dependency ratios which follow from these figures are given in table 3.2.

On this score, it seems probable that the position in York was marginally better than in the nation as a whole during the 1840s, and also closely comparable with the local situation in the 1890s. The high proportion of children has much in common

TABLE 3.2 *Ratio of 'dependent consumers' (0–14 and 60 and over) to 'producers' (15–59); various dates*

York 1841	York 1851	England and Wales 1851	York 1891	York 1961
0.65	0.66	0.75	0.69	0.68

with the situation in many emerging countries today,[5] and it is worth remarking how much the age-composition differed, during the nineteenth century, from the present position achieved as a result of drastic reductions in family size, mainly since 1900.

Against this slightly favourable factor, it is necessary to set some of the characteristics noted in the last chapter; the absence of advanced industry, which elsewhere offered regular employment to children as well as comparatively high wages to adults; the high proportion of females in the population; and comparatively large numbers of domestic servants and general labourers. Moreover, the implications of tables 2.2 and 2.3, showing high proportions in professional employment and 'dealing' on the one hand, and labourers on the other, lead one to suspect that whatever the absolute percentage of poverty in York, the degree of income *inequality* would have been significantly higher than in most manufacturing towns, which tended to be more socially homogeneous in character.[6]

There are many complications, but it is possible to gain an idea of the mid-nineteenth century situation from an extrapolation of Rowntree's methods backwards to the 1840s, making direct comparisons where feasible, and where this is not so, setting out the data in such a way as to make comparison with future census studies possible.

Rowntree attributed primary poverty to the following causes, in order of importance:

    (a) Low wages, in spite of regular work (52 per cent)

    (b) Largeness of families, i.e. more than four children (22 per cent)

    (c) Death of chief wage-earner (16 per cent)

    (d) Illness or old age of chief wage-earner (5 per cent)

    (e) Irregularity of work (3 per cent), which may be coupled with

    (f) Chief wage-earner out of work (2 per cent).

In addition, he drew special attention to the existence of a 'poverty cycle' in the lives of labouring men, which I shall treat here as an additional cause of primary poverty.[7]

(a) Low wages

Rowntree's tables of minimum necessary expenditure at the level of the poverty line in 1899 covered three components; food, rent and sundries such as secondhand clothing, soap, light and fuel. For a family of two parents with three children, 12s. 9d. was allowed for food, 4s. for rent, and 4s. 11d. for sundries, a total of 21s. 8d. Adjustments were made for families of varying size.[8]

A rough idea of the mid-nineteenth century cost of the 1899 standard can be achieved by adjusting his figures according to changes in the (national) retail commodity price and rent indexes prepared by G. H. Wood in 1909, which show that the price of retail commodities moved down from a level of 100 (1850) to 86 (1899), whilst rent increased by 32.5 per cent over the same period.[9] No allowance is made for changes in the price of 'sundries' which appear to have changed very little over the intervening years.[10]

On that basis, the cost of the 1899 minimal standard in 1850 would have been as follows:

Family composition	
Single adult	7s. 2d.
Adult couple	10s. 8d.
Adult couple with one child	15s. 3d.
Adult couple with two children	19s. 6d.
Adult couple with three children	22s. 8d. (Compare 21s. 8d., 1899)

The steps taken to arrive at this schedule are open to many obvious objections, but it is reasonable to suppose that the 1850 estimates will not be in error by more than a shilling or so.[11]

If that argument is conceded, we may go on to examine wage-levels about 1849–50, compared with those of 1899. At the later date, the weekly wages of railway workers (all grades) averaged about 25s. per week. The general run of building craftsmen earned in the region of 38s., with bricklayers and masons on 40s. a week. Common labourers in York earned 18–21s. per week on the average.[12] About 1850, it is certain that the labourers were earning far less, in the region of 12s. a week. At that period building craftsmen, such as carpenters and joiners, bricklayers and masons, were averaging 18s. a week. Railway employees seem to have earned from 17s. (for porters), up to 4s.–6s. a day, (24s.–36s. per week) for engine drivers.[13] Probably, relative to other groups, the railway employees were much better off in the 1840s than at the end of the century.[14]

Thus, making any reasonable allowance for inaccuracies in the foregoing calculations it is obvious that in 1850 not only must *all* married labourers with children have been in poverty all of the time, but even craftsmen's families could easily find themselves well below the 1899 poverty line, which represented, Rowntree argued, the barest standard necessary for the 'maintenance of merely physical health'. They were likely to fall below this level if they lacked supplemental, (wives and children's) earnings, in the event of illness, or if they had anything remotely resembling a large family of children at home, or relatives to support. The conclusion is, therefore, that a much larger proportion of the population were in a vulnerable position, on account of low wages, although no fully satisfactory measurement can be made.

(b) Largeness of family

Here I cannot directly compare my results with those of Rowntree, since his statistics relate to the percentage of families *already in poverty*, which had five children or more.[15] But it is interesting to note the percentage of families in social classes III–V (inclusive), with this number of children, see table 3.3.

TABLE 3.3   *Percentage of families with more than four children, by class, 1851**

	Class					III-V inclusive
	I	II	III	IV	V	
Percentage with more than four children	13.6	4.7	10.1	3.9	10.2	9.0
Mean no. of children of family heads in each class	1.85	1.37	1.92	1.52	1.94	1.80
$N =$	59	107	386	103	98	587

* 1851 Census sample.

Within classes III–V children in these large families accounted for 28.4 per cent of all children: and children in large families (within classes III–V) represented 22.5 per cent of all children in the totality of York households.[16] The interpretation of these results must await further comparable figures, for in the present state of knowledge it is impossible to say whether they are above or below expected average levels.

(c) Death of chief wage-earner

Here again, no direct comparison with Rowntree's findings is possible, but in the 1851 sample, no less than 108 (13.8 per cent) of all households were headed by widows, of whom sixty were placed in social classes III–V (rather a large number, nineteen, were unallocable on the basis of the occupational data given). The 108 widows had charge of sixty children aged under 15, or thirty-six under 10, and in turn these made up 6.2 per cent of all children under 15 and 5.0 per cent of all under 10 in the main household sample. It is true, these estimates have rather large ranges of error, but if the 10 per cent sample results are taken at face value they imply that in York about 600 children aged under 15 lived in households headed by widows at this time, the great majority of whom were in very modest circumstaces. Children of widows among lodgers, visitors, relatives, etc., add about another 180 to the numbers so far calculated, (the ranges of error here are certainly large), so raising the proportion of all children in the care of widows to roughly 7 per cent of all children aged under 15 in the Parliamentary Borough. This may be an overestimate, but it is more likely to be an underestimate, as fatherless children in institutions of various kinds are not included.

(d) Illness of chief wage-earner

Morbidity in 1899 was much greater in what Rowntree called the 'ill-conditioned' parts of the city. In 1898 York had a general death rate of 18.5 and an infant death rate of 175 per 1,000, about the same as the average of the thirty-three largest towns of England and Wales. The range of variation in working-class districts alone is given in table 3.4.

TABLE 3.4   *York death rates in 1898**

	General death rate per 1,000	Infant death rate per 1,000
(a) Poorest section of population, (Walmgate inside the bar, with Hungate), 6,803 persons	27.8	247
(b) Middle section of population, (Parts of the Groves, Nunnery Lane, Leeman Rd), 9,945 persons	20.7	184
(c) Highest section of population, (Small districts in different parts of the city), 5,336 persons	13.5	173

* Rowntree (1902) 205–6.

Rowntree also showed that the height, weight and general physical condition of schoolchildren in these areas varied in a similar manner, and that public health conditions were at their worst in the poorest district, and at their best in the highest section.[17]

He pointed out that 'a high death rate implies a low standard of general health, and much sickness and suffering which is not registered'. Undoubtedly there was even more unregistered sickness and suffering in the 1840s, and much direct evidence shows that the Walmgate area, then as later, provided more than its proportionate share of this. Laycock's sanitary report shows the outlays in respect of sickness on members in different parts of the city, by six friendly societies on behalf of 2,385 members, 349 of whom had received sickness pay during 1843. It will be noticed that the Walmgate area referred to in tables 3.5 and 3.6 (districts 1 and 2) is roughly the same as the 'poorest' district mentioned by Rowntree.

TABLE 3.5 *Number of sick members of six benefit societies in six districts, 1843: duration of sickness and allowance received**

District	Mean altitude of district	No. Sick	Average duration of sick pay (weeks)	Sums paid per head during sickness (average)		
				£	s.	d.
1. Streets and courts adjoining west bank of the Foss	29	54	15.3	3	9	0
2. Walmgate and courts and lanes east of the Foss	31	43	7.9	2	4	8
3. Various streets and courts adjoining the Ouse	34	71	9.5	2	6	8
4. Old streets and courts, imperfectly paved and drained	44	62	9.2	2	6	7
5. New streets, imperfectly paved and drained	46	79	7.9	1	19	4
6. Comparatively well-paved and drained streets	53	40	5.9	1	7	10

* Laycock (1844) 237.

A similar table (table 3.6) showing the distribution of the sick attended by the medical officers of York Dispensary 1839–43, and of the medical officers of the Poor Law Union (1843 only), is equally eloquent.

TABLE 3.6 *Distribution of the sick attended by Medical Officers of York Dispensary, 1839–43, and by the Medical Officers of the Union, 1843**

District	Population	No. attended (with cases under 5 years in brackets – these are additional)	Proportion of all cases to the population
1. New streets and courts partially or wholly unpaved or drained	4,206	1,139 (80)	0.290
2. Old streets and courts partially paved or drained, not adjoining either river	5,565	2,021 (193)	0.398
3. Streets defectively drained, adjoining River Ouse	4,217	1,582 (198)	0.422
4. Streets defectively drained, adjoining Foss (west side)	2,934	1,378 (144)	0.519
5. Walmgate, etc. (east of Foss)	3,905	1,521 (149)	0.428
6. Other streets, generally well-paved and drained	6,603	810 (53)	0.131
	27,430	8,451 (817)	0.388

* Laycock (1844) 246.

(e) and (f) Irregularity of work and unemployment

A major variable governing the amount of poverty in nineteenth-century society was the employment situation. Rowntree attributed only 2 per cent of poverty to unemployment of the chief wage earner, and another 3 per cent to irregularity of work, but it should be remembered that 1899 was on the whole a prosperous and busy year. The only records capable of throwing any light on this question for the earlier period are those of the Board of Guardians. As a means of gauging unemployment they suffer from two defects; they measure expenditure rather than incidence, and naturally, all classes of paupers, not merely the unemployed, are included. Even so, a partial analysis, set against what is known of fluctuations in the local economy, has some value (table 3.7).

The inmaintenance series tells us comparatively little. In 1848 a new workhouse was brought into use after sustained

TABLE 3.7 *York Poor Law Union expenditure (£) 1841–51: City Relieving Officer's District**

Half-year ending	(i) Inmaintenance	(ii) Outdoor relief	
		(a) Settled	(b) Non-settled
Sept. 1841	255	2,767	206
Mar. 1842	247	2,988	260
Sept. 1842	236	2,959	385
Mar. 1843	209	3,428	287
Sept. 1843	251	3,147	361
Mar. 1844	268	3,083	434
Sept. 1844	227	2,949	506
Mar. 1845	252	3,079	591
Sept. 1845	184	2,735	730
Mar. 1846	241	2,564	781
Sept. 1846	243	2,506	841
Mar. 1847	275	3,140	418
Sept. 1847	287	3,680	261
Mar. 1848	314	3,620	250
Sept. 1848	Not available	3,146	249
Mar. 1849	,,	3,306	260
Sept. 1849	358	2,996	363
Mar. 1850	361	2,854	399
Sept. 1850	281	2,709	382
Mar. 1851	285	2,582	390
Sept. 1851	264	2,400	388

* *Sources*: For in maintenance, the General Ledgers of the Board (1848–9 missing). 'Quarterly bills' incurred by various parishes and townships were summed to produce column (i). For outdoor relief, the Minute Books of the Board, giving weekly returns, here summed into half-yearly totals distinguishing between relief given to those with settlements in the union and those who had not. Note that the table relates not to the Union as a whole, but to the City Relieving Officer's District, i.e. the Municipal Borough; in the annual published returns of the Poor Law Commissioners, this element cannot be distinguished.

pressure from the Poor Law Commissioners, so raising capacity to about 50,000 collective days per half year as against 17,000 for the old building. But the number of collective days passed in the workhouse was only about 12,000 in each of the summer half-years in 1841–2 and 1845, and 17–20,000 in the corresponding half-years of 1849–51.[18] The new building was only half-full at the census of 1851, and we may conclude that outdoor relief was vastly more important at all times.

Outdoor relief for those with settlements in the Union closely corresponds with what is known of the state of trade in the city.[19] Thus the years 1841–3 saw a mounting relief bill, as would be expected when work was difficult to obtain and wages were low. This was followed by diminished expenditure from summer 1843 to September 1846, doubtless aided by falling food prices but also reflecting the recovery of business and employment opportunities to which I have referred. From autumn 1846 the cost again rose, partly an artifact due to the reclassification of certain classes of paupers (see below), and partly reflecting an upsurge in food prices following the disastrous harvest of 1846. In addition, although employment opportunities in the city remained very good, there may have been some rise in the volume of *real* relief required, since it is unlikely that wages rose as fast as prices; having drawn attention to the sharp upward movement of food prices Joseph Rowntree remarked that 'with some trades there might have been an advance of wages . . . but the trades formed by far the larger proportion upon which no higher wages were paid'.[20] During the period from summer 1848 to September 1851 the amount fell to rather lower levels; the cost of living was declining, and the fall in real relief would not have been so great. But the employment situation remained generally good, and although there was some pressure on wages, these years evidently saw a real advance in standards of living for the urban working population.

The most striking feature of column ii (b), that is the non-settled (who could be persons who had lived in York for years, or recent immigrants), is the steady rise between summer 1843 and summer 1846. We have seen that these years were propitious for immigration, and if this was accompanied by increased relief for the non-settled, the explanation must lie in over-response; in other words the pull of the town beckoned more immigrants than could be speedily assimilated into employment, or flows were engendered out of proportion to the original disparity of incomes and opportunities.[21] The precipitous fall in 1846–7 merely reflects legislative change. By the Act 9 and 10 Vict., *c.* 66 certain classes of paupers were made irremovable and were henceforth charged to the appropriate York parishes, and by the subsequent measure 10 and 11 Vict., *c.* 110, were to be charged to the union as a whole.[22] Hence also, in part, the rise in outdoor relief to the settled (column ii (a)). From 1849 onwards expenditure on the non-settled was again running at rather higher levels; though employment opportunities were good enough to encourage further immigration, there may again have been some over-response.

In figure 3, the half-yearly totals for the settled (a) are compared with those for all outdoor relief (b). This shows that

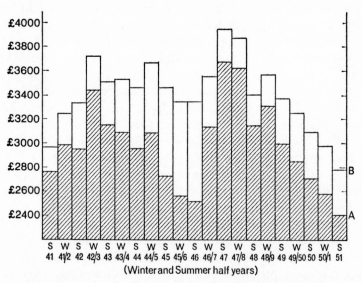

Fig. 3. Out-door relief in the City Relieving Officer's District

in the years 1843–6, the falling relief of the settled was partly offset by the rise in the demands of those whose settlements were elsewhere. Seen against this background, the subsequent rise of the cost of outdoor relief in the city as a whole was not so dramatic, but the marked improvement of the years 1848–51 remains. Certainly this is to be explained to some extent by the price fall of these years, but on the other hand it should not be forgotten that between 1841 and 1851, the population of the City Relieving Officer's District (i.e. the Municipal Borough) rose by 26 per cent. Thus in the round the decade can be viewed as one of improvement in the position of the wage-earning classes.

(f) The poverty cycle

Rowntree also drew particular attention to the 'poverty cycle', as it affected labouring men on basic unskilled wages, i.e. 18–21s. a week.

The life of a labourer is marked by five alternating periods of want and comparative plenty. During early childhood . . . he will be in poverty; this will last until he, or some of his brothers and sisters begin to earn money . . . then follows the period during which he is earning money and living under his parents' roof . . . this period of comparative plenty may continue after marriage until he has two or three children, when poverty will again overtake him. This period of poverty will last . . . [until his children begin to earn] . . . only to sink back again into poverty when his children have married and left him, and he himself is too old to work.[23]

In the 1851 sample, social classes III–V (to which the poverty cycle may be deemed relevant), yielded 1,038 adult household heads and wives, and 1,089 children to be taken into account. A scrutiny of ages and family composition in the enumerators' books permitted the following conclusions to be drawn:

(i) Respecting the 1,089 children: 10.9 per cent were only children and 26.8 per cent were in families of two children or more, where at least half the children were aged 13 or over (i.e. were

59

likely to be making a contribution to family income). *However,* 62.3 per cent were in families of two or more, where more than half the children were aged below 13.

(ii) Respecting the 1,038 heads and wives: 63.6 per cent had one or no children, or had two or more, where at least half were 13 or over. *But,* 36.4 per cent had two or more children where more than half were aged below 13.

(iii) Respecting 104 families headed by persons aged 60 and over (already included in (ii)): 50.0 per cent had at least one child at home (49.0 per cent at least one aged 13 or over). *On the other hand,* 50·0 per cent had no children at home.

This series of crude calculations should not be taken to mean that 62·3 per cent of the children in these classes were *in poverty,* or that 36·4 per cent of heads and wives were so placed, etc. Rather, they indicate the *potentiality for poverty* and enable us to gain some idea of the relative size of the vulnerable classes. This is another instance where comparative tables for other towns could be extremely fruitful, for, other things being equal, the communities with relatively large vulnerable classes defined in this way would be the seats of greater poverty.[24]

(g) Secondary poverty: the drink question

In 1901 the county borough of York had 338 licensed premises, comprising 236 'on' licences, and 102 'off' licences. This represented one licence to every 230 persons, York being seventh in a list of large towns. Rowntree's 'drink map' of York showed that the older streets within the city walls, especially within the areas inhabited by the poorer classes, had comparatively more licensed premises than other districts.[25] *Per capita* consumption of alcoholic beverages is believed to have been higher at the end of the nineteenth century than in the middle decades,[26] but it is quite possible that on the whole, a lower proportion of working-class incomes was spent on drink in the later period, when larger margins over the subsistence level were available.

For local evidence relating to the 1840s, all we have to

work with are the published statistics of persons in relevant occupations. The 1841 Census lists 2 beershop keepers (1 female), 88 hotel and innkeepers (28 female), 91 publicans and licensed victuallers (16 female), 11 spirit merchants (2 female) and 12 wine merchants, in all 204. To these may be added 43 brewers and 13 maltsters, making a total of 260 persons engaged in the drink trade – or, put another way, one to every 110 of the population.

In 1851, the census lists 141 innkeepers, (including 27 females), 75 beershop keepers and licensed victuallers, (18 females) 32 others of both sexes dealing in 'drinks and stimulants', and 41 wine and spirit merchants, in all 289. There were now 92 maltsters and brewers, and the ratio of all engaged in the liquor trade for this date was one to every 95 of the population. It looks as if the expansion of the trade was at least keeping up with the rise of the population, if not surpassing it. Pickwell believed there to have been only 187 public houses in 1835, but how comprehensive his coverage was cannot be judged.[27] If York is compared with the other eighteen towns in Rowntree's 1899 list,[28] in respect of the ratio of persons in the drink trade to total population, the mid-nineteenth century city emerges at the very top of the list. Its ratio of one drink worker to ninety-five population (1851) was unmatched by any other town, the values for the others ranging from 1 : 101 (Bristol) to 1 : 284 (Bradford). Excepting Bradford, all cities lay within the range 1 : 100 to 200. Of course, it is impossible to gauge the total volume of business, but it does look as if York was exceptionally well catered for by the licensed trade, especially when it is borne in mind that the city did not have an unusual proportion of persons engaged in drink manufacture, included in these ratios. No doubt this was partly due to the fact that York had prominent 'central place' functions. As a market town and regional distributive centre, its population was probably augmented very markedly on appointed days. Larger industrial towns may not have demonstrated this phenomenon to the same extent.

Rowntree's 1899 drink map showed that the vast majority of

licensed premises in York lay within one mile of the city centre –
and along certain streets (Walmgate, Micklegate, Goodramgate, etc.), leading out of the city. He remarked on the paucity
of licensed houses in 'the newer and outlying parts of the city',
even in new working-class districts.[29] For 1851, a list has been
made of household heads who were innkeepers, publicans,
licensed victuallers, hotel keepers, wine and spirit merchants,
porter and beer dealers and retailers, by parish. Those who
combined one of these trades with something distinct, (e.g.
tailor and publican), were included, but all 'retired' innkeepers,
etc., were excluded, as were those simply termed 'brewer'.
Ratios of population to the purveyors of drink were then worked
out, grouping parishes into 'concentric rings', with the results
given in table 3.8.

TABLE 3.8 *Ratio of population to drink purveyors in city centre, older suburbs
and new suburbs**

	(a) Population (1851)	(b) Drink purveyors	(c) Ratio (a)/(b)
(1) Intra-mural parishes	18,859	126	150
(2) Older suburbs (outside walls, but within municipal boundary)	17,444	55	317
(3) New suburbs (outside municipal but within parliamentary boundary)	4,056	10	406

* 1851 enumerators' schedules.

Very obviously the pattern which Rowntree discerned was
also prevalent fifty years before. There was an especially heavy
concentration of drink purveyors in the central parishes of All
Saints' Pavement, (one to every 47 of the population), St
Sampson, (1 to 58), Holy Trinity King's Court (1 to 80), St
Crux (1 to 84), and St Michael Spurriergate (1 to 73). These
parishes virtually encompassed the central market area of the
city, which at this period was in Pavement, St Sampson's
Square, and Parliament Street. These were obviously the best
sites for public-houses, and we may also take note of similar,

though less intensive concentrations in St Lawrence, and All Saints Peaseholme, which probably reflected the existence of the extensive cattle market in the former, and hay and wool markets in the latter. The other heavy or moderately heavy concentrations, (St Martin-cum-Gregory, St Dennis, Holy Trinity Goodramgate, St Wilfred, St John Delpike), were all adjacent to or lay along the principal routes leading out of the city, to the north, south, east and west.

Perhaps the most remarkable fact is that various poor and ill-conditioned parishes, such as St Cuthbert, St Saviour, St Margaret, St George, St Peter-le-Willows, did not exhibit a large proportion of drink purveyors. Nevertheless, it would be unwise to assume no connection between drink and poverty – in a city of this size, it would be impossible to point to any area where the nearest ale-house was more than a few minutes' walk away. As elsewhere, a lively temperance movement championed by leading nonconformists set out to expose 'the catalogue of crimes and domestic evils which flow from the tap-room and the beer-shop'; and the membership of the York Temperance Society is alleged to have moved from 363 (1837) to 729 (1841) and to 2,368 in 1852.[30]

STRENGTH OF THE LABOUR MOVEMENT

On its own terms, the tempo of political activity in York during the 1830s and 1840s is interesting enough; traditionally the city was regarded as a Whig stronghold, but the vigorous machinations of one man, George Hudson, achieved a temporary Tory dominance during the years between 1837 and the year of his downfall, 1849. Electoral bribery and corruption were rife, as elsewhere, and for the most part politics had little to do with social questions. In spite of an evident co-existence of poverty with considerable wealth, and major income inequalities, the various elements which historians usually link under the heading 'labour movement' appear to have been weakly represented.

For example, although knots of skilled artisans and tradesmen met from time to time to make speeches and pass resolutions, there was never any basis of mass support for Chartism in York. In July 1839, when signatures were being collected for the National Petition, only 300 or 400 were obtained at a 'sizeable' meeting. A Chartist lecture and demonstration held in June 1841 met with 'strong marks of disapprobation' from the audience, which showed, according to the Whig *York Herald*, that Chartism was 'but at a low ebb in York'.[31] Sporadic activity centred on the Chartist Association Rooms in Fossgate, but even when (at a by-election in May 1848), a curious combination of Chartist, anti-Hudsonian Tory and Radical forces described as 'the Hopwood clique' put forward the candidature of the Chartist leader H. R. Vincent, he secured only 860 votes.[32] By contrast, Nottingham had in the preceding summer elected the comparatively volatile Feargus O'Connor as one of its members.[33]

It is equally apparent that trade unionism was very weak in the area, throughout the nineteenth century. As late as 1899 only 3.3 per cent of the population were trade unionists, as compared with 4.4 per cent over the whole country and no doubt a higher figure than this in most urban areas. Although the railway industry was growing fairly rapidly during the 1840s, there was no trade union for these workers until 1871.[34] During the 1840s few examples of concerted industrial action can be found. In April 1841 journeymen joiners struck against the plan of their masters to extend the Saturday working day by one hour. There is no record of whether or not this defensive stand was successful. In 1846, a year of much better trade and good employment, the joiners struck successfully for a rise of 6d. per day. Later in the same year bricklayers and masons struck for higher wages. Their masters maintained that these demands were 'uncalled for either by the state of trade or the price of provisions', but although the outcome is not known, it is likely that the strike was successful in view of the boom conditions prevailing.[35] Finally, engine drivers and footplate workers on the York and North Midland Railway secured a substantial rise in their already relatively high rates of pay in the spring of

1850, along with the agreement of the directors that a yearly advance of 6d. per day should in future be given every twelve months 'for certain'.[36] This is all that has come to light, in reading the local press.

Co-operation in England had its origins in the activities of trade unionists, Chartists and Owenite socialists in the 1830s. The first permanently successful retail store was founded in Rochdale in 1844, and by 1851 130 Co-operative stores are said to have come into existence, mainly in the industrial districts of Yorkshire, Lancashire and Clydeside.[37] I have shown that York's population contained an unusually large proportion of retail shopkeepers, who could not be expected to welcome such a development. The trade union movement was almost non-existent and the forces of socialism and Chartism, although not entirely negligible, certainly commanded less support than in the manufacturing districts. Thus it is not surprising that York did not have a Co-operative Society until 1858. At that date the York Equitable Industrial Society was formed with 130 members, but even then, according to the historian of the movement, co-operation 'went slowly in York for the first thirty years of its existence'. Throughout the century the society was very largely dependent on the railway workers: sales in the first weeks of 1861 were £145: £97: £133 and £82, the alternation being due to the system of fortnightly pay at the railway works.[38]

In fact the most representative association to which workpeople and small tradesmen were likely to attach themselves was the friendly society, which with its ethos of individualism and self-help, and tendency to social exclusiveness, must be regarded as only very tenuously associated with the labour movement, although trade union historians usually refer to it in some measure.[39] Laycock noted the existence of forty such societies, either local or branches of the great national affiliated orders, in 1845.[40] On various assumptions set out elsewhere,[41] I have suggested that these would have had a total membership of some 3,200, which represents about 29 per cent of all males over 15. This compares unfavourably with a figure of 41 per cent for 1899, the latter being Rowntree's estimate of total membership divided by the 1901 population of males of 15 and over in the County Borough of York. Neither estimate makes any allowance for multiple membership. Very probably the intervening period saw the accession to membership of more labouring men; in the records of one society numbering from 5–600 members in the 1840s, there is a list of members surviving in 1861. The first 'labourer' does not appear until 1827, and only thirty-three are listed for the whole of the period 1827–51.[42]

EDUCATIONAL FACILITIES AND THE EXTENT OF LITERACY

In these respects York was a fortunate city by contemporary standards. In a report prepared in 1836–7 by the Manchester Statistical Society, the fact that only 19.9 per cent of the whole population attended day and secondary schools appeared to contrast unfavourably with proportions of 21.7 per cent for Manchester, 23.4 per cent (Salford), and 28.6 per cent (Bury). On the twin assumptions that 5–15-year-olds made up one-quarter (7,000) of a total population still growing, in 1831–6, at the rate ascertained for 1821–31, it appeared that 67 per cent of the age-group were receiving some form of instruction in various schools, and 33 per cent were not.[43] In fact the impression given by this report is unduly gloomy. To begin with, the proportion of population attending *day* schools was considerably higher in York than in the other communities studied (17 per cent in York, 10 in Manchester, 11.9 in Salford, 13.1 in Bury, and 12.8 in Liverpool), as their own report shows.[44] Moreover, it is clear that the critical assumptions made in estimating the size of the population 'at risk' were seriously in error. If we suppose that the figure for 5–15-year-olds was the same in 1836 as it was in 1841 (a generous assumption), then the true number is 5,698 not 7,000; and the 4,700 scholars in the age-group represented not 67 per cent, but in fact 82.4, or 69.8 per cent even if Sunday and evening scholars are excluded.

Between 1837 and my next point of reference, the Education

Census of 1851, much new school-building occurred in York
and its environs, including church or national schools in Walmgate (1842), Bishopgate Street (1851), Clifton (1841), Dring-
houses (1849); and nonconformist day schools such as Albion
St (Wesleyan, 1840), St Saviourgate (Congregationalist, 1844),
St George's (Wesleyan, 1847), together with St Mary's Girls'
school and St George's Boys' School in Walmgate (Roman
Catholic, 1844 and 1851). Yet between 1841 and 1851 the size
of the 5–14 age-group rose by 1,566 (26 per cent) in the Municipal Borough alone, and there can have been little, if any,
reduction of the 'deficit' revealed in the 1836–7 enquiry.
Briefly, the situation shown by the 1851 census was that in the
Municipal Borough, 5,784 children were being educated in
private or public day schools, i.e. excluding Sunday schools,
because no effort was made to distinguish what proportion of
children attended both.[45] It may safely be assumed that about
83 per cent of these scholars were aged 5–14. There is no
breakdown for York itself, but for England and Wales, the
proportion was 82.47 per cent, for the East Riding including
York 84.10 per cent, and for Lancashire 82.26 per cent, all on
the basis of limited numbers of returns; in the 1836 York survey
the proportion of scholars of this age had been 83.83 per cent.
In York 4,800 scholars (83 per cent of 5,784) were therefore
in all likelihood aged 5–14, which amounts to 66.1 per cent of
the age-group in the Municipal Borough. This figure relates to
the proportion of the age-group 5–14 which attended day
schools, and as such is comparable with the figure of 69.8 per
cent or thereabouts for 1836. Given the assumptions that have
been made, it would be unreasonable to conclude that there
was an actual decline in the proportion of the age-group
undergoing day-school education; rather let us say that so far
as can be seen, there was no great change. School building and
the provision of further places had progressed rapidly in the
1840s, but the expansion of the population in the relevant age-
groups had roughly kept pace with it.

On the other hand, York managed to maintain a better level
of provision than did the nation as a whole and certainly than

the neighbouring industrial towns. The proportion of under-20-year-olds not given a specific occupation in the 1851 published abstracts was 72.8 per cent for males and 82.8 per cent for females, comparable proportions for Leeds being 66.5 and 74.9, and for Bradford 59.6 and 61.6. Those specifically described as 'scholar at home' or 'scholar at school' amounted to 39.4 per cent of the male and 37.0 per cent of the female age-group, but for Leeds only 30.2 and 28.9 per cent, and for Bradford 24.1 and 20.8 per cent respectively. Further confirmation of York's superiority over manufacturing districts is given by table 3.9, which, however, relates to the union (registration district) as a whole.

TABLE 3.9   *Proportion of scholars aged 5–14 to population aged 5–14 in 1851 (Day schools only)**.

	(a)	(b)	(c)	(d)
		No. of scholars aged 5–14		Col. (b) as
	No. of scholars	(84 per cent of col. (a))	Population aged 5–14	percentage of col. (c)
York R.D.	9,034	7,589	11,718	64.8
Bury R.D.	9,821	8,250	20,151	40.9
Manchester R.D.	19,741	16,582	47,128	35.2
Salford R.D.	7,523	6,319	18,557	34.1
Liverpool R.D.	27,627	23,067	51,639	44.7
England and Wales	2,108,592	1,771,217	4,005,716	44.2

* 1851 Educational Census and Age abstract.

From 1839 onwards, the Registrar-General included in his annual reports, literacy data for both men and women derived from the civil marriage registers. In these statistics, signing with a mark is taken to imply illiteracy, and table 3.10 indicates that the levels indicated in the registers of the early 1850s and 1860s, were comparatively low in York Registration District, both for males and for females, although there was everywhere a marked difference between the two sexes.

The trend in all registration districts seem to have been to improvement between the marriages of 1851–3 and 1861–5,

TABLE 3.10   *Illiteracy levels in various districts: proportion of persons signing the marriage register with marks* *

	Males	Females
1851–3		
York R.D.	21.3	32.9
Manchester R.D.	28.4	59.8
Salford R.D.	23.3.	52.4
Bury R.D.	36.7	69.4
Liverpool R.D.	28.1	50.2
England and Wales	30.5	44.6
1861–5		
York R.D.	12.8	21.9
Manchester R.D.	19.4	46.3
Salford R.D.	24.2	50.0
Bury R.D.	24.2	48.2
Liverpool R.D.	24.8	42.1

* Registrar-General's Annual Reports.

which would involve young people educated during the 1840s. How much significance ought to be attached to this is obviously arguable, but at least it can hardly be doubted that the position in the York district remained relatively good. It is true that the figures cover the registration district, and embrace a wide expanse of countryside; but since in 1851, the Municipal Borough had 64 per cent of all scholars in the union, and 62 per cent of all children aged 5–14, there was probably little difference between York itself and the rural part of the union in respect of literacy.

Of course, many of the people covered by table 3.10 would have been educated elsewhere – that is, they were the immigrants discussed in the next chapter; and it is particularly interesting to link these literacy figures with those established for a number of rural East Riding parishes from *parochial* register material of an earlier period. In 1754–60 the proportion of illiterates has been put at 36 per cent for males and 61 per cent for females; by the 1840s the illiteracy level in these parishes was down to 27 and 42 per cent respectively.[46] Educational provision seems to have been well above average in the rural area from which many of York's immigrants were drawn; and if the early decades of the Industrial Revolution are associated with a catastrophic shortfall in regular educational provision and literacy levels elsewhere,[47] increased population and urganization does not seem to have overwhelmed provision in this region.

Naturally, qualifications must be made; whilst the position in York and the results achieved were good by the standards of the time, one must note:

(i) Attendance was never anything like so great as the calculated number of school places. For example, in five of the six government-aided schools in 1850, accommodation (at 6 sq. ft each) was available for 200, 296, 407, 285 and 400 pupils (totalling to 1,588): while average attendance in 1850 was 140, 161, 110, 269 and 268 respectively (totalling 940 or 59 cent).[48] Clearly, the ratio of average attendance to places was much lower than today. No doubt more days were lost in illness by the average pupil in the year, and in a non-compulsory setting the attitude of both children and parents to regular schooling must have differed greatly. Further evidence of the short and intermittent character that a child's educational career could take is given when the age groupings of the pupils at the Manor School in 1849 are scrutinized:[49]

ages of children	7	8	9	10	11	12	13	14
number in school	92	29	59	41	16	17	7	8

(ii) It is clear that the provision of educational facilities within the city varied from district to district. The local Quakers had studied education on a parish by parish basis in 1826.[50] Their findings for the different parishes may be grouped by the registration sub-districts of the future, giving rise to table 3.11.

Similarly, this material data may be related to Laycock's drainage altitude data with the telling results given in table 3.12.

On the other hand we have seen that so far as the schools in the public sector were concerned, the provision of education in the under-privileged parts of the town was receiving more

TABLE 3.11 *Proportion of children attending school in sub-districts, by age-group, 1826**

	Aged 6–10	Aged 10–12	Proportion of household heads in classes I–II (1841)
(a) Micklegate	78.3	74.3	24.1 (±7.2)
(b) Bootham	78.1	70.2	36.6 (±7.4)
(c) Walmgate	70.8	61.8	21.1 (±5.3)

* Manchester Statistical Society (1836) xv, with parish data arranged by sub-districts, as in Statistical Appendix, III. For class composition see notes to table 5.9.

TABLE 3.12 *Proportion of children attending school in parishes of varying drainage altitudes**

	Below 35 ft	35–44 ft	Above 45 ft
(1) Aged 6–10	70.8	74.9	79.7
(2) Aged 10–12	64.1	67.1	72.3

* Manchester Statistical Society (1836) xv; Laycock (1844), Sanatory Table (see figure 4).

vigorous attention in the 1830s and 1840s. In Walmgate the opening of two national schools, St George's Wesleyan and the Congregationalist and Catholic schools provided for nearly a thousand extra schoolchildren by 1851. Yet it must be remembered that the population of 5–15-year-olds in that area must have increased by *at least* that amount in the decade 1841–51, and very probably by more. We do not have data on the age-structure for 1841 at the sub-district level, but there were 4,113 5–14-year-olds in 1851, and if the number had increased over the decade by only 26 per cent,[51] this alone would have filled the extra places, leaving the original problem untouched. There is thus every reason to believe that despite the vigorous efforts of churchmen and nonconformists alike, Walmgate remained an educationally under-privileged sector of the city in 1851.

(iii) Quite apart from the public schools, the distribution of

71

private instruction, boarding schools, academies, etc., was exceedingly skewed. They were to be found almost wholly within the better districts in and around the town. In a directory of 1851, forty such institutions are listed; twenty-two (55 per cent) were in Bootham sub-district, fifteen (37 per cent) in Micklegate, and three (7.5 per cent only) in Walmgate. There were virtually none in the poorest districts of all in the neighbourhood of the Foss.[52]

RELIGIOUS OBSERVANCE

In an age when religious observance was far more widespread than today, church attendance levels in York were well above national levels and much in excess of those found in the great industrial towns. The unique Religious census of 1851 enquired into attendances at each place of worship on Sunday 30 March, and into the number of sittings available. The accuracy of the returns was then and has since been impugned, and there is a growing critical literature on this question,[53] but I shall accept the verdict of *The Times* newspaper and of Inglis, that whatever exaggeration occurred was slight, that it was not confined to the returns for any particular body, and that the returns may be taken as 'substantially accurate and trustworthy'.[54] The chief difficulty in interpreting the results, both on the national and local level, is that no account was taken of those who attended at more than one divine service. This led the official in charge, Horace Mann, to suggest that the formula $1 + \frac{1}{2} + \frac{1}{3}$ of the morning, afternoon and evening services would give a reasonable approximation to the actual numbers attending; although Inglis prefers simply to aggregate the totals (in effect $1 + 1 + 1$ as the weighting factors), in arriving at comparative statistics for different towns.[55]

However the question is approached, it is clear that both provision and attendances in York were very high. Mann calculated that when allowances were made for infants, invalids, the very aged and those engaged in necessary duties elsewhere, provision should be made for 58 per cent of the population:

York had sittings for 65.1 per cent, in which respect it stood third in the list of seventy-two large towns and boroughs, of which only nine attained the suggested 58 per cent.[56] On the Mann formula York had an attendance rate distinctly over the national average (with omission corrections to both), that is 510 per 1,000 against 405 nationally. If Inglis's 'attendance index' is preferred, (sum of all attendances, equally weighted, divided by population), the figure for York (62.3) is again above the national average (61), a distinction shared with only thirteen other large towns (Colchester, Exeter, Bath, Ipswich, Reading, Cambridge, Dover, Cheltenham, Worcester, Northampton, Southampton, and perhaps more surprisingly, Wakefield and Leicester). The average figure for all large towns (49.7) was not attained in any of the eight parliamentary boroughs of London, nor in twenty-one towns which lay within 'the chief manufacturing districts'.[57]

Two qualifying points may be made; first that although in York the Church of England provided 51.5 per cent of all sittings (52.0 per cent nationally), it did not attract a commensurate share of worshippers. Inglis found that nonconformist attendances outnumbered established church attendances in twenty out of twenty-nine towns in the chief manufacturing districts; in a further eleven Roman Catholic attendances prevented either from reaching 50 per cent, and in these church attendances were exceeded by nonconformist in five cases. These were Blackburn, Newcastle, Bolton, Manchester and Preston.[58] Very surprisingly, the same applied in the Metropolitan see and cathedral city of York, where the proportionate attendances, on the same basis, work out to: Church of England 43.2 per cent, Nonconformist 46.3 per cent, and Roman Catholic 10.5 per cent.

Secondly, provision of places and attendances varied widely across the city. Original returns survive at the Public Record Office for seventeen Anglican places of worship, but those for seven more, all in the Walmgate sub-district, have been lost.[59] Total provision and attendance for the Walmgate parishes can, however, be arrived at by deducting Bootham and Micklegate figures from those given for the city as a whole in the printed report of the Religious Census. It is then possible to show that Anglican provision in Bootham and Micklegate (taken together), amounted to one seat for 2.23 persons, whilst underprivileged Walmgate had only one for 4.97. Similarly, in Bootham and Micklegate one person in 1.83 attended Anglican services, against one in 4.14 in the Walmgate parishes. When nonconformist places of worship are treated on the same basis, the differences are less obvious (one place to 3.26 population in Micklegate and Bootham, one to 3.90 in Walmgate; attendances one in 3.40 in Bootham–Micklegate, one in 3.48 in Walmgate), but also less meaningful, since it may be assumed that dissenters would tend to converge on a particular chapel from all parts of the city, according to its sectarian standpoint, (e.g. to the single church of the Society of Friends), which would probably not have been the case to the same extent with the Anglicans.[60]

In general, the selected features of social life which have been reviewed in this chapter may be understood in terms of the pre-industrial character of the town and its relatively sedate pace of development. We have seen that York coped more than adequately (by contemporary standards) with the education question, and the data on religious observance are especially meaningful. In the great towns, lower attendance rates were attributed to the fact that the 'labouring myriads' habitually absented themselves owing to the maintenance of class distinction in church, to a feeling that professed Christians had insufficient sympathy for their social burdens, to a mistrust of the motives of the ministry, and to poverty and overcrowding, 'that condition which forbids all solitude and all reflection'.[61] This complex of causes may have been in evidence to some degree in York as the Walmgate figures suggest, but taking the city as a whole, surely to a lesser extent than in the great manufacturing towns? After all, the proportion of small shop-keepers and petty manufacturers was much higher, and by the same token, that of persons in a distinctively 'proletarian' situation lower; overcrowding may have been less marked than in other towns; ministers of religion must have been familiar figures, bearing in mind their large numbers and the small size of the city; and it is not unreasonable to suppose that the forces of tradition were much stronger in York than in towns where rapid transformation had been experienced.

On poverty the evidence is difficult to sum up except that we can certainly say that it was more apparent than in Rowntree's day though for much the same causes. If it were possible to strike on average *per capita* income level, I should guess that the figure for York may have been on the national level, or even a little above it; but the co-existence of high proportions in public and professional services, and with 'independent means' on the one hand; and above average proportions of general labourers and female domestics on the other, suggests that the degree of inequality of wealth and income would have been higher in York than in, say, the great industrial towns.[62] Yet this did not engender a coherent working-class self-consciousness, as the mild manifestations of workers' political, trade union and industrial action show. No doubt status differences were keenly felt, but these had always characterized the pre-industrial order, and general acceptance mingled with some resentment would, I surmise, be the common attitude. The fact was, that society was composed of groups, the divisions between which were so 'obvious and irrefragable' in Checkland's phrase,[63] that they would have seemed part of the natural order.

Situations of *class* confrontation may be presumed to be fostered by the decisive physical segregation and consequent mutual incomprehension of those whose incomes and life-styles in any case served to set them apart. In some 'advanced' communities of the period, this was indeed the case, as Foster's example of Oldham suggests.[64] It is also perhaps implied in Chadwick's significant remark in his *Report on the Sanitary Condition of the Labouring Population of Great Britain*, 'when Dr. Arnott with myself and others were examining the abodes of the poorest classes in Glasgow and Edinburgh, we were regarded with astonishment; and it was frequently declared by the inmates, that they had never for many years witnessed the approach or the presence of persons of that condition near them'.[65]

York was different, both in its scale and nature. Suburbanization was not as yet more than embryonic, and Thernstrom's description of a small New England city in the early nineteenth century would apply; 'the distinct class-segregated neighbourhoods of the modern city did not exist. There were no working-class ghettoes, nor had the merchant and professional classes abandoned the central business district of the city as a place of residence'.[66] This is not to say that people of all social gradations were randomly intermingled; of course individual streets and courts had their own homogeneity of social status. For that matter, there were broad differences in class-composition between Walmgate sub-district, taken as a whole, and Bootham and Micklegate. Yet, none of these was without a significant representation of higher-class residents on the one hand, and labouring men on the other.[67] In short, with certain qualifications noticed in chapters 4 and 5, the classic description of land-use patterns adumbrated for the pre-industrial city by Sjoberg largely holds true for York, including a persistent tendency for *élite* groups to reside in central districts, the existence of certain finer spatial differences according to ethnic, occupational and family ties, and rather a low incidence of functional differentiation in other land-use patterns.[68]

These configurations, and the nature of the social relationships which they encouraged, had long and tenacious historical roots. No doubt things were different in the great manufacturing towns, but it has been wisely remarked that 'the first effect of early industrialization was to differentiate English communities rather than to standardize them'.[69]

4 The growth of population: migration and natural increase

During the first fifty years of the nineteenth century, many northern industrial towns experienced unprecedented rates of population growth; thus, for example, the censuses show that the population of Bradford grew by 700 per cent between 1801 and 1851, whilst Liverpool, Huddersfield, Manchester and Leeds attained 359, 343, 304 and 225 per cent respectively. York was not in this class, but its overall growth of 112 per cent was distinctly better than that achieved by a number of other old county towns; the increase of population in Exeter over the period was 94 per cent, whilst Norwich, Chester and Shrewsbury managed only 89, 87 and 33 per cent, and even partially industrialized Nottingham grew by only 97 per cent.

TABLE 4.1   *Growth of the population of York, 1801–51**

	Population (York Municipal Borough)	% Increase	Population (York Parliamentary Borough)	% Increase	England and Wales (% Increase)
1801	16,846	–	–	–	–
1811	19,099	12.8	–	–	14.3
1821	21,711	13.7	–	–	18.1
1831	26,260	20.5	–	–	15.8
1841	28,842	9.8	30,152	–	14.5
1851	36,303	25.9	40,359	33.8	12.7

* Census enumeration abstracts, 1801–51.

Table 4.1 indicates that the population of York grew less rapidly than did that of the nation as a whole over the first twenty years of the century, but that the twenties saw a spurt of growth. The city appears to have lost ground once again, relatively, in the 1830s, although this may have been due in some measure to the movement of some citizens into embryonic suburbs, especially Clifton, which fell within the parliamentary limits but outside the Municipal Borough. The decade 1841–51 witnessed the most spectacular rate of growth especially of the Parliamentary Borough.

CALCULATING THE LEVEL OF IMMIGRATION

Breaking down these gross decadal increases into natural increase and immigration components is difficult on the basis of the scanty records of the period: but three methods, albeit crude, may be brought to bear for the period 1801–41:

(A) The parish register abstracts, compiled by John Rickman and published along with successive censuses, 1801–41, may be used as a basis for calculating natural increases (baptisms minus burials) by decade; whilst subtracting the natural increases, so calculated, from the inter-censal population increases will give an indication of net immigration, or emigration. The reliability of the method depends on the degree of omission in the abstracts, which could be considerable,[1] and the data is available only for the calendar years 1801–10, 1811–20, etc., whilst the censuses were usually taken in May. Although the correction is arbitrary, it seems prudent to adjust the baptismal and burial records in accordance with the multipliers suggested by Griffith, prior to performing this calculation; that is, to inflate baptisms by 15 per cent, and burials, by 10 per cent.[2]

(B) One can apply national growth rates to arrive at an estimate of what the city's total population would have been at the end of each decade, had these rates also applied in York. The difference between the estimated and observed population is taken to represent net migration. This is the method favoured by Sigsworth and others.[3] The disadvantage is obvious; York rates of natural increase may have differed very considerably from those recorded nationally, as a result of disparate birth, death or marriage rates, or all three.

(C) A variant on (B), substituting for the national rates of increase the significantly lower rates of natural increase which are implied by the calculations attempted below, in chapters 5 and 6.[4]

Table 4.2 draws together the results of estimates made along these lines.

TABLE 4.2 *Estimated net gains* (+) *and losses* (—) *by migration, York Municipal Borough, 1801–41**

	(i) Method A	(ii) Method B	(iii) Method C
1801–11	+894	—105	+1,035
1811–21	+541	—844	—21
1821–31	+2,085	+1,119	+2,279
1831–41	–	—1,173	—166

* Sources stated in text.

Whichever method is preferred, the conclusion must be that the city's net gains were at best very modest indeed in the years 1801–21; during which period, applying method B, Leeds gained 12,000. Subsequently, after a fairly substantial net gain of perhaps 2,000 in the years 1821–31, York's capacity to attract a positive inflow fell away very sharply indeed; the results for 1831–41 indicate stagnation and possibly a small net loss by emigration.

The decade 1841–51 is the focal period of this study, and it is fortunate that, with the advent of civil registration in 1837, a much superior technique of gauging the net flow can be brought into play.

(D) This method, which was devised by Shannon and Grebenik for the study of historical population trends in Bristol, has been applied to York by Sigsworth.[5] The stages of the calculation are as follows: given that for a registration district, the initial population is known, together with decennial totals of births and deaths, then the rate of increase or decrease can be worked out for the district. In this case the York Union is the relevant registration district, and its rate of increase of population can be worked out using the Registrar-General's statistics of birth and deaths. The registration district includes, as a large part of its population, an urban area (City of York). Assuming little difference in the rate of natural increase between the rural and the urban parts of the area, one can apply the calculated rate of increase for the *district* as a whole to the actual population of the *urban area* at the beginning of the decade. In this way it is possible to estimate what the urban area's population would have been at the end of the decade, had no migration occurred. This figure may be compared with the actual population of the urban area at the end of the decade (the census total), and the difference is deemed to be the result of net migration. For the decade in question, the registration district population was 47,778 in 1841: over the years 1842–1851 (inclusive) there were 16,012 births and 12,741 deaths, yielding a net natural increase of 3,271, or 6.8 per cent. The population of the Municipal Borough, (the urban unit chosen by Sigsworth), was 28,842 at the beginning of the decade, and if the 6.8 per cent rate of growth by natural increase is applied to this figure, then York's population would have increased by 1,970. Since the actual increase was 7,561, Sigsworth concluded that approximately 5,591 of the increase of the urban area derived from immigration, and 1,970 from natural increase.

Once again the deficiencies of the method are obvious. In the first place, registration of births was not explicitly made the responsibility of parents until 1874.[6] Secondly, the unit for which registration particulars are available is, in this instance, considerably larger than the borough; clearly this is a method which would be most effective for cities which directly coincided with registration districts, for example Nottingham or Liverpool. Even so, there are two ways of improving upon Sigsworth's estimate and conclusions for the decade 1841–51. To begin with, the area and population of the York Registration District may be 'narrowed'. It consisted of seven sub-districts, Micklegate, Bootham and Walmgate; and Skelton, Dunnington, Escrick and Flaxton. In fact the urban entity of York (whether defined by municipal or parliamentary boundaries), extended only into the first three of these sub-districts. (see map 1.) Since there is data on births and deaths at sub-district level, the purely rural elements may be dropped from the calculation. Secondly, Sigsworth analysed the population increment of the Municipal Borough only for the decade 1841–51. It is difficult to see why, for he continued the calculation using the parliamentary boundaries from 1851 onwards,

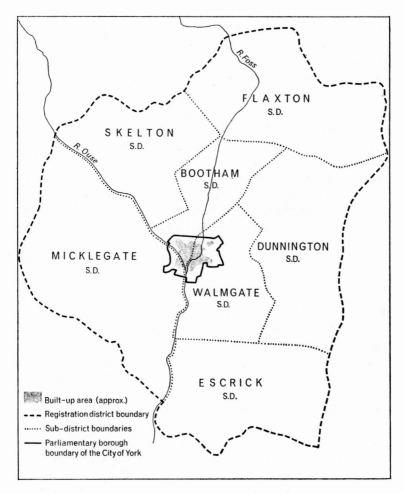

Map 1. York Registration District

and the 1841 census does give a total population for the Parliamentary Borough.

Using the same basic method, a recalculation may be performed. Our registration district (now comprising only Micklegate, Bootham and Walmgate sub-districts), had a population of 38,406 in 1841. In the years 1842–51, 10,945 deaths and 13,273 births occurred, giving a net natural increase of 6.1 per cent for this area. This figure is not, as it happens, markedly different from Sigsworth's estimate for the Registration District as a whole (6.8 per cent).

The 1841 population of the Parliamentary Borough was 30,152. Applying the 6.1 rate of natural increase figure to this, the natural increase would have been 1,819 by 1851. The net increase as represented by census figures for that unit was 10,207, which suggests that the Parliamentary Borough experienced a net increase of 1,819 by natural increase, and 8,388 by net inward migration. If applied to the Municipal Borough, the 6.1 per cent rate of natural increase seems to suggest that a slightly lower proportion of the net population increase came from natural increase, and a slightly higher proportion from immigration, than Sigsworth allowed. In this case, the total population increase was 7,561 (as we have already seen), but we can now estimate the natural increase as being about 1,759: and the net increase by migration as 5,802.

It is hardly necessary to repeat Sigsworth's strictures on the nature of the approach. The modifications of the method have shown that his estimates for the Municipal Borough remain substantially correct, even when various refinements have been made. On the other hand, our attention is drawn to the expansion of the Parliamentary Borough, which showed a more dramatic rise in population resulting from immigration than had been suspected. Of course, all calculations carried out on these lines are dependent on the assumption that the rate of natural increase in the Registration District did not differ materially from that of the Municipal Borough (in Sigsworth's calculation): or that the rate of natural increase in a large proportion of the Registration District did not differ markedly from that of the Parliamentary Borough (in my revision). The assumption may be checked by reference to the rate of natural increase in the rural sub-districts of Flaxton, Dunnington, Escrick and Skelton. Did it differ markedly from the 6.1 per cent figure for the rest of the York Registration District? In these sub-districts, 1,796 deaths and 2,739 births occurred, giving a percentage increase of 10.1 for the period 1841–51, on a base population of 9,372.[7] This conclusion underlines the scepticism with which one must treat all such calculations, but justifies the attempt to 'narrow' the size of the Registration District which has been used to derive the rate of natural increase. Only 60.3 per cent of the population of the entire registration district lay within the Municipal Borough, and 63.1 per cent within the Parliamentary Borough, the unit Sigsworth declined to use. In my 'narrowed' registration district, 75.1 per cent of the population lay within the Municipal Borough and 78.5 per cent in the Parliamentary Borough.

We are now in a position to conclude that during the 1840s York was gaining immigrants on an unprecedented scale. Indeed, the influx bears comparison with that indicated by applying method B to Leeds township (+ 8,550) or Hull (+ 7,600). Never again, during the remainder of the century, did the net immigration gain approach these levels, for as Sigsworth has shown by extending the Shannon–Grebenik method forward, the most favourable decade was 1871–81 (+ 3,632) and the worst 1881–91 (− 66).[8]

One fundamental objection may be made to the various calculations performed so far, even including the Shannon–Grebenik technique: it is that all natural increase is in effect attributed to the original population at the commencement of each decade, as if to suggest that the immigrants were both immortal and impotent. In reality they themselves accounted for some unknown proportion of the natural increase. One is led to ask, would the population of York have grown at all, had it not been for immigration?

To answer this question, it is necessary to have knowledge of the age–sex composition of the initial population, and the rates of mortality and fertility which applied, which is not the case until the 1840s. By this date, projecting these rates makes it possible to arrive at a rough estimate of the total such a closed population would have reached by the end of a ten-year period, had no migration occurred and had vital rates remained unchanged. Once again, the method would work best where registration district and urban area were identical; for York age–sex distributions exist for the Municipal Borough only, and the published vital rates are obtainable only for the larger, registration district which of course contained a substantial rural minority.

Nevertheless, something is to be gained from a projection of trends in the borough, by performing a series of simple calculations, in three stages:

(i) Starting with the male age-distribution of 1841, we have 1,680 individuals aged 0–4, 1,436 aged 5–9, etc. Because it is not known how the 1,680 individuals were distributed within each age-group, and in order to simplify the arithmetic, the first 1,680 are assumed to be aged 2, on the average; in the same way the 1,436 5–9-year-olds are assumed to be 7, etc. Next, one can read off, from the *English Life Table No. 3*, the chances of 2-year-olds surviving 10 years to age 12, 7-year-olds to 17, etc. This assumes that York mortality rates were much the same as national levels for 1838–54, on which the life-table is based; in general, except for York's somewhat higher infant and child mortality, they were.[9] Thus, for males, the following steps occur:

(a) Age Group	(b) No. in 1841	(c) Assumed mean age	(d) Life table survival factor (2 to 12 : 7 to 17, etc.)	(e) Survivors in 1851 (b) × (d)	(f) Actual Nos. in census	(g) Difference (f) − (e)
0–	1,680	2	0.872	1,465	1,816	+351
5–	1,436	7	0.942	1,353	1,610	+257
10–	1,312	12	0.939	1,232	1,516	+284
15–	1,214	17	0.921	1,118	1,454	+336
20–	1,327	22	0.910	1,208	1,326	+118
25–	1,163	27	0.900	1,047	1,140	+ 93
30–	1,176	32	0.888	1,044	1,042	− 2
35–	854	37	0.871	744	845	+101
40–	812	42	0.846	687 ⎫	1,099	− 30
45–	546	47	0.810	442 ⎭		
50–	892	55	0.719	641	734	+ 93
60–	601	65	0.503	302 ⎫	368	− 9
70–	336	75	0.223	75 ⎭		
				11,358	12,950	+1,592

A similar series of calculations may be performed for females, with the abbreviated results given below.

(a) Age group	(b) No. in 1841	(e) Survivors in 1851	(f) Actual Nos. in Census	(g) Difference (f) − (e)
0–	1,713	1,494	1,823	+329
5–	1,500	1,410	2,015	+605
10–	1,450	1,357	2,010	+653
15–	1,590	1,458	1,756	+298
20–	1,690	1,529	1,457	− 72
25–	1,453	1,302	1,271	− 31
30–	1,258	1,116	1,133	+ 17
35–	874	765	900	+135
40–	897	772 ⎫	1,382	+116
45–	590	494 ⎭		
50–	1,064	796	949	+153
60–	826	445 ⎫	695	+120
70–	513	130 ⎭		
		13,068	15,391	+2,323

(ii) Next, an estimate of the number of births which would have accrued to the initial population must be made, however roughly. We have no detailed knowledge of age-specific fertility in York around 1841, but the number of births occurring per 1,000 women aged 15–44 at that time for the York registration district as a whole was 114, as against 135 for England and Wales.[10] Now, the number of women actually at risk would be (approximately) 7,967 – this is a simple average of the number of females in the age-group 15–44 in 1841, and the projected comparable figure for 1851. In ten years (on the rate of 114 per 1,000 given above) these would produce

$$\frac{7,967}{1,000} \times 114 \times 10 \text{ births, i.e. } 9,082$$

or 908 per annum.

(iii) These children would range between 0 and 9 years of age in 1851, but some account must be taken of child mortality in thinning their ranks. I assume that the births can be equally distributed over ten years, and, by reference to the *English Life Table*, calculate the proportion of 908 births (of 1841) surviving to age 10 (in 1851); of 908 births (of 1842) surviving to age 9 (in 1851), etc. On the basis of these calculations, there would have been 6,783 0–9-year-olds in York in 1851. As it happened, the actual number enumerated in 1851 in this age-group was 7,982, implying that an unchanging native population could have provided the majority of children, but that the (net) adult immigrant inflow accounted for the presence up to about 1,200 of the 0–9 age-group in 1851, who presumably would have been too young, in all but the most exceptional cases, to have arrived there independently.

It would be possible, even now, to refine this calculation to a very considerable extent in considering towns which were themselves entire registration districts, in that one could utilize published local age-specific mortality rates to construct an appropriate life-table, as against relying on national rates; and in time to come, if free access to the Registrar-General's original records of births, deaths comes to pass, it will become worthwhile to improve the precision of the method out of all recognition. But with all its evidence crudities as employed here, it succeeds in showing that:

(i) Given the existing age–sex structure of 1841, and assuming no changes in mortality and fertility, York had some, though limited potentiality for population growth, migration being left out of account. Summing the projected population figures for 1851 (11,358 males and 13,068 females of 10 years and over, plus 6,783 0–9-year-olds) yields 31,209, as against a total census population of 28,842 in 1841.

(ii) The greater part of the actual inter-censal increase in the Municipal Borough can however be ascribed to net immigration, that is 5,114, or 68 per cent.[11]

(iii) The attractions of York were somewhat greater for females than for males, since a net gain of 2,323 females aged 10 and over is implied, as against 1,592 for males. One is reminded of Ravenstein's seventh 'law of migration', that females are more migratory than males, at least over short distances.[12]

(iv) In the case of both sexes, the gains were most obvious among those aged 10–29 in 1851 (see column (g) in each case). Indeed, these accounted for some 80 per cent of the total adult immigration gain (i.e. those age-groups covered in the tables). That migration was normally age-selective is of course well-known, but few attempts have as yet been made to measure to what extent this was so.

In concluding this analysis, it is important to emphasize that I have framed the discussion in terms of *net* gains and losses rather than gross flows. In point of fact the *turnover* of population must have been far greater than any of these calculations imply. No account has been taken of mortality among immigrant adults, though clearly they were mostly of an age where rates would be comparatively low. Much more important is the point that emigrants leaving York are not considered. Accordingly, when one examines by means of the 1851 census sample, the birthplaces of household heads and their wives by age-group (table 4.3), it is obvious that York must have drawn immigrants on a substantial scale throughout the first half of the nineteenth century; correspondingly, there must also have been some very significant outflows, especially in the decades when the net migration gain was slight, or even non-existent (1811–21, 1831–41 for example).

TABLE 4.3 *Birthplaces of household heads and wives recorded in 1851, by age-group (Parliamentary Borough)**

	Household heads		Wives	
	Percentage born in York	Percentage immigrant	Percentage born in York	Percentage immigrant
20–	41	59	42	58
25–	36	64	31	69
30–	31	69	24	76
35–	35	65	24	76
40–	35	65	30	70
45–	44	56	23	77
50–	35	65	32	68
60–	32	68	24	76
70–	23	77	18	82

* 1851 Census sample. $N = 781$ household heads, 541 wives.

SOURCES OF IMMIGRANTS

An examination of the relevant data in the census volumes for 1841 and 1851 suggests that most migration into York was on a short-distance basis (table 4.4). Such a finding is in line with Redford's pioneering study,[13] and is unremarkable.

TABLE 4.4 *Birthplaces of the inhabitants of York Municipal Borough in 1841**

Birthplace	No. of persons	No. of persons as percentage of total population of M.B.
City and Ainsty of York	25,724	89.2
Elsewhere in England and Wales	2,239	7.8
Scotland	245	0.9
Ireland	429	1.5
Foreign parts, colonies, etc.	57	0.2
Not specified	148	0.5
Total	28,842	100.1

* 1841 Census. Enumeration Abstract, Pt. 1.

Little reliance may be placed on some of the proportions shown in table 4.4. It will be recalled that householders were asked to state whether or not they were 'born in the same county', and it is unlikely that the average householder realized that the City and Ainsty of York would be regarded by the census authorities as a county in itself.[14] It is therefore probable that a large proportion of the 25,724 enumerated as having been born in the City and Ainsty were in fact born outside it, but within the county of Yorkshire taken as a whole.

The return for 1851 is much more detailed and explicit.

TABLE 4.5   *Birthplaces of the inhabitants of York Municipal Borough in 1851* *

Birthplace	No. of persons	No. of persons as percentage of total population
1. York (M.B.)	16,750	46.1
2. Elsewhere in Yorkshire	13,277	36.6
3. London	571	1.6
4. Surrey, Kent, Hants, Sussex, Berks.	202	0.6
5. Middx, Herts., Bucks., Oxon., Northants., Hunts., Beds., Cambs.	140	0.4
6. Essex, Norfolk, Suffolk	136	0.4
7. Wilts., Dorset, Devon, Cornwall, Som.	190	0.5
8. Gloucs., Herefords, Shrops., Staffs., Worcs., Warwicks.	296	0.8
9. Leics., Rutland, Lincs., Notts., Derbys.	598	1.6
10. Lancashire and Cheshire	531	1.5
11. Durham, Northumberland, Cumberland and Westmorland	989	2.7
12. Wales	55	0.2
13. Scotland	473	1.3
14. Ireland	1,928	5.3
15. Islands and British seas, colonies, foreign parts, at sea	167	0.5
Total	36,303	100.1

* 1851 Census. Population Tables II (2).

If the 1841 figure of 25,724 is accepted as referring to persons born in the whole county of Yorkshire, it is possible to perform a rough calculation to link the data of the two censuses together, throwing some light on the birthplaces of those who came to York in the years 1841–51.

TABLE 4.6 *Birthplaces of the inhabitants of York: two censuses compared**

Born in	1841	1851	Percentage increase (1841–51)
Yorkshire	25,724	30,027	16.7
Rest of England and Wales	2,239	3,708	65.6
Scotland	245	473	93.1
Ireland	429	1,928	394.4
Foreign parts, etc.	57	167	193.0
Not specified	148	—	—
Total population of York (M.B.)	28,842	36,303	25.9

* Sources as for tables 4.4 and 4.5.

From table 4.6, it is clear that the largest immigration increment to the population of York in absolute terms continued to be from the surrounding countryside.[15] Possibly the increased proportion of persons born elsewhere in England, Wales and Scotland was encouraged by improvements in travelling facilities, but the combined total of these categories remained quite small, at 11.8 per cent.

The most striking feature of the table is the increase in the numbers of Irish-born inhabitants of the city, which was significant both in absolute and percentage terms. Indeed, although the proportion of Irish-born persons in York in 1851 was naturally much lower than the extreme proportions encountered in some Lancashire towns (Manchester and Salford 13.0 per cent, Liverpool 22.3 per cent for example), at 5.3 per cent it was nevertheless unexpectedly high compared with other large towns in the central and north-eastern districts of England (Lincoln 1.3, Hull 3.5, Nottingham 2.7, Derby 3.2, Sheffield 3.3, Leeds 4.9 per cent, etc.).

Thus the city of York, like other towns of the period, was

predominantly composed of immigrants. The figures cited to support this in table 4.5 relate to the whole population, and it is obvious that, if adults alone are considered (table 4.7), the immigrant proportion was still higher.

TABLE 4.7 *Birthplaces of adults (persons over 20): York Municipal Borough, 1851**

Birthplace	Absolute No.	Percentages
Municipal Borough	6,650	31.58
Yorkshire (outside York M.B.)	9,910	47.06
Surrounding northern counties	1,324	6.29
Rest of England and Wales	1,344	6.38
Scotland	354	1.68
Ireland	1,350	6.41
Foreign parts, etc.	125	0.59
Total over 20	21,057	99.99

* 1851 Census. Population Tables II (2). The figure for 'surrounding northern counties' includes 127 born in Notts., 66 in Derbys., 55 from Cheshire, 282 from Lancashire, 218 from Lincs. and 363 from Durham. To these was added Northumberland (213), although this is not a contiguous county; but those born in Westmorland (25 only) were added to 'Rest of England', in view of the small numbers involved and distance from York.

SOME SOCIAL CHARACTERISTICS OF IMMIGRANT GROUPS

Little work has been carried out on the fortunes of urban immigrants in the period. It is therefore of some interest to relate household heads' birthplaces to the social classes in which they found themselves, by 1851.

A number of conclusions, significant both in an historical and statistical sense, may be drawn from table 4.8.

(i) Native-born citizens of York were distributed across the class structure in very much the same proportions as the community at large.

(ii) Immigrants tended to fall into two categories. Those drawn from more distant parts (northern counties; rest of England) were disproportionately well-represented at the upper end of the social hierarchy, whilst local immigrants drawn from the agricultural North and East Ridings,[16] and of course the Irish,

TABLE 4.8 *Birthplaces and social class of household heads, 1851**

	Percentage in classes			
Birthplace	I and II	III	IV and V	$\mathcal{N} =$
(a) York (Parliamentary Borough)	20.8	54.3	21.6	269
(b) North and East Ridings	17.6	45.2	33.0	221
(c) West Riding	23.7	47.4	25.7	152
(d) Surrounding northern counties	26.8	55.4	16.1	56
(e) Rest of England and Wales	35.9	48.7	12.8	39
(f) Northern counties plus rest of England	30.5	52.6	14.7	95
(g) Ireland	8.0	24.0	56.0	25
(h) All household heads	21.3	49.4	25.7	781

* 1851 Census sample.

tended to cluster in classes IV–V. No doubt the reasons for such differences were that in general (except in the case of the Irish) those who travelled farther would tend to be people with more education, skill and capital, deriving commensurate critical advantages.

Of course, except the Irish, in every case a larger proportion was to be found in class III than either I–II, or IV–V, and it would be possible to read too much into these differences. No doubt contemporaries were well aware of the disadvantageous situation of the Irish (even if they thought it well deserved), and may have perceived that an above average proportion of the upper class had originated elsewhere. It would seem less likely that the marginal relative disadvantages experienced by most local immigrants would have made much of a mark upon the popular consciousness, especially since a good many successful local worthies were known to have originated from the local countryside.[17]

DISTRICTS OF SETTLEMENT

Given that, on the basis of the 1851 sample, 65.4 per cent of all household heads, 72.0 per cent of wives, 74.1 per cent of lodgers and 78.8 per cent of domestic servants were immigrants, it is safe to speak as if the city were three-quarters made up of immigrants, so far as adults were concerned. Understandably, this was the case in all areas of the city, although table 4.9 presents some slight evidence of assortive residential patterns.

TABLE 4.9 *Birthplace distribution of immigrant heads and wives by wards of the Municipal Borough* (%)*

	East/North Ridings	West Riding	Northern counties	Rest of England and Wales	Ireland
$N =$	398	269	90	70	44
(a) Micklegate	36.1	33.1	18.3	5.9	3.6
(b) Castlegate	42.7	38.2	6.7	4.5	3.4
Wards wholly or partly south-west of river	38.4	34.9	14.3	5.4	3.5
(c) Bootham	49.4	29.4	4.7	8.2	–
(d) Guildhall	46.3	29.6	13.0	9.3	1.9
(e) Monk	47.6	27.8	10.9	9.0	0.9
(f) Walmgate	42.3	26.4	5.3	8.2	15.4
Wards wholly north-east of river	45.8	27.7	8.1	8.6	6.3

* 1851 Census sample. For composition of wards see Statistical Appendix III.

Pooled estimate tests show that there were significant if slight differences between these two groups of wards. Those to the north and east of the Ouse had a significantly larger proportion of East and North Riding born among their immigrants than the wards wholly or partly to the south of the river, which looked towards the West Riding (i.e. the value 45.8 per cent is significantly different from 38.4 per cent). The difference is a very bare one indeed, however. A pooled estimate test on the West Riding percentages shows that significantly more West Riding heads were to be found in the wards south-west of the river than in those to the north and east of it, when the values 34.9 and 27.7 per cent are compared. Note however, that it is possible that even in the Micklegate and Castlegate

wards, there were *absolutely* more immigrants from the North
and East Ridings (i.e. when the figures 38.4 and 34.9 per cent
are compared) though it is not possible to assert significance
of difference here. This is to be expected, and simply reflects
the fact that there were more stronger urban centres of attraction than York in the West Riding. In sum, in so far as West
Riding migrants went to York, they were marginally more
likely to abide south and west of the Ouse: North and East
Riding migrants were more likely to settle north and east of
the river – but even on the other side there may well have been
proportionately more of them.

A further feature of interest in table 4.9 is the very high
proportion of Northern Counties born heads in Micklegate
ward (18.3 per cent). This reflects the high proportion of
skilled railwaymen found there, many of whom came from
Durham and Northumberland.[18]

Lastly, it is clear that the high proportion of Irish indicated
in Walmgate ward (15.4 per cent) certainly reflects the known
centres of settlement, which were principally the parishes of
St George, St Margaret, St Peter-le Willows, St Dennis (all in
Walmgate ward), along with the Bedern, which lay like a
sort of irritating ant-heap in the otherwise respectable district
of Bootham.[19]

'Social class' was clearly another variable influencing the
place of residence of native-born and immigrants alike; only
the Irish were an homogeneous group likely to be in the same
(low) social classes wherever they were encountered. The small
size of the sample severely limits what can be said here, but
table 4.10 attempts to show how the class composition of
native and Yorkshire (ex-York) born household heads varied,
over very broad areas of the city.

There is a significant difference between the proportion of
successful (class I–II) York-born heads living in Micklegate
and Bootham on the one hand, and insalubrious Walmgate on
the other (when the values 28.5 and 12.0 per cent are compared). Walmgate nevertheless contained a higher proportion
(63.2 per cent) of class III heads, primarily skilled working-

TABLE 4.10   *Class-structure of household heads in various sub-districts**

	Class			
Sub-district	I–II	III	IV–V	$N =$
(i) *York-born*				
(a) Micklegate	27.3	43.6	25.5	55
(b) Bootham	29.2	48.3	19.1	89
Micklegate and Bootham	28.5	46.5	21.5	144
(c) Walmgate	12.0	63.2	21.6	125
(ii) *East, North and West Riding-born*				
(a) Micklegate	22.3	44.7	28.7	94
(b) Bootham	23.8	47.6	25.7	105
Micklegate and Bootham	23.1	46.2	27.1	199
(c) Walmgate	16.7	46.0	33.3	174

* 1851 Census sample. Note that this table refers to those substantial parts of the registration sub-districts which lay within the Parliamentary Borough boundaries.

men. None of the differences in the second part of the table are statistically significant at the 95 per cent confidence level, but it is not unlikely that the more successful immigrants, like the native-born, showed some tendency to shy away from the Walmgate area.

These were the underlying patterns of settlement, and hint at the existence of *tendencies* rather than clear-cut segregated areas of the city, either on a 'birthplace' or for that matter a 'class' basis, a feature no doubt due to the mixed commercial and residential nature of much the greater part of the city.[20] Further research would probably reveal marked assortive residential patterns at the street or court level, as distinct from the broader sub-districts taken here, which was certainly the case with the Irish and railway employees, but that is another question. In any case, the trends which I have been able to disengage here disregard short-distance movements within the city, which were considerable and frequent. In the meanest districts, it was found that nearly 27 per cent of families had not resided one year and 37 per cent had been less than two years in their present residences in the early 1840s, according to statistics collected by Dr Laycock.[21]

MOTIVES FOR AND FLUCTUATIONS IN IMMIGRATION

So far as upper-class householders were concerned, this represents no problem. A large proportion were consumers rather than producers. To fund-holders, annuitants and individuals with private means, York must have been an attractive place to live. The city was still, in the 1840s, an important social, ecclesiastical and military centre, even though there had been some decline of fashionable and aristocratic patronage. When the establishment of a provincial school of design was being considered in the early forties, the arguments put forward in favour of York were that it was 'a gentlemanly place . . . being a place retired, in a certain degree, from manufacturing districts'.[22] Domestic servants were readily available, many of the shops were noted for their quality, and the opportunities for literary, antiquarian and recreational pursuits were outstandingly good.

Nor is there any mystery concerning the appearance of large numbers of Irish during the decade. The general reasons for the Irish influx into Great Britain in the 1840s are too well known to bear lengthy repetition. The great potato famine of 1845–9 is believed to have carried off by death about 700,000 persons, and caused about a million more to leave the country. Liverpool alone landed 280,000 immigrants in 1846 and nearly 300,000 in 1847. Somewhat under a half moved on to America, but from this and other main points of entry 'the horde of starving vagrant Irish pushed on into the interior of the country'.[23]

A rather larger proportion found their way to York district than might have been expected however. The district had frequently seen a seasonal augmentation of the agricultural labour force, and it is not surprising to notice that an extremely large proportion of the York Irish described themselves as agricultural labourers in the census of 1851; York had 145

persons so described in 1841, 541 in 1851. B. S. Rowntree
later wrote that the Irish 'were probably attracted to York
by the prospect of obtaining work in connection with the
cultivation of chicory, for which the district was then noted'.
Benson, a local historian, states that 'chicory was introduced
about 1840, and eventually a thousand acres were under
cultivation and 400 persons employed at Dunnington. With
the imposition of a duty in 1860 the cultivation of chicory
gradually declined to twenty acres'.[24] The importance of this
industry is legendary, but there are many different versions of
the story. In later years Lancelot Foster, an ex-Lord Mayor of
York, led a crusade for the revival of the industry; in 1885 he
read a paper on the chicory duty to an assembly of interested
farmers, and called for its reduction.[25] There exists a Board of
Agriculture Report on the industy which was 'instituted in
consequence of representations made to the Board by Mr
Lancelot Foster . . . supported by several Yorkshire agricultural
societies'.[26] It seems clear that in the 1840s and 1850s there
was an increasing demand for the root, and that its cultivation
was extremely profitable. More significant in this context, the
growing of chicory obviously necessitated the availability of
a considerable labour force. The one imperative condition for
the crop was that the land should be thoroughly and effectively
cleaned;[27] at a later stage the harvesting of the crop furnished
employment for large numbers of women and labourers, argued
Foster. There is evidence to show that to a large extent, the
Irish provided this labour. If the industry could be revived, he
observed in 1885, 'it would be the means of finding employment
for large masses of the Irish and labouring classes'.[28] Several
references from our period show that the Irish had been directly
associated with the growing of this crop.[29]

Of course, this was not the only outlet for Irish labour.
Obviously they would work seasonally in agriculture
generally;[30] take casual jobs in the town and around the
markets, and perhaps tend to spend a disproportionate amount
of their time doing little but draw relief, if the complaints of
the Poor Law Guardians are to be believed.

Another exceedingly interesting development of the forties was the way in which York drew upon the North-Eastern counties for railway workers, especially in the skilled grades. In the 1851 sample, out of 59 railway workers, 43 (73 per cent) were immigrants; and of the immigrants, 19 (44 per cent) were from the two counties of Durham and Northumberland. This seemed to be worth further investigation, and the entire complement of railway workers' households in Oxford Street, Cambridge Street and three minor adjuncts was examined (45 households in all, comprising 243 persons). Over half of the household heads (51 per cent) had in fact been born in Durham and Northumberland, 34 per cent in Yorkshire (only 8.5 per cent in York itself), and 15 per cent elsewhere. These household heads were on the whole fairly young men (81 per cent aged 39 or under), so that a good many are likely to have migrated when single. This would explain why York-shire-born wives (48 per cent), predominated slightly over those born in Northumberland and Durham (41 per cent) or elsewhere (11 per cent). Average family size (4.3), and mean number of children (2.3), were, as might be expected, well above those generally prevailing in the city.[31] Each household contained on the average 0.7 lodgers and/or relatives, nearly all employed on the railway. Of these 34 per cent were born in Northumberland and Durham, 28.5 per cent in Yorkshire, 31.5 per cent elsewhere. Most of the workers in these streets were skilled men – engine fitters, drivers and clerks. Intermediate grades such as guards and pointsmen, and lower grade workers such as engine cleaners, porters and labourers were scantily represented there. It seems likely that while the lower-grade jobs could be filled by local men and boys, during the early years of railways in York, skilled men had to be attracted from elsewhere – from the oldest railway district of all, in fact. The wages earned by drivers and fitters undoubtedly secured them a notable place in the artisan *élite* of the city.[32]

To refer back to table 4.5 however, it is clear that in absolute terms, by far the greatest number of immigrants in the 1840s still came from the surrounding countryside, as no doubt they had always done. The forces of attraction and repulsion which affected the majority group demand particular attention. It was once assumed that rural populations tended to remain rooted and immobile over time. 'Not an estate in this district, or other neighbouring ones, can be pointed out where the same families have not remained for generations on it, perhaps for many generations . . . estates may be shewn, where not a family has been changed, or a new one introduced, in the memory of man.' This comment, drawn from Tuke's *General View of the Agriculture of the North Riding of Yorkshire*[33] was perhaps intended to refer to farmers, but cannot be an accurate description of the mobility of pre-industrial populations in general, which had long been very considerable. In support of this view, Chambers has marshalled evidence not only from the seventeenth and eighteenth centuries, but even for the fifteenth; so that 'the picture of a mobile country population incessantly engaged in the process of moving for the purpose of improving their condition, above all seeking their future in the towns, is now firmly established'.[34]

It is one thing to assert this as a general principle, but quite another to measure its extent. In the present context, we are fortunate to have a recent detailed study upon which to draw. Holderness has recently documented personal mobility in ten parishes within, or bordering on the Plain of York, through scrutinizing baptismal entries in various published volumes of the *Yorkshire Parish Register Society* between 1777 and 1812, which carry unusually full details of the places of origin of the parents. 'Among farmers', he writes, 'the pressures to move about the countryside were somewhat less powerful than among other social groups. A high proportion [54 per cent] lived where their fathers had lived, and where they themselves had been born.' In the same way, an established and steady livelihood among tradesmen acted as an incentive to stability, and 'inheritance obviously played a considerable part in maintaining the comparative constancy of the "commercial" population of rural communities'. Of this group 48 per cent were found to be located in their original villages of origin. By contrast, 'the group described as labourers was more volatile with respect to its geographical mobility', only 32 per cent appearing in their respective parishes of origin, although more labourers, proportionately (30 per cent) were immigrants from within a range of ten miles, as against 18 per cent for farmers and 20 per cent for tradesmen. Farmers' and tradesmens' wives, incidentally, were more mobile than their spouses, only 38 and 36 per cent coming into observation in their parishes of origin; but labourers' wives, *per contra*, appeared there in 35 per cent of cases, that is, a figure slightly higher than for the labourers themselves.[35]

The relevance of this study here is that it illustrates the high turnover rate in the countryside, and for the first time, succeeds in measuring it with an approach to accuracy. The cycle of family life among the agricultural labouring class is especially interesting, and has been sketched out by Holderness, and by Shepherd, in the following terms: rural labourers tended to have large families (whether larger than those of other social classes is unknown), and since cottages tended to have only two bedrooms, children left home at the age of 12 to 14, the girls entering service, the boys joining the ranks of farm servants, living in. Farm service remained a regular feature of agricultural employment north of the Humber and Dee until late in the nineteenth century, and in the intervals between engagements single men moved freely about the countryside to find or change employment, usually at hiring fairs. After perhaps ten years in this capacity, the farm servant married, so changing his status to agricultural labourer, living out independently in a cottage. His mobility would tend to be much reduced at this juncture, but as his own children reached adolescence, the cycle of mobility would be renewed.[36] Obviously, there were many potential points of leakage from this rural merry-go-round, with young men and women departing for the towns at various stages.

There existed, in rural Yorkshire, as elsewhere, a number of pressures which would tend to influence them to do so:

(i) Population pressure: this was perceptible in the North Riding (of which, in 1800, it was remarked that 'all parts of this Riding, except the moorlands, are as fully peopled as the nature of it will admit'),[37] where nevertheless the total population rose by 35 per cent between 1801 and 1851; whilst in the East Riding (excluding York and Hull) population rose by 52 per cent in that period, and in the West Riding the registration districts of Ripon, Pateley Bridge, Knaresborough, Selby and Tadcaster (the more or less agricultural parts of the Riding), increased, as a whole, by 41 per cent.

This argument is in accordance with modern interpretations of rural poverty; against the older view which overemphasized the role of enclosures, Chambers and Mingay affirm

that the fundamental factor was the great upswing of population. Population increase . . . was expanding the labour force at a rate faster than agriculture could absorb it, and the growth of numbers, of landless and sometimes unemployable labourers, was observable both in enclosed and the still open villages . . . population growth was the main factor in the increase in a landless, as well as a partially workless, labour supply in the countryside.[38]

There is reason to believe that this factor was reflected in a tendency for the cost of poor relief to mount in Yorkshire (table 4.11), although the comparatively high level of farm workers' wages (for which, see below), and the wider availability of alternative employment in the West Riding, served to keep down *per capita* expenditure to a level well below that encountered elsewhere.

TABLE 4.11 *Poor Law relief per head, by counties, 1802–31 (shillings and pence)* *

	1802		1812		1821		1831	
	s.	d.	s.	d.	s.	d.	s.	d
Yorks., E.R.	7	6	12	6	13	0	11	11
Yorks., N.R.	6	5	8	4	9	6	8	9
17 other Speenhamland counties	12	10	19	7	16	3	14	8
Yorks., W.R.	6	6	9	11	8	2	5	7
23 other non-Speenhamland counties	8	3	11	3	10	8	8	7

* Blaug (1963) 178–9.

(ii) In general, farm workers' remuneration in Yorkshire was noticeably higher than in the south, throughout the first half of the century, as indicated by table 4.12, and by numerous contemporary statements.

TABLE 4.12 *Weekly money wages of agricultural workers, 1795–1850 (shillings and pence)**

	1795		1824		1833		1837		1850	
	s.	d.	s.	d.	s.	d.	s.	d.	s.	d.
Yorks., W.R.	11	0	12	5	11	5	12	0	14	0
Yorks., E.R.	11	3	11	8	11	0	12	0	12	0
Yorks., N.R.	10	0	10	3	11	4	12	0	11	0
England and Wales as a whole	8	11	9	7	10	8	10	3	9	6

* Blaug (1963) 182–3.

Yet at no stage did farm wages compare with what could be earned for similar work in the towns. For example, agricultural wages in the York district stood at 10–12s. a week in 1850, whereas railway porters earned about 17s. and brickmakers the same, to mention two fields where no apprenticeship bar existed. And in 1842, an exceptionally bad year, the wages of 'labourers' in the city were alleged to be 12s., but those of country labourers in the surrounding area, 7–8s.[39] Moreover, it should be remembered that the demand for farm labour was by no means constant. Local sources of labour would fall short of requirements at harvest-time almost as a matter of course, and farmers' estimates of their requirements were notoriously apt to fluctuate with their own sense of well-being and expansiveness. Their incomes tended to be larger in times of high prices, even though their harvests might be small, the demand for grain being inelastic. Conversely, when prices were low, Jones writes, 'farmers tried to economize the volume of labour they employed, and more strenuously the rate at which they paid for labour'.[40] Therefore, as a result of pressures on the supply side and seasonal fluctuations in demand, farm work offered far less security of employment than might perhaps be assumed.

(iii) Obtaining cottages was a difficult matter, and what was to be had was often unattractive. R. Brown's *General View of the Agriculture of the West Riding of Yorkshire* (1799) referred to 'a great want of dwelling houses for husbandmen and labourers', attributable to the operation of the Poor Laws, and to 'the want of a little land laid out to cottages in every parish'; whilst John Tuke described the cottages of the North Riding in 1800 as 'generally small and low, consisting only of one room, and, very rarely, of two ... [and] damp, and frequently very unwholesome'.[41] Although, according to the evidence of H. R. Strickland, the habitations of labourers in the East Riding were more comfortable (two up, two down) than in many parts of England, and rents low, there was 'a great want of habitations for the labourers'. 'It is much to be regretted', he went on to say, 'that the practice of suffering cottages to fall into decay, and the disinclination to build new ones, should be so prevalent in this part of the Kingdom.'[42] Even so, Shepherd points out, on the Wolds the effort to keep poor rates low by this means continued for many years, many labourers being in the position of having to walk three or four miles to and from their place of work in the 1840s.[43]

As a general rule, even if it is accepted that rural labourers were not 'driven' off the land as a consequence of a general deterioration in their prospects as a result of enclosures and associated social changes, there was little positive inducement to attract the labourer to remain on the land. As far as can be discerned, the regulator of migration was the possibility of obtaining employment in the towns.

Chapter 2 advanced the argument that the twenties saw a rapid advance of York's prosperity on the basis of the substantial demand of the relatively well-off farming classes. Urban employment opportunities were thus created, and as table 4.2 shows, migrants were forthcoming to fill them. By contrast farming demand in the thirties was stagnant, since on the whole the farmers seem to have been less prosperous. The growth of York was therefore checked, and the possibility of finding jobs there must have narrowed considerably. Hence, as table 4.2 indicates net migration to the city fell away.

This study is especially concerned with the 1840s however, and there is no need to rest content with a decadal generalization for these years. An attempt will be made to show how far, and under what influences, particular years were favourable to immigration into York from the surrounding rural areas.

1841–2–3

1841 was the last of a series of poor harvests; those of 1842 and 1843 were good, and the price of grain sank nationally and locally.[44] We must infer that the demand of farmers for non-agricultural goods and services would be stagnant if not declining. Respecting the condition of the labouring population in York Union, the Clerk wrote to London to say that 'there is a great want of work and much distress in consequence ... this was much about the state of affairs last year'.[45] Later in the year it was noted that at the York Martinmas fair hirings were poor; 'those servants who had the good fortune to obtain masters we understand had to submit to lower wages, and many had to go unhired'.[46] Railway building had come to a temporary halt with the completion of the Great North of England line in 1841, and although in the summer of 1843 there were new signs of activity in the industrial towns, York did not exhibit them; 'in all towns where there is no manufacture, the state of trade continues painfully depressed'.[47] Clearly this must have been an unpropitious time for immigration into York.

1844

The situation for farmers was still poor, prices remaining low; farm servants were still finding it difficult to obtain jobs. Of the Martinmas fair, it was remarked 'though some servants were hired at good wages, we believe that generally speaking, wages were low'.[48] Nationally however, the trade cycle began an upswing on the basis of railway speculation, in which York shared. The York–Scarborough line was authorized in 1844 and the York and North Midland purchased the Leeds and Selby line; several competing plans for a direct line from London to York were under discussion, and the Leeds–York line was authorized in 1845 followed by York–Market Weighton and York–Knaresborough in 1846. The local press was speaking of 'the late commercial depression' by April,[49] and we may infer that immigration would have recommenced.

1845–6–7–8

Although as a speculative boom the 'Railway Mania' was checked in the autumn of 1845, the construction of lines authorized during 1844–6 went on until 1848, in the York district.[50] In the city these were years of very good trade and employment, actually seeing (a rare event) strikes for higher pay among joiners and building workers in February and June 1846.[51] Hudson declared in November 1846 that there was 'more work to be done than hands could be secured to execute'. He had recently requested a contractor to engage another 500 men, and had been told that it was impossible to get them.[52] Generally the district does not seem to have been much affected by the cyclical downturn of 1847–8, for again in January 1848, Hudson remarked that railway building projects were being neglected 'for want of workmen ... although the contractor had offered to the masons 27s. a week'.[53]

On the land poor harvests in 1845, 1846 and 1848 were partially offset by high imports; agricultural prices remained low.[54] Yet it seems that in so far as farmers required labour in these years, they had to offer good terms. 'High wages were required and received by farm servants' at the Martinmas hirings of 1845, as was also the case on the corresponding occasions in 1846 and 1848.[55] Jones has referred to a 'shortage of farm labour produced in many districts by the sudden demand for navvies to build the railways'[56] of which we are perhaps witnessing a local manifestation. In these expansive circumstances, we may presume that immigration into the city would have run at high levels.

1849–50–51

The agricultural interest, unprotected against foreign corn since the abolition of the Corn Laws in 1846, now sank into a state of considerable gloom.[57] With large importations now entering the country the price of grain commenced to fall, in good and bad harvest years alike.[58] Reports from all the agricultural areas around York attested to a 'great scarcity of work' on the land and wage decreases were variously stated as '25 per cent' or 'one-sixth' according to locality.[59] In the non-agricultural sector, railway-building was now slackening, but employment opportunities in the city itself seem to have remained reasonably good. The fact that the cost of living had sunk so far may have meant that a much enhanced number of urban consumers now had a greater margin than ever before over and above the cost of basic necessities, and this probably helped to maintain the level of demand in the city. Although the *Yorkshire Gazette* alluded to a 'want of employment' in York in the January of 1850,[60] this is likely to have been seasonal. In the previous summer, Assistant Commissioner Hawley wrote to the Poor Law Board as follows: 'York is not a manufacturing city, and though among the retail traders there is a general complaint of stagnation in business, distress among the labouring classes does not appear to be the consequence, as employment is by no means scarce and very few able-bodied workmen are applicants for parochial relief.' During the following months wage reductions were made in a number of trades in the area, but Hawley believed that provisions had fallen more in price.[61]

To conclude, there can be little doubt that the years 1841–3 were unfavourable to immigration. It seems likely that a renewed influx began in 1844, and in view of the fact that the employment situation in the city remained quite good throughout, immigration may well have continued at a high level down to 1851. We cannot, of course, gauge exactly how the volume of immigration fluctuated from year to year, and to this extent there remains a gap in our knowledge of the demographic development of the city in this period. This is inevitable and unfortunate, but not wholly disastrous. Obviously it would have been desirable to arrive at a precise estimate of the size of the population in the inter-censal years in order, in subsequent chapters, to calculate birth rates and death rates. I have had to assume that the net immigration increase of the three mainly urban sub-districts (6,905) can be split into ten equal parts, adding in one-tenth per annum. These increments cannot be distributed along a curve (which might be in some ways preferable to a straight line) because the data is not adequate.[62] But the estimates of birth and death rates, which follow in subsequent chapters are not likely to be more than 1 or 2 per cent out in particular years between 1841 and 1851; i.e. the absolute size of the denominator is not much affected by being two or three hundred in error.

5 *Mortality*

In a recent article Cowgill has calculated a series of mortality rates for sixteenth-century York that can only be described as horrendous. On the basis of studying six parishes, she estimates that almost half the children born died before attaining the age of one, whilst 35 per cent of females and 38 per cent of males survived to reach 5, 21 and 31 per cent to 10, and only 11 per cent (for each sex) to 40.[1] However, a number of critics have argued that these levels of mortality are over-estimated; attention has been drawn to the fact that only 36 per cent of sixteenth-century births were traced to correspond-ing entries of deaths, and one cannot assume, as Cowgill does, that the ages of death of the remaining 64 per cent were distri-buted in the same way, since 'there is . . . a much better chance linking a baptism entry to an early death than to later deaths'.[2]

Even so, it is known that the infant death rate in the well-favoured parish of St Michael-le-Belfrey in 1571–86 stood at 235 per 1,000 live births, which compares unfavourably with a rate of 189 established for the British aristocracy for the same period, and with a figure as low as 120–40 for the rural parish of Colyton in sixteenth-century Devon.[3] Infant mortality is of course a major component of total mortality, and in the first half of the eighteenth century English death rates as a whole are unlikely to have been lower than the 32.7 per 1,000 put forward by Brownlee, that is, three times as high as the death rates of the 1960s, which varied between 11.2 and 12.2.[4] Urban death rates were no doubt higher than the national mean; Deane and Cole have suggested a rate of 48·8 for the London area in 1700–50, while for York, a contemporary estimate for 1728–35 is 46 per 1,000.[5]

The primary difficulty of establishing valid rates in the eighteenth century is, of course, that in the absence of censuses before 1801, the necessary base populations are unknown, or can only be very approximately estimated; whilst paradoxically by the time more or less firm decennial census figures commence, there is reason to believe ecclesiastical registration had deteriorated sharply at least in towns, thus affecting the published record of vital events. Therefore, only tentative suggestions can be made about the movement of death rates in York or elsewhere, prior to the beginning of civil registration in 1838.

Nevertheless, there are grounds for presuming that some improvements in the crude level of mortality took effect from about the mid-eighteenth century. On the basis of data collected from the parish registers by Drake for 1728–35, and William White for 1770–6, it can be seen that the average annual number of baptisms in the City of York rose by 36 per cent (from 350 to 475) and the number of burials by only 4 per cent (from 436 to 453).[6] Using the 1801 *Parish Register Abstract* Allison and Tillott have shown that regular surpluses of burials over baptisms gave way, after 1750, to excesses of baptisms, in most years.[7] Thus we may speak with some justification, of the occurrence of a 'vital revolution' in eighteenth-century York, which was paralleled, *inter alia*, in London, Nottingham, Manchester, Exeter and Leeds – all of which gave evidence of baptismal surpluses coming into being during the second half of the century.[8]

In the case of York, if base populations prior to 1801 are calculated (i) on an assumption that the crude birth rate was constant at 31 (the baptismal rate of 1800–2) (ii) on the assumption that the marriage rate was constant at the 1800–2 level of 12·8; and using census figures from 1801, the course of crude death rates down to 1820–2 is as set out in table 5.1.

These calculations, although entailing some heroic assumptions, reveal how the course of mortality in York probably reflected the national trend, as it is accepted by most historians; that is, to lower mortality rates in the second half of the

TABLE 5.1   *Course of crude death rates in York, 1700–1820–2**

	(1) Assumed birthrate 31	(2) Assumed marriage rate 12.8	(3) Base population from censuses
1700	42.9 ⎫		
1710	33.8 ⎪		
1720	38.2 ⎬ 39.4		
1730	32.4 ⎪		
1740	52.3 ⎪		
1750	36.6 ⎭		
1760	30.5 ⎫	31.2 ⎫	
1770	28.9 ⎪	30.9 ⎪	
1780–2	33.0 ⎬ 30.8	35.2 ⎬ 32.8	
1790–2	30.9 ⎭	33.6 ⎭	
1800–2			30.4
1810–12			23.8
1820–2			19.4

* *Parish Register Abstracts*, 1801–31; Censuses 1801–31.

eighteenth century and first 20 years of the nineteenth. Little difference would be made to these conclusions by applying the multipliers suggested by Talbot Griffith to correct for under-registration. On a national basis, he found that multiplying burials by 1.10 and baptisms by 1.15 smoothed the jump in rates observed when the ecclesiastical system of registration gave way to civil registration after 1837.[9] If such corrections were applied to the long-run data for York, the effect would be merely to raise the absolute number of deaths, but also the base populations to which they are related in the calculation of crude rates, the net effect being to slightly lower mortality throughout the period covered by table 5.1. On the other hand, it has been argued that English parochial registration probably reached its nadir in the first twenty years of the nineteenth century,[10] from which it follows that the national rates calculated by Griffith for 1806–16 and 1816–26 (19.98 and 20.33), as well as the York rates given here for 1810–12 and 1820–2 could be inordinately low. But the remarks accompanying the 1831 *Parish Register Abstract* for York City and

Ainsty mention that the coverage of registers was complete ('it is believed that no return whatever remains due'), and refer to a handful of only seven unregistered births and baptisms.[11] This gives the impression of comparatively good registration, which is consistent with the finding that in 1839–40, when the twin systems of ecclesiastical and civil registration overlapped most effectively, ecclesiastical registration in the East and North Ridings was among the best in the country; the comparison suggests that burials needed to be raised by only 2 per cent, and baptisms by 7 or 8 per cent, to agree with the results of civil registration.[12] Tinkering with the rates set out in table 5.1 would therefore probably make little difference to these general conclusions.

It is worth summarizing the reasons for this apparent improvement in death rates, as understood by contemporaries and by modern historians; although pending more detailed work on the course of mortality, it is impossible to give an order of importance, or to pinpoint the improvements by time, district, social class or cause.

Environmental improvements

William White referred to street improvements and the taking down of some old houses; as well as to new paving and street drains, making the city 'drier and cleaner than formerly'.[13] While the physical extension of the city was slight in the eighteenth century 'red-brick buildings took the place of half-timbered houses and shops in many streets within the city walls and in the old suburbs outside the walls', state Allison and Tillott, going on to catalogue instances of house demolition and rebuilding, street widening, the Corporation's zeal in enforcing the obligation of citizens to maintain the paving before their houses, and attempts to regulate dung traffic on the River Ouse. The Corporation would, in some circumstances, contribute from its own funds to street widening and to the construction of drains, and by 1825 nearly seven miles of city streets had been paved.[14] These developments parallel those outlined by Dorothy George for London, where, it is said, perhaps with a touch of exaggeration, 'the change both in appearance and sanitation was immense'.[15] White also believed that the construction of Naburn Lock, four miles down river, in 1757, had a favourable effect: 'before this the river was frequently very low, leaving quantities of sludge and dirt in the very heart of the city, also the filth of the common sewers which it was unable to wash away ... the lock has effectively prevented this for the future, by the river being kept always high, broad and spacious'.[16]

Improved medical facilities

White mentioned as a further cause of mortality reduction improvements in the treatment and cure of several disorders and 'the general use of antiseptic medicines and diet'.[17] Major new institutions extending medical services to a much wider range of people than before included York County Hospital (1740) and the York Dispensary (1788). An increase of medical skills and facilities in the eighteenth century has traditionally been given considerable weight by students of population history, such as Griffith, in his *Population Problems of the Age of Malthus*. About fifteen years ago, McKeown and Brown, in a striking article, appeared to have demolished this argument by calling into question the medicinal properties of many of the drugs then in use, and pointing to the lack of effectiveness, from the patient's point of view, of advances in surgical and midwifery techniques in the absence of proper antiseptic procedures. Indeed, these authors went so far as to reverse the traditional view, arguing that 'the chief indictment of hospital work at this period is not that it did no good, but that it positively did harm'.[18] A number of historians have felt that this is exaggerated, and in an article of special interest in this context, Sigsworth has criticized their view on the basis of the records of York County Hospital. He points out that only fifty-two of the 1,708 patients treated between 1740–3 actually died in hospital; that 90 per cent of 26,023 patients admitted between 1740–83 and 89.5 per cent of the 35,326 admitted between 1784–1842 were discharged as 'cured' or 'relieved', and that attempts were made to segregate patients to avoid cross-infection.[19] All in all, in the light of these records, 'one can only suggest, either that the hospital was served by successive generations of arithmetical incompetence, or chronic liars – doctors, surgeons, trustees and governors engaged in a perpetual and successful campaign to deceive an utterly gullible public', or that further investigation into the role of hospitals is required before one can accept that they positively worsened mortality, as McKeown and Brown implied.

In the light of this new evidence, it seems probable that the County Hospital made a positive contribution, although precise measurement is impossible. Probably the same was true of the Dispensary, which treated no fewer than 94,589 cases between 1788 and 1844. 'In times of sickness no charitable institution meets their wants more completely or more speedily', wrote its historian, and in the mid-1840s it treated an annual average of 2,119 patients as against 974 at the County Hospital – at less than half the cost.[20]

Finally, it should be noted that, for better or for worse, the ratio of doctors to population was far above the national average in York in the 1841 census (1 to 424 persons against 1 to 930), and that there is evidence of the practice of inoculation against smallpox through the Dispensary, which White states was 'the means of saving a few lives'.[21] Whether or not inoculation was a significant factor is unknown; for many years historians tended to dismiss it, but Razzell has recently maintained that this factor was of major importance in reducing mortality on a national scale.[22]

The retreat of epidemic diseases

In recent years a number of distinguished scholars have argued that epidemic disease was much less in evidence after about 1740, and have become disposed to regard this as an autonomous factor influencing levels of mortality, operating largely independently of food supply, indeed as fortuitous from an economic point of view. In a notable analysis by Chambers, population growth in Nottinghamshire after about 1750 has been represented as 'an upswing of an entirely new order. The forces of demographic growth were now on the move, mainly as a result of the changing incidence of epidemic disease.' Reference is made to the effects of economic growth through the provision of alternative employment and better clothes, houses, and diet in accounting for greater resistance to disease, but 'in view of the fact that it was becoming effective in many parts before these environmental changes had made much impact ... allowance must also be given for those changes in virulence and resistance upon which human effort had no influence'.[23] In the same vein, Eversley has remarked that

If people lived longer, it must have been partly because they were cleaner, partly because some effective medical practice was known, partly because famines were no longer severe, but *mostly* [my italics] because the great killer epidemics failed to return, for reasons which might not be connected with human actions at all.[24]

York had certainly suffered its share of the bubonic plague in the distant past: the *Victoria County History* notes occurrences in 1349, 1361, 1375, 1378, 1485, 1538, 1550, 1604, 1631 and 1645, which will not be an exhaustive listing. Chambers has pointed out that when the plague vanished from England after 1666, a number of other epidemic diseases continued to scourge the population periodically[25] and it is certain that these were in evidence in York during the following seventy-five years.

The city appears to have suffered constantly from epidemics: between 1715 and 1735 smallpox, measles, and influenza followed or accompanied one another almost without intermission. In the same period a variety of fevers 'seemed to be everyday diseases': cholera, dysentery, intestinal inflammation, 'putrid fever', 'sweating sickness'. Disease was intensified by severe winters. The high death-rate of 1740 for example, probably reflects the bad winters of 1739–42: in 1740 the Ouse was so deeply frozen that booths were set up and football played on the ice.

Thus Allison and Tillott characterize the position in the first half of the century.[26] But it is notable that no further reference is made to the occurrence of epidemic disease in York until the nineteenth-century outbreaks of cholera and typhus discussed below: nor does Creighton's *History of Epidemics* indicate any unusual mortality at York. On the basis of Wintringham's *Commentarium Nosologicum, morbos epidemicos et aeris variationes in urbe Eboracensi* . . . (1739), he notes eight references for the period 1715–39; thereafter there is nothing until a notice of epidemic influenza in 1842. This is of course, negative evidence, but we may assume that any major outbreaks of epidemic disease between 1740 and 1832 would not have gone unnoticed in Creighton's compendium.

Although much of the supporting evidence is circumstantial, and none beyond dispute, it seems probable that the second half of the eighteenth century and first twenty years of the nineteenth saw declining mortality and increased expectation of life. Thereafter, there seems to have been a halt to the trend to improvement, which is suggested by comparing the crude mortality of 1820–2 (19.4 in table 5.1), with the average level in the three York urban sub-districts in the 1840s (24.9, see table 5.4 below). By this time the life-saving factors referred to above would have worked themselves out; indeed the appearance of cholera in 1832 may be seen as a reversal of the retreat of epidemic disease. Moreover, York was becoming more crowded; by 1821 29 per cent more people dwelt within the constant boundaries of the Municipal Borough than in 1801, and by 1831, 56 per cent. Griffith's calculations of the course of the national death rate indicate a slight rise after about 1820,[27] a view which accords well with the impressions of contemporaries such as Farr and McCulloch, who wrote in 1847, 'it appears probable, however, that the rate of mortality had been reduced to a minimum in 1815, and that it increased somewhat in the interval between that and 1830'.[28] Buer has listed a range of possible causes ranging from economic depression and dislocation in agriculture in the years after 1815 to Irish immigration and 'a natural ebb in the tide of public health reform'.[29] But the critical factor was probably the continued growth of towns, which was faster both absolutely and proportionately after 1821 than before;[30] that is to say, of the element which, in spite of eighteenth-century improvements, continued to experience rates of mortality somewhat above those prevailing in the countryside. Everyone is familiar with the spate of sanitary reports and enquiries of the 1840s, and it might be assumed that their very existence implies a concern with deteriorating public health conditions, or at the very least, a recognition that no improvement had been seen for twenty years or more.

Thus, if further reductions in York mortality ceased to occur after about 1820, this would be in accordance with the national experience, especially with regard to towns. Indeed, all the developments described here are in accordance with national trends and their causes, as these are understood by the vast majority of historians.[31] However, it is only right to point out that there is another view respecting the tendencies of these years, and perhaps by implication, developments in York. Krause has argued that the ecclesiastical record of births and deaths worsened far more than most historians have believed, between 1780 and 1820, but thereafter improved. This, if true, means that in the post 1780 period, birth rates and death rates are both grossly understated by using the *Parish Register Abstracts*, and he propounds the view that, on a national scale, a rising birth rate rather than a falling death rate was the principal motor of population growth.[32] Latterly, his arguments have been buttressed by Hollingsworth, who, having settled on a series of national rates of population growth for each decade in the period 1780–1821, fits a number of appropriate model life-tables to the age-distribution ascertained by the 1821 census, with a view to reading off the vital rates. This procedure enables him to suggest that fertility in the years down to 1821 (44 per 1,000) was about a quarter as high again as most historians have believed, and therefore, by implication, given the known rate of growth of population, the death rate must also have been high in the same period (it is put at 32.25). When these levels are compared with birth and death rates derived from civil registration data for the 1840s, the indications are that fertility had dropped to about 35, and the death rate to 22.[33] This interpretation, which tends to reverse established conclusions on the course of national death rates both before and after 1821, may be correct, and could apply to such country towns as York. But it is based on assumptions that are just as sweeping as those employed earlier in this chapter, and does not accord at all well with the views of contemporaries, and well-authenticated historical impressions.[34]

Pending further enquiries into the course of mortality in York, I shall therefore provisionally conclude that it was falling between 1750 and about 1820, and thereafter tended to stabilize: the remainder of this chapter will be devoted to a closer examination of patterns of mortality in the 1840s, based on the far more reliable evidence available after the commencement of civil registration, together with the factors which explain them. The first relevant factor is environmental.

THE SANITARY STATE OF YORK IN THE 1840S

Drainage

'The locality of the city is situated in a great flat, extending for miles and rising nowhere more than 100 feet above the river.' So stated James Smith of Deanston, the prominent drainage engineer and sanitarian, in introducing his *Report to the General Board of Health* on the state of York.[35] The natural drainage was into the River Ouse, and its tributary the Foss, so that all constructed drains passed into them. The Ouse was subject to flooding from time to time, affecting North Street, Skeldergate and other adjacent streets. But the privations of those who resided by the Ouse were as nothing compared with those who dwelt by the Foss. The Foss had been canalized under an act of 1793, and was an economic failure from the very beginning. As part of the engineering works a lock had been constructed at Castle Mills, where the river joined the Ouse. The general effects of the lock were to hold the level of the Foss about 7 ft above that of the Ouse, and the consequence was the existence of a considerable sheet of 'stagnant water, replete with vegetable and animal matter', in the centre of the low-lying districts of Walmgate, Hungate, Foss Islands, Layerthorpe, etc.[36] The vestry of one affected parish (St Cuthbert), memorialized Smith of Deanston in 1849, saying that the natural drainage of the locality was entirely lost 'by the artificial means used in raising the level of the River Foss to a higher elevation than the adjacent lands, by which cause our parish is almost surrounded by a stagnant marsh or bog on the one side . . . and on the other by the stagnant river itself, which is now and has been for years, a source of danger to human life'.[37] Into the Foss poured the fetid contents of the drains, and hard by its unwholesome banks, the proprietors of dung and sellers of night-soil maintained their principal stockpiles.[38]

Mention has been made of the drains and sewers actually carrying refuse to the rivers, which all writers on the York sanitary problem criticized extensively. The City Commissioners laid about 6,000 yards of drains over the years 1830–45, but their work had been inadequate.

It is much to be regretted that . . . the regard for economy which it has been thought requisite to observe has materially lessened the utility of what has been done . . . The whole of the drains built during the last twenty years are laid on vegetable soil, which is of a spongy or boggy nature, and fails in giving that support necessary to enable the drains to retain their form and level . . . The fall of the drains per lineal yard is about half an inch, and sometimes less; and, on account of the spongy bottom, and the slight and open nature of the brickwork, I believe, the majority are in a very inefficient state.[39]

Not all areas had the dubious benefits of even these main drains. 'Inefficient as the sewerage of the city is, it is rendered more so by the fact that back courts and streets, and many dwellings have no side drains communicating with the main sewers already formed . . . To some cottage tenements lately built there is no drain or sewer in the street.'[40] Laycock went on to describe the general character of cleansing. While the houses of the higher classes and 'all the more respectable houses recently built' had water-closets emptying into the drains or into cesspools, the houses of the poorer classes had only midden privies. These were cleansed by scavengers. 'The night soil is retained, giving off its impurities until a sufficient quantity is accummulated, when it is removed from the yard during the night in barrows . . . and put out into the street; from thence it is carted away to large dung-hills within the city.' Numerous examples were given by Laycock and others.

In the newly-built ranges of cottage tenements, one privy is appropriated to from four to eight, twelve, and even fourteen families . . . the position of the privy is selected evidently without any reference to the health or comfort of the inhabitants. In a new range of cottages in Long Close-Lane, there may be seen the door of a common privy at one end exactly opposite to the door of a tenement . . . In 'Plow's Buildings' the privies of the houses are in front. The soil-holes are usually open, and run over and flood back courts (as in Court No. 46, Hope Street, Beedham's Court, Skeldergate, etc.). In St John's-place, Haver-lane, during wet weather the privies have to be emptied by buckets into the open channel in the middle of the street. In the Water-lanes there are several houses *without* privies, so that the inhabitants have to use those of their neighbours by stealth, or go into the street.[41]

Again and again the theme of the inadequacy of the system recurred in the debates of the period. Some argued in favour of the 'principle of water-closet piping through the entire sewerage' for the houses of all classes, while others dismissed such ideas as utopian. In 1850 the water company claimed to supply 600 water-closets,[42] and since the 1851 census gave the total number of inhabited houses in York as 7,077, only about 8 or 9 per cent enjoyed this superior system. While later efforts were made to improve the state of privies, there remained many more of these than of water closets in York right down to the 1890s.

A subsidiary irritation, under this general heading, arose

from animal refuse. Canon Harcourt commented adversely upon 'the slaughter-houses, dung-heaps, pig-sties, etc., which unfortunately subsist in the heart of the town, are represented in several instances as pouring their solid contents into open drains, and the effluvia to be sometimes such as might alone suffice to generate contagion'. The Shambles was

a narrow row of houses in a nest of narrow streets in the heart of York, filled with small butchers' shops, in which animals, driven through these streets, are slaughtered. At the back of these there passes a shallow drain with a bad fall, partly covered and partly open . . . into this channel the drainings from the privies, and the runnings from the slaughter-houses, are washed or swept, while the more solid offal is thrown on the soil holes (to which there is no access but through the shops), or collected in tubs.[43]

This was a continuing complaint throughout the period.

Inadequacy of water supply

Owing to the lack of high land around York, upon which rain water could have been collected in reservoirs and fed into the city by gravitation, the water supply had to come from either the Rivers Ouse and Foss, or from springs and wells which occurred at various points in the city.

In this period most York consumers were provided with Ouse water, by a waterworks company first set up in the 1670s. A steam engine was in operation to draw the water from the river and in the early 1840s it was distributed across the city by means of iron mains of 11 inches and 3 inches in the principal streets. Lead service pipes led from the main to individual houses, and it was estimated in 1844 that about 3,000 houses (out of some 7,000 in the City) were supplied. The middle and higher classes filtered the water coming into the houses, but the poorer classes, often dependent on taps in the yards, did not. Charges were estimated at about 9d. or a shilling in the pound of the rental, so that they would vary from 3s. to 5s. for a two-roomed cottage rented at £4 or £5 per annum. The water of the Ouse was said to be of very pure quality, being taken from the river above the point where the first of the city drains disgorged itself, and the only general complaints against the service seem to have been that the supply was sometimes intermittent, and liable to have a muddy appearance at times of flooding, due to the high amount of alluvium held in suspension.[44]

The other source of water, still used by perhaps half the York households in 1845, was from wells and springs. 'Had the inhabitants of York to depend exclusively for their supply of water, as a beverage, upon the springs, their complaints of bad water would be well-founded ... water from this source is most generally of a very indifferent quality, containing an unusually large amount of calcereous and nitrogenous salts in solution', commented White. The great peculiarity found in York spring water was the existence of the nitrates, and White alleged that these arose from the decomposition of organic matter – two springs close to St Cuthbert's and St Sampson's churchyards respectively, had a 'very large amount of organic impurity'.[45]

Fortunately, the supply of water from the Ouse was much improved after the formation of the York New Waterworks Company in 1846. New works were set up at Acomb Landing, consisting of two reservoirs, three filter beds of the latest design, a supply reservoir at Severus Hill, and two pumping engines. This plant was in operation by 1849, and by 1850, the company claimed to supply nearly 6,000 houses.[46] In June 1849, when James Smith of Deanston was working on his *Report to the General Board of Health*, he was able to speak with approbation of the new works, which would secure to York 'an ample supply of river water well filtered', to replace a supply which hitherto had been 'very scanty and of inferior quality'.[47]

Graveyards

'The state of the parochial burial-grounds of York must have a considerable and noxious influence on the atmosphere within the churches and on that of the city generally, and on the

water. The greater number of these grounds are of extreme
antiquity, and must have been buried over very often. In
fact, many of them are raised above the street level from the
accumulated remains of generations.'[48] Much more sensational
descriptions of the 'disgraceful and revolting' state of the York
graveyards were delivered by A. E. Hargrove, in a lecture to
the Health of Towns Association in 1847. It was apparently
impossible to bury the dead without committing acts of
'indecency and desecration' by this date: five of the twenty-
four churchyards had already been closed, but horrific facts
were ascertained in relation to the others. The graveyard of
St Martin-le-Grand had been 'twice buried over during the
last quarter century', and like St Sampson's was often water-
logged. At St Michael-le-Belfry and St Mary Bishophill Junior
funerals could scarcely ever take place without exposing sound
or decayed coffins, with bones. At other churches, conditions
were less disgraceful, although at one, Hargrove knew of an
instance of a dog having run off with a leg-bone with fragments
of flesh still adhering; and certain children in Walmgate had
'become possessed of the greater part of a skeleton'. Hargrove
argued that these things were not only sacrilegious, but also a
great menace to the health of the living, through their effects
on air (stench), and water. 'Hundreds of unsuspecting individuals are daily drinking the filterings of human corruption,
to their present injury, and hastening the arrival of a premature
death.' His recommendation was that the citizens should press
for closure of the burial grounds forthwith – even of the Dissenters' burial grounds, which were in nothing like so grievous
a state.[49]

By 1850, Smith of Deanston discerned 'a general feeling' in
York for the closure of the churches and churchyards for burial.
'The clergy in general are favourable to the discontinuance
and some of them express a desire that the graveyards and
churches should be closed against interments of any description.' He commended a graveyard set up by the York Public
Cemetery Company in 1837, as roomy, well-situated and drained, and tastefully laid out, with a 'proper air of propriety'

about it. Burials within the city churchyards were in fact discontinued by an Order in Council of 1854, and it was laid down that no new burial grounds were to be established in the city or within two miles of the boundary.[50] So ended, in York, 'the baneful custom of interment in towns'. It is true that the 'miasmatic' or poisoned air theory on which the arguments of Hargrove and other reformers depended, has now been discarded in favour of bacteriological explanations of the transmission of disease. But ground-water collected through strata of interment soil may be bacterial to a high degree. Would-be improvers were right in seeking an end to the custom, even if their theory was wrong. Indeed it was as well that even in the 1840s, few York inhabitants drew their water from wells adjacent to graveyards.

The smoke nuisance

Reference was frequently made to this alleged nuisance by would-be reformers. Laycock calculated that 123 industrial and commercial premises discharged smoke into the atmosphere, and declared that 'the quantity of soot which falls is very great . . . the pollution of the air from this source must be extremely great, and injurious to the health'.[51] In a pamphlet published by the York Health of Towns Association (1852), it was argued that the few isolated efforts of manufacturers to co-operate had hitherto been comparatively useless, that commercial and industrial interests would not suffer greatly if they adopted more perfect methods of combustion, that there was no longer any reason why the nuisance should continue in the city, and that there should be a vigorous effort to improve the situation on the part of the Town Council and local manufacturers.[52]

However, it does not seem likely that York suffered to an unusual degree from this type of pollution. The 123 establishments mentioned in Laycock's report were generally small-scale in character, and the total volume of smoke and soot which they produced would almost certainly be less than that produced by the coal fires of some 7,000 houses. 'Coal is cheap in York ... and it is the usual fuel of the people', as Laycock himself remarked. This is not to argue that there was no smoke nuisance in York, but rather that as compared with manufacturing towns, it was of smaller importance. 'Few places of its magnitude have less occasion to complain of atmospheric vitiation from this source', wrote William White, in the course of preparing a paper which inclined to take a rather more complacent view of the sanitary condition of York than did some of the others mentioned above.[53]

The Irish problem

The disorderly habits of the Irish immigrants were viewed at the time as an additional cause of poor public health conditions. Their very ways of life, it was thought, helped to create an unwholesome environment. The inhabitants of York were on the whole seen as 'a cleanly people ... it was pleasing ... to see in passing along the streets, the thoroughly clean cottage, the bright window frames, the scrupulously clean door step, stoned to whiteness with great precision, and forming a margin to the well-washed red-brick floor'. The principal exception to this was 'the unfortunate sons and daughters of Erin, whose national habits are less orderly'.[54]

The principal enclaves of Irish settlement have been noted above – Bedern, the Walmgate district (parishes of St Dennis, St Margaret, St George and St Peter-le-Willows), with additional streets elsewhere, such as the Water Lanes in St Mary Castlegate. In all, the number of Irish-born persons in York reached 1,928 (1851); from the enumerators' returns I counted 333 in Bedern, 412 in St George, 159 in St Margaret's parish, 144 in St Peter-le-Willows and 223 in St Dennis. The rest were scattered through the city. Within these parishes and districts there was still more intensive colonization of particular streets or blocks of buildings. Notably, Snarr's, Pulleyn's, Jackson's and Henderson's buildings in the Bedern, had between them 292 Irish-born persons, and Long-close Lane in St George, 308.

The Irish were of course, grossly over-crowded. The houses in Long-close Lane contained up to twenty-one inhabitants and seventeen lodgers. Irishmen tended to be 'packed close as herrings in a barrel', wrote Richard Thomas, particularizing rack-renting in Long-close Lane in his account to Smith of Deanston.

There are 20 houses, I believe, there, and the original rent was fixed at the rate of 1s. 6d., and in no case did it exceed 1s. 9d., per week. He let the houses to the Irish; he charged an extra rent which got to 2s. and 2s. 6d. I believe nine of the houses have been taken off his hands, and instead of charging 1s. 6d., as he did originally, he is now, with 11 houses charging 4s. a week, whereby he receives as much rent from them as he did formerly from the 20 houses. I believe, positively, he could get twice that amount of rent.[55]

I have attempted to examine the Irish by means of a Bedern sub-sample, consisting of the whole of the inhabitants of Snarr's Building (referred to by Thomas as 'the monster nuisance in York'), Pulleyn's, Jackson's and Henderson's buildings. These consisted of apartment dwellings, usually of one room, thus average household size was not so large as that encountered elsewhere, in Long-close Lane for example. Even so, these buildings contained 350 persons, of whom 323 were in households headed by Irish-born heads. The average size of households in this scanty accommodation was 6.1 (or 7.7 in the case of the 42 Irish headed households); that is, quite significantly higher than the city average of 4.70. The average size of Irish-headed nuclear families was 4.9, again higher than the city average of 3.45, although very significantly the ratio of children aged 0–4 per 1,000 married women aged 15–49 in the Irish-headed households was as low as 560 (city average 836). This last ratio, taken in conjunction with the fact that the average number of heads' children (of all ages) was very high in these Irish households (3.07 compared with 1.76 for the city as a whole), suggests that whereas the fertility of the Irish was above average, the incidence of infant mortality amongst their offspring was extremely high.[56]

A miserable physical environment was obviously one cause

of the unfortunate position in which the Irish found themselves. Another was poverty, if the two things can be distinguished. Of the Irish-born 72.3 per cent aged 12 or over returned their occupations as agricultural labourer, a relatively ill-paid occupation, and as many as 82.4 per cent of the Irish male household heads were so described. Not surprisingly, they found it necessary to admit lodgers into their miserable apartments and the average number of lodgers or visitors in households with Irish heads was 2.43, as compared with 0.61 for the city as a whole. There was also a strong degree of localization of origin: 70.6 per cent of the Irish-born were from Mayo, 17.8 per cent from Sligo, 7.8 per cent from Roscommon, and 3.7 per cent from the rest of Ireland, in this sub-sample.

In the worst cases, these unfortunates slept on straw or shavings and could not be persuaded to wash either their clothes or their persons. 'We always put them into a bath, and the Irish so strongly objected, that we were obliged to use physical force to make them. One old woman made the most hideous yells when put into the bath. She said that it would almost certainly kill her, and that she had never been washed since she was an infant; at any rate she could not remember the time.'[57] The Irish were generally viewed with hostility for their wild ways, their alien religion, and in their personal and household habits, were looked upon as an affront to public decency.

PATTERNS OF MORTALITY IN THE 1840S

Crude, child and infant death rates

Crude death rates have been estimated for York Registration District in the period 1841–51. After computation of annual rates, the mean rate for the period was 24.0 for the Registration District, 24.9 for the three urban sub-districts. This compares with 22.3 (a simple average of the annual crude death rates) for England and Wales, over the same years.[58] By this date, however, it is possible to provide more detail in the form of age-specific death rates; there exists a valuable table of mortality for the years 1838–44, which is compared in table 5.2 with that for England and Wales in the same period.

TABLE 5.2   *Age-specific mortality rates per 1,000: York Registration District, 1838–44**

	Males		Females	
	(1) York R.D.	(2) England and Wales	(1) York R.D.	(2) England and Wales
0–	213.8	205.1	163.1	154.4
1–	56.6	67.1	58.2	63.9
2–	33.9	35.3	38.4	34.9
3–	23.2	25.2	24.5	24.8
4–	19.1	18.5	24.6	18.3
0–	73.5	70.7	64.8	60.4
5–	11.9	9.3	10.3	9.0
10–	4.5	5.0	5.3	5.5
15–	7.7	8.1	7.2	8.3
25–	11.1	9.7	10.5	10.1
35–	14.2	12.5	12.4	12.4
45–	20.4	17.8	15.4	15.5
55–	32.2	31.4	26.9	27.8
65–	69.6	66.1	60.2	58.9
75–	156.7	143.9	128.1	132.0
85–94	276.9	296.5	307.8	275.6

* Appendix to the 9th Annual Report of the Registrar-General, Pt. III.

The most important conclusion to be drawn from table 5.2 is that infant mortality within York Registration District was worse than the national experience, by 4.2 per cent for males under 1, by 5.6 per cent in the case of girls. This meant that York mortality was worse in the overall 0–4 age-groups. (By 4.0 per cent for males; 7.3 per cent for females.) From the age of 25 and upwards, mortality among males again seems to have been rather higher in the York District, since every single age-group (except 85–94) had a higher mortality factor than the national, although this was not the case with females.

Of course, these figures include the rural surround, since they relate to the Registration District as a whole. A child mortality rate (0–4) for the years 1839–41, has been calculated from Laycock's data covering the Municipal Borough, and works out to 95.2 per 1,000, undifferentiated by sex. This in turn was an average, covering child death rates of 84.0, 100.9 and 104.1 for the parishes comprised within the municipal parts of the three sub-districts of Micklegate, Bootham and Walmgate respectively.[59]

Comparable age-specific mortality rates have been computed for the years 1851, and 1850–2, using 1851 census data to obtain the populations at risk within the various groups. Once again, a comparison is made with England and Wales.

TABLE 5.3   *Age-specific death rates, 1851 and 1850–2**

	(1) York R.D. 1851		(2) York R.D. 1850–2 (average)		(3) England and Wales 1850–2 (average)	
	Males	Females	Males	Females	Males	Females
0–	92.4	83.4	76.2	67.9	71.8	61.8
5–	7.0	8.4	6.5	7.0	8.7	8.5
10–	3.5	4.6	3.3	4.0	5.0	5.2
15–	7.9	6.2	8.0	7.4	7.7	8.1
25–	10.6	12.0	10.3	10.2	9.4	10.0
35–	12.1	11.7	14.1	12.3	12.2	12.1
45–	16.4	15.2	19.8	15.8	17.6	15.2
55–	33.6	20.9	34.3	25.2	30.2	26.6
65–	80.2	65.6	71.8	60.1	63.5	57.4
75–	138.9	142.6	151.2	135.8	141.4	128.9
85–	160.0	218.0	266.0	311.5	291.3	274.7

* 1851 Census and Registrar-General's Annual Reports for 1850–2.

Column (1) merely shows the dangers of generalizing from one year rate, but incidentally draws attention to the effects on the child death rate of the measles outbreak of 1851, said by the Registrar-General to have been particularly prevalent in Yorkshire (see below, p. 144). When columns (2) and (3) are compared, it is clear that the tendency for the child death rate to surpass the national rate was still evident. This time the York rate was 6.1 per cent higher for males, 9.9 per cent for females, in the 0–4 group. Perhaps York's position was worsening *vis-à-vis* the national situation; at all events, it is clear that it was not improving. Nor had there been any improvement in York since 1838–44, as is obvious when tables 5.2 and 5.3 are compared. It is also interesting to note that still, in 1850–2, York mortality rates in all male groups of 15 and upwards were rather higher than average, although once again, this was not consistently true of the female age-groups.

So far I have shown that in so far as York mortality was worse than that of the nation as a whole, higher infant mortality was mainly to blame. If the deaths under one year of age, are related to the sum of half the births of the given year, plus half the births of the preceding year, the mean infant mortality rates (per 1,000) arrived at for 1842 and 1845–51 combined are:

	Male	Female	Persons
York Registration District	209.0	174.7	192.9

By comparison, a simple average of the national infant death rates for these years works out at 156·3.[60] Birch later gave the infant death rate for York as 157 for the period 1841–70 taken as a whole, and mentioned that his figures were drawn from the Registrar-General's returns. This figure has been repeated in the *Victoria County History*, where it is also stated that the 157 rate was applicable to the 1840s.[61] It is in fact clear that the infant death rate was much higher than 157 in this decade, and served to keep the general (crude) death rate for York rather above the average for England and Wales.

Variation of mortality between different districts

Table 5.4 indicates sizeable differences in crude mortality between the various sub-districts composing the York Registration District.[62]

Micklegate sub-district exhibits lower rates throughout than the other two mainly urban sub-districts, which is probably attributable to the fact that of the three Micklegate was that with the largest rural minority (33.9 per cent of its inhabitants lived outside the boundaries of the city of York, as compared

TABLE 5.4   *Crude death rates in various sub-districts, 1841–51 (Deaths per 1,000 persons)* *

	(1) York R.D.	(2) York – 3 urban sub-districts	(3) Boot-ham S.D.	(4) Mickle-gate S.D.	(5) Walm-gate S.D.	(6) Rural Surround	(7) England and Wales
1841	21.7	21.8	21.9	20.3	23.0	21.6	21.6
1842	23.3	24.1	27.3	21.6	23.3	19.6	21.7
1843	21.1	22.1	25.9	18.4	21.8	16.9	21.2
1844	22.1	23.2	22.7	18.9	26.8	17.7	21.6
1845	20.7	21.4	20.1	20.1	23.2	18.1	20.9
1846	24.9	25.7	24.1	23.4	28.2	21.9	23.0
1847	30.8	32.4	28.0	27.4	39.1	24.3	24.7
1848	25.8	27.4	25.9	23.9	30.7	19.1	23.0
1849	26.7	28.8	32.0	20.7	31.7	17.7	25.1
1850	20.4	21.3	21.7	18.1	23.0	16.9	20.8
1851	24.4	25.6	24.3	22.3	28.4	19.2	22.0

* Registrar-General's Annual Reports; Mitchell and Deane (1962) 36.

with 5–15 per cent for Walmgate, and 5–25 per cent for Bootham, according to whether the Municipal or Parliamentary Borough boundary is taken). However, it is clear that even the crude death rates experienced in Micklegate were generally somewhat higher than those of the surrounding wholly rural sub-districts (Skelton, Escrick, Dunnington, Flaxton). The rates for Bootham are rather higher than those for Micklegate, and present some interesting differences – notably the rise in 1842–3, and another in 1849, driving the death rate up beyond the level reached in 1847. Finally, Walmgate death rates seem to have been consistently higher than those of both other sub-districts, at least after 1843. Throughout 1846–9 there were very high death rates, with a peak in 1847; again in 1851, the Walmgate rate (like the others, but with more force), moved upwards.

Unfortunately, these inter-district comparisons cannot be placed on an age-specific basis, for lack of data on age at death at the sub-district level. However, a re-working of Laycock's data for 1839–41[63] points to the existence of interesting differences between those parts of these districts which lay within the borough, is respect of child death rates, pulmonary and epidemic death rates (table 5.5). Table 5.6 is the result of further analysis on the basis of wards of the Municipal Borough.

TABLE 5.5 *Deaths per 1,000 at risk by sub-districts, 1839–41**

	(i) From all causes	(ii) From Epidemics	(iii) From Pulmonary diseases	(iv) Child death rate, 0–4
Urban part of				
(1) Bootham sub-district	25.4	4.5	5.0	100.9
(2) Micklegate sub-district	25.6	5.3	6.2	84.0
(3) Walmgate sub-district	27.7	5.9	6.0	104.1

* Laycock (1844) 235. See Figure 4.

TABLE 5.6 *Deaths per 1,000 at risk by wards, 1839–41**

Ward	(i) From all causes	(ii) From Epidemics	(iii) From Pulmonary diseases	(iv) Child death rate, 0–4
(1) Bootham	23.5	4.6	4.9	94.2
(2) Guildhall	21.1	4.3	4.0	78.4
(3) Walmgate	28.1	5.8	6.8	107.6
(4) Monk	27.9	5.8	5.7	104.7
(5) Castlegate	29.8	7.0	5.8	119.3
(6) Micklegate	23.7	4.2	5.9	65.2

* Laycock (1844) 235. See Figure 4.

Walmgate sub-district emerges as the worse of the three sub-districts, on balance; among the wards, the two which substantially made up Walmgate sub-district (Walmgate and Monk), were similarly bad. Castlegate had the worst record of all the wards: since this ward came partly under Bootham and partly under Micklegate sub-district, it is clear that we have here a component tending to worsen the records of these two sub-districts. If Castlegate ward were excluded then the differences between Walmgate sub-district on the one hand, and

Bootham and Micklegate sub-districts on the other, would be enlarged.

If the urban part of Walmgate sub-district was on the whole less healthy than its neighbours to what factors must we look to explain this phenomenon? An orthodox approach is to look to ratios of overcrowding, persons per acre, or persons per house. But when such calculations are made, Bootham sub-district turns out to be the most crowded in terms of inhabitants per acre, houses per acre, and inhabitants per house. In point of fact such calculations tell us little; all these registration sub-districts included tracts of countryside, and in any case houses varied greatly in size. The best indicator, persons per room, is not obtainable from the census statistics of this period.

We thus have little to go on in respect of overcrowding. Laycock recorded that the highest proportion of families having only one room for all purposes was in the Bedern (Bootham sub-district, 68 per cent). This was certainly as inferior, Irish neighbourhood and a danger to public health; but the other extreme in the city was St George (2 per cent).[64] St George lay in Walmgate sub-district and was by no means a healthy parish. as Laycock's 'Sanatory Table' shows. In addition, it is probable that grouping parishes by sub-districts or wards is not the most illuminating permutation. We should therefore be well advised to follow closely the arguments of this excellent Laycock, who had access to a great deal more material than is available to the modern historian.[65]

Laycock believed that the variations in mortality within different parts of the city arose from differences of drainage. This in turn, was related to their mean altitudes. 'The natural drainage ... or in other words, the varying altitude of the different parishes ... may (though not without exceptions) be taken as the standard. Even when two districts are closely contiguous and sewered alike, and inhabited alike, a difference in the fall ... will be accompanied by a difference in the viability of the people in the two parishes, for the lower lying parish will ... receive the drain water of the upper, as well as its own.'[66]

No. 5.—A SANATORY TABLE for York; calculated on the Census of 1841, and the Entries of Deaths in the Registries of the York District during 1839, 1840, 1841.

Parish.	Population in 1841.	Mean Altitude.	Inhabitants per Rood.	Inhabitants to One Birth Annually.	Inhabitants to One Death Annually. From all Causes.	From Epidemics.	From Pulmonary Diseases.	Per Cent. living aged under 5 Years.	Per Cent. dying aged under 5 Years.	Per Cent. of Deaths of Labourers.	Per Cent. of Deaths of Artizans.	Average Age at Death, 1839-40-41.	Difference above or below the General Meanage.	Difference above and below the Mean Ratio of Death.	Difference above or below Epidemic Ratio.
Holy Trinity, Micklegate	1,212	61	24	84·75	52·69	404	281·8	9·04	17·39	8·7	24·5	42·58	+10·37	+15	+117
St. Martin with St. Gregory	554	50	32	49·02	41·93	213	346·2	7·40	32·16	24·3	18·9	41·89	+9·68	3	+27
St. Helen, Stonegate	607	48	38	45·63	43·35	360	404·3	8·40	23·80	11·9	21·4	39·95	+7·74	+6	+117
Holy Trinity, King's-court.	685	53	43	38·92	47·80	171	207·5	9·05	34·88	16·2	39·5	38·07	+5·86	+10	-16
St. Martin-le-Grand	553	44	30	50·27	48·83	332	184·3	7·23	26·47	8·8	1·4	37·18	+4·97	+8	+118
Minster Yard	542	54	16	(a)	95·75	821	416·9	9·59	35·29	5·8	41·01	35·47	+3·26	+58	+414
St. Giles (d).	1,228	48	31	43·37	39·81	358	147·2	10·60	29·63	6·1	34·5	35·30	+3·09	+3	+171
St. Nicholas	182	..	19	45·5	54·65	(e)	605·6	7·18	20·08	10·0	20·0	34·30	+2·09	+17	..
St. Michael, Spurriergate	499	40	41	32·67	27·72	150	249·5	9·62	37·03	35·1	18·9	33·35	+1·14	-10	-18
* St. Maurice (f)	1,424	40	22	36·37	42·72	356	178·0	13·11	33·00	20·0	27·0	32·54	+0·33	+5	+149
St. Mary, Bishophill, Junior	1,757	48	35	39·39	37·38	210	125·5	12·85	31·91	17·7	24·1	31·51	-0·70	par	+32
St. John, Delpike	351	47	62	28·53	23·1	117	117·0	10·08	46·66	17·7	37·7	30·95	-1·26	-14	-79
All Saints, Pavement	417	47	23	23·9	62·61	313	1390·0	10·09	40·00	10·0	45·0	30·30	-1·91	+15	+175
St. Wilfrid and Mint Yard	336	50	13	44·59	75·96	357	593·3	6·46	35·55	5·5	22·2	30·18	-2·03	-39	+189
St. Mary, Castlegate	952	36	42	34·69	30·49	286	151·1	11·02	47·29	43·2	27·2	29·69	-2·52	-7	+98
St. Olave, Marygate (g)	563	46	39	19·68	28·93	175	154·3	12·09	45·83	38·4	26·07	29·35	-2·86	-2	-17
St. Michael le Belfrey	1,218	54	32	35·07	37·00	143	287·9	9·37	43·87	15·3	25·5	28·27	-3·94	par	+3
* St. Lawrence	981	42	22	32·73	40·32	737	105·4	13·25	39·72	26·02	20·5	27·31	-4·90	+3	+550
St. Sampson	761	52	39	43·23	53·10	254	253·6	10·77	46·51	9·3	27·9	27·09	-5·12	+16	+66
St. Mary, Bishophill, Senior	1,123	40	31	34·44	41·05	196	153·8	12·91	40·24	19·5	34·1	26·61	-5·60	+4	+9
* All Saints Peaseholm	373	34	33	(b)	48·66	225	286·1	14·20	47·82	4·3	60·8	26·47	-5·74	+11	+37
* St. Margaret	1,207	37	50	25·68	27·62	125	165·3	13·58	47·69	23·8	33·8	25·94	-6·27	-10	-63
St. Peter the Little	573	47	70	28·65	44·07	172	286·5	11·69	43·59	20·2	38·4	25·28	-6·93	+7	-15
* Beddern	368	49	59	(b) 29·13	27·06	110	102·2	12·22	52·50	40·0	15·0	24·12	-8·09	-10	-77
* St. Andrew	318	44	33	(b) 23·56	28·95	318	95·0	8·50	44·11	11·7	39·2	24·09	-8·21	-9	+111
Holy Trinity, Goodramgate	551	52	46	28·11	44·59	275	183·6	15·24	45·94	24·3	35·1	23·89	-8·32	+7	+88
* St. Saviour	1,995	39	50	29·51	37·22	142	231·9	13·95	57·87	16·8	48·7	23·62	-8·59	par	-6
* St. Crux	910	43	38	57·38	45·5	227	211·6	10·10	45·0	18·3	31·6	23·26	-8·95	+8	-72
St. John, Micklegate	1,026	33	131	29·31	30·78	114	132·2	11·98	50·49	29·7	27·0	21·36	-9·34	-7	-73
St. Cuthbert	1,138	36	40	25·65	25·67	103	120·1	14·70	57·94	24·03	34·8	22·47	-9·74	-12	-15
* St. Dennis	1,314	35	38	22·57	36·18	172	146·0	12·25	52·25	24·7	28·4	21·36	-10·85	-1	-15
* St. Helen-on-the-Walls	444	40	35	(b)	66·66	334	740·0	14·18	57·89	26·3	47·3	19·52	-12·69	+29	+88
All Saints, North-street	1,199	39	143	24·82	36·40	100	164·2	14·76	55·10	23·4	55·1	19·56	-12·65	-1	-86
* St. Peter-le-Willows	497	39	40	27·89	27·61	93	115·5	16·70	59·25	18·5	57·3	19·9	-13·12	-1	-88
* St. George	1,024	37	40	(c)	38·88	140	147·7	15·13	60·67	14·6	61·7	18·07	-14·14	+1	-8
Total and Averages	28,932	44	37	33·87	37·77	187	181·	11·76	42·16	21·68	33·36	32·21	..	..	..

(a) Minster Yard and Beddern, (b) All Saints Peaseholm, St. Cuthbert, and St. Helen-on-the-Walls, and (c) St. Dennis and St. George are respectively united. No return of the births in the parish of St. George could be obtained. (d) Exclusive of the asylum. (e) No deaths of this class. (f) Exclusive of the hospital. (g) Exclusive of the workhouse.

Note.—The parishes which are marked * have a declination exclusively to the Foss; and as the level of that river is 7 feet higher than the Ouse, their true drainage altitude = the mean altitude - 7; thus the true drainage altitude of St. George is 30, or 37-7.

Fig. 4. Dr Laycock's 'Sanatory Table', 1844

He conscientiously listed in the 'Sanatory Table', the drainage altitude of each York parish, and from this data it is possible to compute the mean drainage altitudes for the urban parts of the three sub-districts, (Micklegate 45 ft, Bootham 47 ft, Walmgate 31 ft), which clearly has a bearing on the results of table 5.5. Laycock however, ignored the conventional sub-district boundaries and grouped the parishes according to the state of their drainage, so producing the data in table 5.7.

Not surprisingly, the worst-drained parishes were those on the banks of the two rivers – the Ouse and, more particularly, the Foss.[67] Laycock was clearly correct in drawing attention to drainage altitude as a key factor in determining death rates. Moreover, the 'worst-drained and ventilated' parishes of York

TABLE 5.7 *Mortality characteristics according to drainage district**

| | Mean altitude (feet) | Population per sq. rood | Mean age at death | Inhabs. to 1 death annually | | |
				(a) All causes	(b) Epidemic diseases	(c) Pulmonary diseases
(a) Best drained and ventilated parishes	50	27	35·3	54·3	347·7	334·2
(b) Intermediate parishes	43	40	27.8	41.4	247.2	219.7
(c) Worst drained and ventilated parishes	33	63	22.6	32.2	129.4	153.0

* Laycock (1844) 235.

coincided largely with the urban part of Walmgate sub-district, where every parish without exception was ill-drained. This explains of course, the relatively high death rates recorded for the district in tables 5.5 and 5.6.

Class differences in mortality

We have seen that of the three registration sub-districts, the most healthy, owing to its substantial rural content, was Micklegate and the least healthy was Walmgate. Moreover mortality has been shown to have varied markedly according to drainage altitude. What is the evidence on class differences in mortality, and could it not be argued, on the grounds that environment, nutrition, etc., were functions of class, that this was the critical variable?

It is true that there were marked inter-class mortality differences both within the city and outside it, as Laycock showed. His table (given in abridged form as 5.8 below), leaves much to be desired in respect of technique: 'average age at death' is a poor measure when the differing age-struc-

tures of the various social groups are not taken into consideration. But for all that, it is worth reproducing his statistics, since
he alone has enjoyed the opportunity of scrutinizing the entries
of deaths in the local registers, and was able to group the entries
by social status.

TABLE 5.8 *Abstract of deaths in York Registration District, 1839–41**

	Total no. deaths	Percentage aged under 15	Percentage from epidemic and contagious diseases	Average age at death	
A. York city					
(1) Gentry and professional with their families	146	23.3	11.6	48.6	
(2) Tradesmen, etc.	429	46.4	22.1	30.8	32.2
(3) Artisans, etc.	798	57.9	25.1	22.1	
(4) Undescribed	521	34.7	11.6	35.8	
(5) Labourers, etc.	504	56.9	21.2	23.8	
B. Suburbs					
(1) Gentry and professional with their families	40	15.0	12.5	49.2	
(2) Tradesmen, etc.	104	30.8	14.4	39.5	36.4
(3) Artisans, etc.	64	54.7	23.4	20.7	
(4) Undescribed	87	25.3	10.3	41.9	
(5) Labourers, etc.	188	44.7	26.6	30.7	
C. Rural population					
(1) Gentry, landowners, etc., with their families	29	13.8	20.7	44.9	
(2) Farmers, village tradesmen, etc.	243	32.5	19.8	39.1	38.7
(3) Agricultural labourers, etc.	279	40.9	15.0	32.0	

* Laycock (1844) 229.

Moreover, it must be conceded that within the borough, the
relatively favourable mortality levels for the higher classes in
York owed something to the fact that they tended to live in the
better-favoured districts from a sanitary point of view. To
demonstrate this, one can compare the class composition of

various districts and adduce further evidence in respect of rateable values and the *per capita* assessment of house property to Property and Income taxes.[68]

TABLE 5.9 *Socio-economic character of three sub-districts, related to their mortality experience*

	Micklegate	Bootham	Walmgate
Percentage of household heads in classes I–II (1851 sample)	24.2 (±6.2)	27.9 (±5.8)	15.8 (±4.9)
Annual value of house property assessed to Property and Income Tax (1842–3) divided by population (1841)	£3.10	£3.35	£2.41
Percentage of all rate assessments £10 or over (1850–1)	35.7	56.2	15.3
Average crude mortality rate, 1841–51 (table 5.4)	21.4	24.9	27.2
Child mortality rate, 1839–41 (Laycock) (table 5.6)	84.0	100.9	104.1

N.B. The proportions of Class I–II householders can be shown to have differed significantly when Walmgate and Bootham, and Walmgate and Micklegate sub-districts are compared. From the 1841 sample the proportions of household heads in Classes I–II for the three areas works out at 24.1 (±7.2) per cent for Micklegate, 36.6 (±7.4) per cent for Bootham, 21.1 (±5.3) per cent for Walmgate. Significant differences can be asserted between Bootham and Walmgate and (after a pooled estimate test) between Bootham and Micklegate.

Walmgate presents a clear association between high mortality and low socio-economic composition, and we know that it also had the most notorious public health problems. Bootham was on average a relatively affluent area, as all the socio-economic indicators show, but in addition to several very high class streets it happened to contain most of the crowded commercial and market district of the city, and certain confined enclaves (e.g. the Bedern), whose squalor and poverty was not surpassed even by the worst parts of Walmgate. Micklegate, although intermediate so far as these socio-economic indicators are concerned, was very largely the abode of the lower middle class and the respectable artisans (e.g. railway workers), and it also contained a substantial rural minority. These factors seem to have given it a better mortality record than Bootham (as a whole), and a much superior record to that of Walmgate.

It is also useful to reconsider Laycock's drainage districts in terms of the same socio-economic characteristics.[69]

TABLE 5.10   *Socio-economic character of well, intermediately and badly drained parishes related to their mortality experience*

	Best drained	Inter-mediately drained	Worst drained
Mean drainage altitude (feet)	50	43	33
Percentage of household heads in classes I–II (1851 sample)	29.8 (±5.8)	20.0 (±11.7)	16.1 (±3.6)
Annual value of house property assessed to tax. (1842–3) divided by population (1841)	£4.30	£5.45	£2.41
Percentage of all rate assess-ments £10 or over (1850–1)	45.5	53.4	18.1
Inhabitants to one death annually, from all causes, 1839–41 (Laycock)	54.3	41.4	32.2

N.B. In respect of proportions in social classes I–II, a significant differ-ence can be asserted between the best drained and worst drained districts, but not between the others. For 1841, the class I–II distribution was 36.7 (±6.9) per cent for the best drained district, 39.0 (±14.9) per cent for the intermediately drained, and 18.6 (±4.4) per cent for the worst drained. In that case one can assert a significant difference between the worst drained district and both other categories.

Once again, according to table 5.10 there is an obvious con-junction between the *worst* drainage, the highest death rates, and the presence of the highest proportion of lower class, poorer households. In the other categories the position was more complex. The best-drained district (and the least mortal), appears to have had a somewhat higher proportion of upper-class households, but this is not certain, since the ranges of error overlap considerably when the values 29.8 per cent and

20.0 are compared. On the other hand, the other socio-economic indicators seem to point to *the existence of a richer community, on the average, in the intermediately drained area of medium mortality.*

The last finding has particular significance. It is possible to state with certainty that there were clear connections between high mortality, poor drainage, and low-class, low income social parameters in York at this time. Walmgate sub-district was characterized by all these features. But it has also been shown that (a) the sub-district where the highest social classes were proportionately over-represented, and where *per capita* wealth was probably largest (Bootham) had somewhat *higher* death rates than the sub-district which was rather less well-placed from these points of view (Micklegate – see table 5.9); (b) conversely, the least mortal sub-district (Micklegate) was not, on the average, that where *per capita* wealth was highest and where most upper-class households were situated[70] (see table 5.9). On the other hand, we have already seen that (c) there was *always* a clear connection between drainage altitudes and mortality levels (tables 5.7 and 5.10).

From these findings, it can be argued that place of residence was more important in explaining differential mortality than social class and wealth and income *per se*, once a certain level of adequacy in respect of incomes, nutrition, etc., was achieved. It is probable that commercial factors operated to keep some higher-class residents in districts which, while certainly not the most deficient from a sanitary point of view, were not the best either. Coney Street and Spurriergate for example, were high-class streets of substantial trading families, and the principal thoroughfares of the parishes of St Martin-le-Grand and St Michael Spurriergate, which (along with St Mary Bishophill Senior) constituted the intermediately drained zone.[71] On the other hand it is very clear that the *worst* drained and most mortal areas were likely to be inhabited by households whose incomes and standards of nutrition were lowest. Below a certain level, all these phenomena were inextricably linked, and one cannot say whether relative deprivation or physical environment ought to be given primacy in explaining higher rates of mortality. These hypotheses are provisional in character, but cannot be improved upon unless detailed civil registration material is made available to historians in time to come.

Fluctuations in mortality

Table 5.11 sets out the annual fluctuations in crude and infant death rates over the period 1841–51, which were considerable.

TABLE 5.11 *Crude and infant death rates: York Registration District, 1841–51**

	Crude death rate per 1,000 (all ages)	Infant death rate per 1,000	Crude death rate excluding infant age-group
1841	21.7	178.1	17.3
1842	23.3	197.2	18.2
1843	21.1	Not available	–
1844	22.1	Not available	–
1845	20.7	157.3	16.7
1846	24.9	216.7	19.0
1847	30.8	191.4	25.9
1848	25.8	210.6	20.2
1849	26.7	186.7	21.6
1850	20.4	163.6	15.8
1851	24.4	221.2	18.0

* Registrar-General's Annual Reports; no separate information on deaths below 1 at the R.D. level in 1843–4.

The general impression given by table 5.11 is that the two rates probably moved up or down together in the years 1842, 1845, 1846, 1850 and 1851. But in 1847 the infant death rate fell, the crude death rate (excluding infants) moving up sharply; in 1848 the infant death rate rose as the general death rate fell, and in 1849 when the infant death rate fell quite sharply again, the general death rate remained fairly steady. Apparently the association between the two is weak, and the forces bearing on infant and adult mortality are thus likely to have differed.

Food prices as such[72] do not seem to have been critical in determining levels of mortality, contrary to the Malthusian supposition that high prices would bring into play the positive checks of famine and attendant disease. Admittedly the data run is short, indeed almost absurdly so, but for what it is worth the correlation of prices with crude mortality levels is r = 0.43, and with infant mortality no better. Only in 1846–7 is there any sign of a possibly significant relationship; flour prices began a rapid ascent in the last quarter of 1846 reaching a peak in the summer of 1847. On the base 23.9 (the mean rate of crude mortality for the whole period) = 100, mortality stood at 117, 116, 121 and 162 in the four quarters of 1847, and at 136 in the first quarter of 1848. This reflected primarily typhus, affecting mainly the lower classes, and may well have owed something to a weakened resistance among the poorer elements in the population. On the other hand, the other remarkable rise in mortality in summer 1849 (index 155, primarily due to cholera), appears to have owed little to factors of this sort, since prices had been falling for some time.

But as a general rule, no consistent relationship between prices and mortality is in evidence during these years, and in considering alternative explanations of fluctuations in mortality, the following points need to be borne in mind:

(i) It is known that weather influences the spread of some diseases by lowering the resistance of the human body. Yet different types of weather are conducive to different diseases, and in the 1840s it was already realized that while cold and wet weather had a marked effect on respiratory diseases, a hot summer tended to favour diseases of the digestive organs.[73]

(ii) Many diseases have a close connection with poverty, overcrowding and undernourishment (typhus, measles). One factor that may be relevant to the human condition is the price of food, for although I have ruled out the hypothesis that the cost of subsistence was the *general* regulator of fluctuations in the York death rate, there is no doubt that this could be important for certain classes at certain times.

(iii) Yet other diseases can be brought in from outside, and spread by contagion or infection even though other factors (weather, subsistence situation, etc.) are reasonably favourable (e.g. cholera, typhus).

(iv) Mortality levels in a community do not necessarily reflect the volume of sickness, since case fatality differs from disease to disease, from class to class, and according to the physical state of the population under attack.

In order to proceed further, it is necessary to examine seasonal fluctuations in the death rate on a systematic basis. To begin with, we may note some interesting changes in the general pattern of seasonal death rates over time. Back in 1770–6, according to White, the first quarter of the year had been most mortal (averaging 918 burials), as against 816 for the second quarter (April–June), 642 for the third (July–September) and 759 for the fourth (October–December).[74] Table 5.12 below, setting out seasonal mortality of the 1840s suggests that in most years the rate of mortality continued to be highest in the first quarter of the year, which is supported by the contemporary judgement of William Guy, who wrote that 'the mortality

TABLE 5.12 *Seasonally adjusted indexes of crude death rates (York Registration District)* *

	First quarter	Second quarter	Third quarter	Fourth quarter
1841	94	90	88	92
1842	102	112	89	88
1843	85	104	78	88
1844	85	91	83	113
1845	98	99	73	76
1846	100	96	110	111
1847	109	119	123	167
1848	127	105	98	101
1849	110	97	159	84
1850	94	82	86	79
1851	94	105	109	100
Mean for period 1841–51	25.55 per 1,000 (=100)	23.17 per 1,000 (=100)	23.57 per 1,000 (=100)	23.28 per 1,000 (=100)

* Registrar-General's Annual Reports, with base populations calculated quarterly on the principle described in note 58.

... in non-epidemic years will be chiefly dependent on the temperature, varying in the several seasons inversely as the temperature'.[75] He referred in explanation to bronchitis, affecting the lungs of the aged, but modern medical science also distinguishes hypothermia, or excessive cooling, which is particularly liable to affect infants and those over 60, and even today is directly responsible for many more deaths than is commonly realized.[76]

The comparison also shows that summer mortality (third quarter), from being easily the lowest in 1770–6, had moved up to rough parity with the second and fourth quarters by the 1840s (23·57 against 23·17 and 23·28). This was due to the very high mortality of 1847 and 1849, and to a lesser extent for 1846 and 1851. It would be interesting to know if this is encountered in other towns, for it looks important. A comparative increase in diseases of the cholera–diarrhoea–dysentery group, common in towns and favoured by hot weather may well have occurred in the swollen English towns of the 1821–51 period; and if this was so, it would certainly be a factor supporting what has been assumed, here and elsewhere, about the course of urban death rates after about 1820.[77]

There is much interest in trying to account historically for seasons of above average mortality indicated in table 5.12. Allowing for some margin of error in the statistics, if we take (say) an index figure of 108 as representing seasons of above average mortality, the following evidence is available:

(a) Second quarter, 1842; there is a report of epidemic influenza in York in March.[78] Possible explanatory circumstances include local mention of a very severe winter (1841–2), and the fact that unemployment was high and wages low, these being factors which would lower resistance to the spread of the virus.

(b) Fourth quarter, 1844; no evidence.

(c) Third quarter of 1846, through 1847 to the first quarter,

1848; the period opened with very hot weather, leading to widespread summer diarrhoea in Hull, Leeds and York, children being the chief sufferers.[79] In the last quarter of 1846 the Registrar-General referred again to excessive mortality in York, noting that 'the diarrhoea of the summer quarter was succeeded by fever'.[80] Early in 1847 local doctors reported the widespread incidence of typhus in the low districts of the town, especially those inhabited by the Irish. Throughout the year typhus deaths were exceedingly heavy. We cannot ignore the fact that in the twelve months preceding the harvest of 1847, prices of food were very high. Although employment remained good, there is contemporary reference to the failure of wages to keep up with the price rise.[81] Some degree of deprivation, especially in a setting of over-crowding and vile sanitary conditions, provide ideal conditions for the spread of a disease of this type.[82]

In the last quarter of 1847, with typhus still going strongly, though perhaps past its peak, an influenza epidemic occurred, lasting into the first quarter of 1848. This occasioned another paper by Laycock, who stated that at the peak, between one-half and one-third of the population were affected. He particularly remarked that good food, a well-drained locality, sound health, etc., were no guarantee against it.[83] In this, an influenza epidemic contrasts sharply with typhus and cholera, the incidence of which always affects the poorer classes most.

(d) First quarter of 1849; no evidence.

(e) Third quarter of 1849; this was an attack of cholera, and part of a national outbreak beginning in Scotland the previous autumn. So far as can be discerned, cholera was brought into York from outside, and spread by infection in lower-class neighbourhoods. No apparent connection with food prices (low), or employment opportunities (good), can be discerned. Nor does the weather seem to have been a significant factor, for the summer was average in temperature and rainfall, according to the Registrar-General's local meteorological observations.[84]

(f) Third quarter of 1851; in York, table 5.11 shows a high infant death rate for this year. Nationally, deaths from measles rose quite sharply, and since fatalities tend to occur with very young children (under two years of age), these facts are probably connected.[85] The Registrar-General's Report refers to a measles epidemic in Yorkshire towns (including York), in the second quarter but also to summer diarrhoea and scarlatina in the third.[86]

Our enquiry into the causes of fluctuations in mortality suggests that in general, standards of living had by this time passed the stage where simple relations between the economic state of the population and death rates could have been expected. The peaks in the death rate are accountable for in terms of outbreaks of epidemic disease, at least at the first level of analysis. As Chambers has argued in another context (eighteenth-century Nottinghamshire), 'It is clear that an epidemic, without the assistance of food shortage, was an effective form of change: it is not certain that the same could be said of food shortage [i.e. acting alone] ... epidemics could do their own work without its aid.'[87] At a deeper level of analysis there can be no doubt that the incidence and general consequences of some outbreaks were at least in part explicable by changes in the physical condition of population, but by and large we have insufficient information to measure this condition accurately and sensitively. In matters of this kind, the historian can be little more than chronicler.

EPIDEMICS IN YORK DURING THE 1830S AND 1840S

The epidemics are worth further attention not only for their intrinsic interest and importance, but also for the light they throw on the attitudes and activities of the bodies concerned with their mitigation. As elsewhere, the appearance of such epidemics, particularly where they followed one another in quick succession in 1847 and 1849, engendered a public furore, much newspaper discussion, and on the whole, helped to bring about an atmosphere which was more favourable to sanitary improvement.

The cholera of 1832

Medical men had for some time been aware that cholera was making its way from its endemic seat in India, across Europe to England. A great number of medical treatises drew attention to the danger, and the Council took the unprecedented step of setting up a temporary Board of Health which suggested various preventive measures and the setting up of local boards in the great towns. York had such a board, comprised principally of medical men. Such measures did not prevent the cholera from gaining a foothold in Sunderland and the north-east in November 1831, whence the disease spread into many other districts.[88] Before arriving in York, the disease had been raging at Goole, Hull, Selby and Leeds for some weeks. Precautions had been taken in the city, and there is mention of food, clothing, blankets being given to the poor: filth was destroyed, and there was much white-washing, cleaning of privies, etc.[89]

The first example of the new pestilence appeared just after the races of May 1832. A 21-year-old male living in a court in Skeldergate, 'intemperate and destitute', who had been engaged in ferrying people from Selby, Hull, etc., across the river, was struck down.[90] The precise location was Beedham's Court ('the Hag-Worm's Nest'), situated in the locality already marked out as the habitat of the pestilences of 1551 and 1604, and by 17 May ten cases had been treated in that filthy court.[91] From this family the disease spread to their relatives, some of whom lived in First Water Lane, just across the river, and 'by the 21st, 30 examples of the disease had occurred in that district'. By the 15 May cholera had made its way into Copper-gate, Hungate, Walmgate and Fossgate north of the river, and into Tanner-row and North Street on the south. By 22 October the disease had passed on; the total number of cases had been 450, of which 185 died and 265 recovered.[92]

In all one in fifty-six of the population had been attacked. The areas most affected had been the 'low-lying, illkept and badly ventilated parts of the city', hence a miasmatic explanation appeared to be the correct one to Laycock.[93]

It is of interest to compare the mortality in York with that experienced elsewhere during the epidemic. Creighton gives a list of 'places with the highest mortality' in each county of England and Wales.[94] The figure cited is the absolute number of deaths in each case. York (with 185 deaths) is the nineteenth town in the list, this number of deaths being exceeded in Plymouth and Devonport, Exeter, Bristol, Bilston, Tipton, Sedgley, Wolverhampton, Nottingham, Liverpool, Manchester, Salford, Leeds, Sheffield, Hull, Sunderland, Newcastle, Carlisle and Whitehaven. But among these towns when population is taken into account,[95] York is fourteenth. The order then reads as follows, (in terms of population to one cholera death): Bilston (21), Tipton and Newcastle (53), Plymouth and Devonport (71), Exeter (73), Carlisle (75), Sunderland (79), Sedgley (89), Bristol (94), Whitehaven (104), Liverpool (108), Hull (110), Wolverhampton (128), York (137), Nottingham (157), Leeds (176), Salford (189), Manchester (201), and Sheffield (228).

Clearly the 1832 cholera epidemic was a serious matter in York, but although the outbreak created a great deal of commotion and concern for some months, public interest soon waned, and it is clear from the subsequent history of public health in York that appropriate conclusions were not drawn at this stage.

The typhus of 1847

Typhus and the enteric fevers (typhoid and paratyphoid) were not distinguished by the Registrar-General in his 'causes of death' until 1869. Typhus, often referred to as 'putrid malignant fever', is louse-borne, transmitted by the bite of the insect; with typhoid, sometimes referred to as 'slow nervous fever', the bacteria gain entry through food or water and live in the large intestine. In either case the symptoms are similar – toxaemia, high temperature and rash. Gale, from whom this brief description of the disease is taken, also remarks that epidemic louse-born typhus is perhaps the best example of a disease associated with the depths of human misery . . . but . . . when once an epidemic has started it can spread to the more prosperous members of the community'. Outbreaks of typhus in the nineteenth century were often associated with the Irish immigrations which followed the potato famines. In England generally, the bad years were 1847–8, the areas most affected being Lancashire and Cheshire, Liverpool being the town with the highest incidence.[96]

York, with its own sizeable colony of Irish, did not escape what was popularly known as 'the Irish fever'. William Proctor, Surgeon to the York Poor Law Union, and the Revd Thomas Billington, a Roman Catholic priest, discovered the existence of typhus fever 'to a serious extent' in Walmgate in March 1847. Several members of the York Health of Towns Committee thereupon visited Butcher's Yard, Walmgate, already described by Proctor as 'foul, dirty and loathsome'. In an ill-ventilated yard stood an open privy, 'used by about fifty persons, in a state of great filth and ruin . . . next are two dilapidated pig-sties . . . adjoining a slaughter-house'. All the drainings of the yard fell into a central open gutter ending in a choked gully and a fetid pool of water. Here stood three lodging houses and a row of thickly populated cottages, occupied by the Irish. The Health of Towns investigators found great overcrowding; 'The number of beds in the lodging houses showed that when filled, the rooms must necessarily be much crowded . . . two families consisting of eleven persons occupy one small room, about twelve feet square and not eight feet high.'

No doubt concurring with Proctor's 'serious apprehensions of its spreading to a fearful extent' the Committee immediately passed resolutions to the effect that fever cases must be removed to a house of recovery 'inasmuch as the fever is of a contagious character' and that the condition of localities such as

Butcher's yard must at once be attended to 'inasmuch as it has been established that from such places fevers may also spread to those districts of the town which are in a superior sanitary condition'. Copies of the report were sent to the City Commissioners and to the Board of Guardians.[97]

Ponderously the Board of Guardians wheeled to meet the new danger. At the meeting of 25 March 1874, a sub-committee was set up to 'look out for and hire some empty house . . . to be used as a fever hospital'. An election for a new board having intervened, the meeting of 29 April empowered its sub-committee to take the rooms adjoining the Vagrant office for this purpose, 'to meet the extraordinary number of Irish cases now pressing upon the Board'. Nothing having come of this, they decided to advertise for suitable premises (6 May), and finally (13 May), it was resolved to erect a temporary building, at a cost not exceeding £600.[98] The hospital, situated in a field in Heslington Lane, appears to have come into operation in about the middle of June 1847. An unsuccessful attempt to borrow tents to extend provision had to be made in July. Between the opening and 11 August, 249 patients were admitted, of whom 15 died, and 188 were discharged cured. Throughout the following months the number of patients actually in the fever hospital at any one time stayed at 40–50, and weekly admissions at 20–30. The surgeon in charge of the hospital reported weekly to the Board, and his reports and miscellaneous comments illuminate the further progress of the disease, and the attitudes of the Poor Law guardians and City Commissioners to the problem. *12 August*, 'I have to report a general decrease both in the number of cases of fever and the virulence of the disease.' *19 August*, Admissions continued to take place, from the Bedern for example. Convalescent patients were employed in teazing oakum. *26 August*, Mention of cases from Snarr's Buildings (Bedern). 'It consists of about 16 tenements in every one of which the inmates have more or less been affected.' *2 September*, 'I have again to speak of the much milder form and far less fatal character of the disease.' *16 September*, 'Hospital superintendent has died.' *23 September*, 'Water-lanes have furnished a very considerable number ... and several have also been sent from Knavesmire, where sickness still prevails and where great numbers of Irish remain encamped in a state of intense destitution and suffering.' *7 October*, 'I must impress upon the board the necessity of withholding outdoor relief in all cases of fever where the patients can with safety be removed to the hospital but refuse to do so.' *14 October*, 'A greater number of admissions this week, owing to the gradual extension of the fever from the Irish to our own inhabitants in the various localities in Walmgate, Water Lanes, Long-close Lane, Bedern, etc.'. This owed 'in good measure to the fact of no step having been taken where sickness exists, either by the owners, or any private or public body entirely to eradicate the disease'. *17 October*, 'In consequence of the decision of the board not to allow a supply of shirts to the hospital, a very great proportion of the male inhabitants are necessarily confined to bed in a state of nudity ...' *4 November*, 'The number of cases admitted ... continue to be large ... arising unquestionably in a great measure from the non-interference of the legally authorized body within the city to modify or remove the causes now operating to perpetuate the disease.' *18 November*, 'It may indeed be deemed a matter for your consideration whether in many instances where the jurisdiction of the Commissioners does not extend, the exercise of the power with which you are vested, will not result in a great and unexpected good ... The improvement of the sanitary condition of the poorer classes tends to greatly remove the causes of destitution and pauperism ...' *2 December*, 'Smith's-buildings, Long-close Lane provided most cases in the last week.' *9 December*, 'The gradual approach of the winter has caused the want of extra bed-clothing ...' *23 December*, 'As one might have expected, the appearance of ... influenza ... its affecting so seriously the aged and those already suffering from disease, would not be likely to leave a place circumstanced as your hospital is, unscathed.' *6 January*, 'The maximum force of the disease has now been attained,' and 'the improvement of the state of the atmosphere is having an important influence in checking and causing its decline.' *13 January*, 'A gradual approach to the usually healthy state of the Union.'

From about the turn of the year, in fact, the numbers being admitted were significantly reduced. There were thirty-five patients in the hospital during the last week in January; eighteen in the last week of April. This figure was constant for some time, and on 16 July a motion was carried to the effect that the hospital be discontinued in one month's time. Presumably the 15 remaining patients were removed to the workhouse, the inadequate size of which had necessitated the erection of the fever hospital in the first place.

In all, during the two quarters ending September and December 1847, 632 persons were admitted to the fever hospital. The parishes of some 400 of them were later stated by Richard Thomas with useful comments. It is a representative list of the most low-lying, crowded, ill-drained, insanitary and generally unwholesome districts of the city (table 5.13).

Unhappily, there is no exact record of the mortality experi-

TABLE 5.13 *Principal parishes affected by typhus fever, 1847**

St George	'Crowded by Irishmen and generally very badly drained'	99
St Dennis	'Another low parish in Walmgate'	96
St Margarets	'Another Walmgate parish ... at the time to which I refer, it was one of the worst of the parishes'	88
Minster-yard and Bedern	'Fever is constantly prevalent there'	39
St Mary Castlegate	'Includes the Water-Lanes'	39
St Sampson	'Contains a great number of low places and slaughter-houses'	25
St Michael Spurriergate	'Contains one of the Water-Lanes'	17
	Total	403

* Smith (1850) 9–10.

enced in this epidemic; causes of death are not available at the registration district level, and the epidemic was not productive of a government report. But analysis of the deviations from normal patterns of mortality in York, several other registration districts, and England and Wales enables us to draw some useful inferences.

TABLE 5.14 *Percentage by which the mortality of 1847 was above* (+) *or below* (−) *the average mortality of 1845–8, by season**

	First quarter	Second quarter	Third quarter	Fourth quarter
York R.D.	+1.6	+14.9	+22.7	+47.5
Leeds R.D.	+23.0	+20.7	+13.6	+18.6
Hull R.D.	+8.7	−3.5	+6.9	+32.9
Manchester R.D.	+13.2	+34.1	+33.8	+16.4
Salford R.D.	+2.7	−4.3	−8.3	+5.1
Chorlton R.D.	+2.9	+2.8	−6.5	+7.7
Liverpool R.D.	+26.0	+84.7	+77.5	+37.6
England and Wales	+10.3	+10.6	+4.5	+7.4

* Registrar-General's Annual Reports. An average of the deaths occurring in each quarter of 1845, 1846, 1847, 1848 was made for each district. The table gives the percentage, for each season and each district, by which deaths exceeded the calculated average. The districts selected for comparison were mentioned in connection with typhus by the Registrar-General in his Tenth Annual Report xxiiff.

Table 5.14 raises several interesting points, showing that

(i) Mortality in York rose by far more than did national mortality in that year.

(ii) The peak season in York, (last quarter of 1847) saw relatively higher mortality than was experienced by any other town on the list except Liverpool, which with its many thousands of starving Irish, was something of a special case.

(iii) The upward trend in York mortality (from the second quarter to the fourth), ties in perfectly with the literary account of the epidemic.

(iv) There is an interesting suggestion of a west to east movement in the progress of the disease, since Liverpool and Manchester experienced their highest (above average) deaths in the second quarter of the year; York and Hull reached peaks in the last quarter of the year.[99] If this was so, it might be explained by the eastward drift of Irish immigrants.

The cholera of 1849

The second great outbreak of Asiatic cholera began in Scotland in October 1848, but did not gain a firm foothold in England till June 1849. In terms of the numbers actually dying, this was the most serious of all nineteenth-century cholera epidemics, since approximately 53,000 cholera deaths were registered for England and Wales, as against about 20,000 in the previous outbreak.[100]

The first cholera deaths in York took place in January 1849, in the workhouse and in Bilton St, Walmgate. No further deaths took place until July, from which point the disease was said to be 'severely felt'. In the Bootham sub-district the last death took place on 14 October and eighty-eight deaths were attributed to cholera, including twenty-seven in the workhouse, which was being used as a hospital. Friargate, Middle Water Lane and King's Staith, in the parishes of St Mary Castlegate and St Michael Spurriergate, were most affected.

In the healthier Micklegate sub-district only eighteen died from cholera, though in the list of streets affected Beedham's Court once again appears. In Walmgate, sixty-one died of cholera during the epidemic, Church Lane, Union Buildings, Duke of York St and Wenlock St being particularly affected. The four rural sub-districts of Flaxton, Skelton, Dunnington and Escrick (with 16.6 per cent of the population of the Registration District in 1851), furnished only seven cholera deaths.[101]

The Board of Guardians had taken note of the re-occurrence of cholera in York on 5 July, and set up the infirmary of their new workhouse as a hospital for cases that could not be dealt with at home. During the following months the Medical Officers of the Union attended several hundred cases of suspected cholera. By 18 September the cholera was noted by the board to be 'on the decrease', and the services of Mr Allen, an assistant medical officer apparently engaged for the duration of the epidemic, were dispensed with. On 27 September it was resolved to close the hospital and Allen's payment and gratuities recommended by the Health Committee for the extra services of the union medical officers were reduced by the Board.[102] The last deaths from cholera did not occur until some three weeks after these steps were taken.[103]

In all, cholera mortality in the York Registration District in 1849 was 36 per 10,000 living inhabitants (or 275 living per death). This was only just above the national average figure (33 cholera deaths per 10,000 inhabitants), and within Yorkshire alone, the York cholera death rate was surpassed at Hull, (287 deaths per 10,000 inhabitants – the highest rate in the country), Sculcoates (181), Leeds (162), Hunslet (111), Selby (74), Goole (59), Wakefield (53), Thorne (46), Howden (41), Pontefract (39) and Dewsbury (37).[104] It can therefore be said that the district as a whole escaped fairly lightly on this occasion, which may owe something to the fact that by this date, a greatly increased proportion of York citizens were supplied with river water from higher up the Ouse. Far fewer must have used water from wells than in 1832, which may have special significance in that cholera infection is usually water-borne.[105]

6 *Marriage and Fertility*

In general it is agreed that the marriage returns are likely to be the most accurate data in the *Parish Register Abstracts* compiled between 1801 and 1841. Indeed I have already used this material in establishing base populations for the eighteenth century, for the purpose of calculating mortality rates.[1] However, from 1801 the existence of census material permits the calculation of a series of independent crude marriage rates (table 6.1), which in York appear to have been consistently in excess of those put forward by Griffith for the nation as a whole.

TABLE 6.1 *Crude marriage rates: persons married per 1,000 population, 1799–1823**

	City of York	England and Wales	Percentage superiority of York
1799–1803	26.5	17.3 (1795–1805)	53
1809–13	22.8	16.5 (1806–16)	38
1819–23	19.3	16.2 (1816–26)	19

* *Parish Register Abstracts*; Griffith (1967) 34.

Similarly, calculations of crude birth rates can be made, incorporating Griffith's suggested adjustment of an addition of 15 per cent to the baptisms, with the results given in table 6.2.

TABLE 6.2 *Crude fertility rates: births per 1,000 population, 1799–1823**

	City of York	England and Wales	Percentage superiority of York
1799–1803	36.7	34.2 (1796–1806)	7
1809–13	37.1	33.8 (1806–16)	10
1819–23	33.5	33.4 (1816–26)	–

* *Parish Register Abstracts*, baptisms × 1.15; Griffith (1967) 28.

It will be seen that York's superiority was much more evident for marriage than for fertility. Thus, the ratio of baptisms per marriage is on the low side, compared with Griffith's findings for England and Wales (table 6.3).

TABLE 6.3 *Ratio of baptisms to marriages, 1780–1824**

	City of York	England and Wales
1780–9	2.89	3.73
1790–9	2.70	3.63
1800–9	2.71	3.73
1810–19	3.20	3.88
1820–4	3.44	3.74 (1820–9)

* *Parish Register Abstracts*; Griffith (1967) 31. The procedure is to divide marriages into the uncorrected number of baptisms five years later, using averages to reduce the effects of abnormal years. Dates given are those of the marriages.

These elementary calculations yield only fragile conclusions, especially on the fertility side. Whereas (assuming no significant net gains or losses by international migration), it is not unreasonable to relate all English baptisms to all English marriages, it cannot be supposed that this holds good for York, which obviously was not 'closed' in the same sense, i.e. one cannot be certain that the baptisms of table 6.3 accrued to the corresponding cohort of marriages five years earlier. Also, both the national and local calculations assume the veracity of the parish register returns of baptisms, which have been severely impugned by some historians; on the other hand, what evidence there is on the state of the York returns suggests that they were not so grossly deficient as is sometimes assumed.[2]

On face value, table 6.3 suggests a comparatively low level of marital fertility in York; these baptism/marriage ratios are generally lower than those given by Cowgill for the period 1538–1751 (3.29 or 3.56, depending on how calculated),[3] and some tenuous supporting evidence of comparatively low fertility is given by the 1821 census fertility ratio (number of children aged 0–4 per 1,000 females aged 15–49) which is as low as 475 for York, compared with 677 for the industrial counties (West Riding, Lancashire, Cheshire, Staffordshire) and 580 for the remainder of England and Wales.[4]

Thus it appears that rising fertility can have played little part in generating population increase in York, but clearly the matter is far from settled. We can however speak with some confidence of a discrepancy between an apparently high marriage rate and the existence of fertility levels that did not fully correspond; all the more so because we shall meet the same situation again in the 1840s. Apart from under-registration of births, possible explanations include late age at marriage, the celebration of marriages in York by persons not normally resident there, or emigration of newly married couples. For this period there is no available evidence to test these hypotheses, but of the existence of another relevant factor, a quite abnormal sex-distribution, there can be no doubt. The ratio of females per 1,000 males stood at 1,301 in 1801, 1,247 in 1811, 1,181 in 1821 and 1,190 in 1831; the presence of a substantial number of unmarried women would certainly have tended to depress crude birth rates, as well as the 1821 census fertility ratio mentioned above, whatever the true level of marital fertility.

MARRIAGE PATTERNS OF THE 1840S

In this period, the more detailed and less suspect evidence of the Registrar-General's returns can be turned to account. To begin with, crude marriage rates were still significantly above the national levels.

The annual average for York Registration District (19.8) was higher than the national rate at any point, whilst only in four years (1845–6, 1850–1) did the national rate even equal the lowest recorded for York (1844) (see table 6.4).

It is true, the local age-structure was comparatively favourable to marriage; in 1841 47.8 per cent were aged 15–44 and 18.8 per cent 20–9, against 46.1 and 17.8 per cent nationally, but this factor by no means accounts for the marked difference

TABLE 6.4 *Marriage rates in York Registration District and England and Wales, 1841–51: persons married per 1,000 population**

	York District	England and Wales	Percentage superiority of York rate
1841	18.4	15.4	19
1842	18.4	14.8	24
1843	18.0	15.2	18
1844	17.2	16.0	8
1845	20.4	17.2	19
1846	20.2	17.2	17
1847	21.2	15.8	34
1848	21.4	16.0	33
1849	20.6	16.2	27
1850	20.6	17.2	20
1851	20.2	17.2	17

* Registrar-General's Annual Reports with base populations calculated according to chapter 4, note 58; Mitchell and Deane (1962) 45.

in marriage rates. If all marriages of 1841 are attributed to these groups, then the marriage rate works out to 19.3 per 1,000 aged 15–44 or 49.8 per 1,000 aged 20–9 for York; 16.7 and 43.4 for England and Wales. Exactly the same holds true in 1851; the age-structure still favoured marriage in York Registration District, but once again, it may be shown to have accounted only in part for the difference in marriage rates.[5] These calculations have to be made for the registration district as a whole, since the Registrar-General's *Annual Reports* do not give marriage data at the sub-district level, but it may be noted that the age-structure of the Municipal Borough was still more favourable to marriage than that of the district as a whole,[6] and that therefore the city of York may have experienced marriage rates still higher than the national.

Much interest attaches to seasonal and annual fluctuations in the marriage rate, although of course the run of data I am considering is short. Cowgill has studied the seasonality of marriage in York between 1538 and 1812, discovering that in the sixteenth century the number of marriages was at a minimum during March (the Lenten season) and at a maximum in November, as Christmas approached. Evidence of a change in this pattern during the Puritan ascendancy of the seventeenth century is explained by the hypothesis that 'religious festivities no longer set the rhythm of the people's year', yet the graphs illustrating the last two sub-periods (1701–52, 1752–1812) appear to suggest some reassertion of the old pattern.[7]

Although we have to move to a basis of quarterly percentages, such a pattern was still apparent in the later 1840s. In table 6.5, the seasonality of English marriages in 1845–51 is compared with that of York Registration District.

TABLE 6.5   *Seasonality of marriage, 1845–51**

| | Percentage of marriages taking place in quarters ending last day of: | | | |
	March	June	September	December
England and Wales	20.6	25.3	24.1	30.1
York District	23.0	23.3	23.5	30.2

* Registrar-General's Annual Reports.

York was sufficiently closely geared to the agricultural cycle of activity to experience the normal flood of marriages late in the year.

At that season harvest wages and the cash which farmers obtained from their first post-harvest sales of grain injected the biggest flush of money of the year into the countryside. Debts to tradesmen were paid off . . . winter supplies were bought in . . . [and from the fairs and markets] . . . a backwash of money flowed to the town tradesmen, hucksters, hawkers and travelling salesmen, and so back to set the consumer goods industries on work.[8]

Undoubtedly such influences were favourable to employment and marriage. On the other hand, York marriages did not reflect the less important stages of the agricultural year, and one can surmise that while business in York would be significantly affected by the rise in orders at and following harvest-time, such orders were more or less steady over the rest of the year.

So far as annual fluctuations are concerned, it is generally agreed that 'of the three short-term regulators of population, marriage is the most sensitive to economic change, birth the second and death the least'.[9] During the period 1789–1815, on the national level, there was a clear inverse relationship over the short period in respect of wheat prices and fluctuations in the absolute number of marriages.[10] It is thus worth relating the cost of subsistence in York in 1841–51 (as measured by flour prices)[11] to the general marriage rates given in table 6.4, and to the proportions of both males and females marrying under full age, set out in table 6.6 below. The following coefficients of correlation emerge:

(a) Between flour prices and the marriage rate, $r = -0.06$, i.e. an inverse correlation, but of a quite negligible order.

(b) Between flour prices and proportion of males marrying under full age, $r = -0.44$. This is only a very moderate correlation, although inverse, as expected.

(c) Between flour prices and the proportion of females marrying under full age, $r = -0.58$, inverse as expected, and again, not really strong.

Perhaps these weak associations were to be expected; Gayer, Rostow and Schwarz state that nationally, the inverse correlation between wheat prices and the marriage rate broke down after 1822, and that the state of industrial activity appeared to increase in its importance as a factor influencing marriage.[12] From 1856, it has been shown that marriage rates were very sensitive to movements in real wages, yielding a correlation coefficient of 0.86 when crude marriage rates for England and Wales were compared with Kuczynski's real wage index.[13] Unfortunately we lack a real wage index for York in this period, and it would be an exceedingly difficult task to construct one. However, something is to be gained from a simple grouping of the annual marriage figures. The year 1845 seems to have marked something of a watershed in York, for the average crude marriage rate was 8.99 per 1,000 between 1841 and 1844, and 10.35 thereafter. Moreover, the proportion of youthful marriages seems to have been much higher from 1845 onwards (see table 6.6).

The rise in 1845 paralleled a national upswing of marriages noted by the Registrar-General to be especially marked in

Stability and Change in an English County Town

TABLE 6.6 *Proportion of persons married 'not of full age', 1841–51; York Registration District**

Year	Males	Females
1841	2.1	6.6
1842	2.2	11.4
1843	3.4	9.1
1844	0.7	7.8
1841–44	2.1	8.8
1845	3.0	9.7
1846	2.1	10.4
1847	2.5	11.3
1848	4.7	12.9
1849	2.8	12.0
1850	3.7	16.2
1851	10.8	19.0
1845–51	3.8	13.1

* Registrar-General's Annual Reports.

London, Birmingham, Lancashire and Yorkshire. He ascribed it to the fact that railway building was more active there, and to the anticipated benefits of tariff changes. Moreover, periodical epidemics of speculation were often seen to be accompanied by an increase of marriages, as 'the apparent improvement in the position of small capitalists, the increased wages of the working classes ... and perhaps the spirit of speculation itself, lead many to embark on matrimony'.[14] Although the anticipated benefits from tariff changes are not likely to have been important in York's case, we have already seen that railway building from 1844 onwards profoundly affected the district, and that as a generalization, the years 1845–51 were much more favourable for working-class employment and incomes than the earlier years of the decade.[15] These findings in respect of marriage rates are highly consistent with the view put forward earlier. It is especially interesting to notice that although there was a sharp check to the national marriage rate

160

in 1847–8,[16] the York series in table 6.4 does not exhibit this, which is consistent with the view that employment in the area remained good despite high food prices during the pre-harvest months of 1847.[17]

Distribution of marital status

If crude marriage-rates in the York District remained on the high side, the proportions ever-married observed at various mid-nineteenth-century censuses were, somewhat paradoxically, low. In 1851, the position is given in table 6.7, which shows that there were relatively more bachelors and especially spinsters, and fewer married persons, either male or female, than in the nation at large.

TABLE 6.7 *Proportion of single persons, married or widowed in 1851, per 1,000 aged over 20**

	Bachelors or spinsters	Married (husbands or wives)	Widowers or widows
York Registration District			
Males	32.2	61.0	6.8
Females	33.4	53.4	13.3
England and Wales			
Males	30.3	62.6	7.1
Females	28.3	58.7	13.0

* 1851 Census. Population Tables II (2)

An opportunity to make fuller comparisons with other districts of a different socio-economic character presents itself for the first time with the publication of the next census, of 1861 (table 6.8).

For males, the chief conclusion must be that marriage tended to take place significantly later in York than in any of these manufacturing or mining districts, and a higher proportion ultimately never married. For females the position is somewhat more complex. Hewitt has shown that the widespread contemporary view that female textile factory operatives married very young has no sound foundations,[18] and it is interesting to observe that the proportions ever-married at all age-groups up to and including 25–34 were much the same in York as in Bradford or Preston, although the proportions ultimately marrying were certainly higher in the two textile towns. On the other hand, the mining and hardware districts of Barnsley and Sheffield both exhibited a much greater incidence of early marriage than York, and higher proportions ultimately marrying.

TABLE 6.8   *Proportions ever-married, by age group: various registration districts in 1861**

	York	Bradford	Preston	Leeds	Barnsley	Sheffield
15–19						
Male	0.3	0.6	2	0.7	0.8	1.1
Female	3.0	2.7	3	3.9	7.6	7.7
20–4						
Male	20.6	28.3	31	26.6	30.5	33.8
Female	30.8	32.8	29	38.0	52.1	53.0
25–34						
Male	66.3	74.6	73	72.1	73.4	76.6
Female	68.5	68.8	64	73.0	83.2	83.4
35–44						
Male	82.5	89.7	88	88.2	87.0	88.6
Female	79.4	84.9	84	86.1	91.9	91.4
45–54						
Male	86.9	92.1	94	91.9	89.7	91.1
Female	84.0	92.1	90	91.2	94.4	95.0
55–64						
Male	88.3	94.3	95	93.9	92.7	91.7
Female	84.4	93.9	92	92.7	94.4	94.0

* 1861 Census. Population Tables II; proportions for Preston from Anderson (1972a) 133.

Further evidence on the question of age at marriage, serving to confirm these findings, has been derived by analysing 724 marriages of the period 1838–65 for five York parishes in which, by chance, exact statements of age happen to be given in the registers.[19] For males in general the mean age was 28.68, and for first marriages 26.96. These means are certainly higher than those calculated on the basis of a limited sample of returns by the Registrar-General for England and Wales as a whole during the early years of civil registration; he gives figures of 27.3 and 27.9 for all marriages in 1838–41 and 1871, and 25.5 and 25.8 for first marriages in the same periods. For females, the York means are 25.77 for all marriages, 25.25 for first marriages; these may be compared with national averages of 25.4 and 25.7 for all marriages, and 24.3 and 24.4 for first marriages relating to the years 1838–41 and 1871.[20] In general it would appear that the first marriages of females in York took place about a year later than the national norm, and some eighteen months later with males.

Slightly later age at marriage in York, especially in the critical area 24–6, is part of the explanation of the apparent incongruence between the buoyant marriage rates recorded in table 6.4 and the comparatively low proportions ever-married in the younger age-groups of table 6.8. In addition, marriages occurring in York included a significant proportion of couples rather obviously unlikely to live there. In particular, seventy-five bridegrooms in the collection (some 10 per cent) were described as farmers who would rarely have lived within the borough boundaries and in many cases outside those of the Registration District, such as William Fenwick, a farmer of Topcliffe near Thirsk who married Alice Rhodes at Holy Trinity Micklegate on 13 March 1841. His marriage would count in the York district returns, but if the couple remained at Topcliffe, they would not figure in the return of married persons at subsequent censuses.[21] Nor need this have been confined to farmers; in the light of what has been said of the high rate of turnover of population, it is not difficult to imagine that those who left York to take new situations could have included an above average proportion of newly marrieds, although there is no evidence on that point.

Lastly, the unusual sex-structure was still relevant in explaining the position of women (table 6.9).

TABLE 6.9 *Number of females per 1,000 males, 1841 and 1851**

	England and Wales	York R.D.	York Municipal Borough
1841			
(i) At all ages	1,030	1,101	1,153
(ii) Age groups 20–39	1,052	1,114	1,167
1851			
(i) At all ages	1,027	1,082	1,138
(ii) Age groups 20–39	1,042	1,132	1,191

* 1851 Census. Population Tables II (2); 1841 Census. Age Abstract (for the borough) and Registrar-General, Pt. III of Appendix to the 9th Annual Report for the 1841 registration district).

Such a remarkable sex-distribution would permit the co-existence of both a high marriage rate and a low proportion ever-married. We have already seen that the situation was one of long standing, traceable back to 1801 at least.

Class differences in marriage habits

On the basis of the 1851 household sample covering 543 couples, the husband was older than the wife in 321 cases (mean difference 5.31 years), whilst fifty couples were of the same age, and in another 172 cases, the wife older than the husband (by 3.42 years, on average). If the latter are treated as negative values, the mean difference for the city as a whole was 2·06 years in favour of the husbands.

Within these averages, there were apparent differences when class I householders were compared with class V, as table 6.10 indicates.

Since the absolute number of cases in table 6.10 is small, especially for class I, these comparisons are far from conclusive. Yet in pointing to a larger difference between the ages of spouses at the top end of the social scale than at the lower end, they accord closely with findings derived from the collection of marriage data mentioned above. To begin with, a higher proportion of white collar and professional men were re-marrying than labourers (23.1 compared with 14.6 per cent), which would probably have tended to raise the age-gap between

TABLE 6.10   *Age differences between household heads and wives; extreme classes compared**

	Class I (N = 33)	Class V (N = 70)
(i) Percentage of cases where head older than wife	76	57
Mean age difference	+6.48	+5.67
(ii) Percentage same age	6	6
(iii) Percentage of cases where wife older than head	18	37
Mean age difference	−3.16	−4.27
(iv) Mean difference (incorporating i, ii, iii)	+4.33	+1.66

* 1851 Census sample.

husband and wife; but in any case, as table 6.11 shows, even at first marriage, there was a difference of some five years between the average age of white collar and professional men (together with farmers) and labourers, with the great majority of bridegrooms (here denoted as the 'middling' class) somewhere between the two. For brides, the differences were slight, by comparison (table 6.11).

TABLE 6.11   *Mean age at first marriage by socio-economic category of bridegrooms**

Bridegroom's category	Mean age of bridegroom	Mean age of bride
White collar, professional	30.4	25.2
Farmers	29.8	26.9
'Middling'	26.4	25.2
Labourers	25.4	24.4

* Mid-nineteenth-century marriage data collection. The numbers of cases on which these means are founded is as follows: white collar and professional, 48 grooms (61 brides); farmers 57 (61); 'middling' 366 (395) and labourers 80 (84). Note that there is insufficient detail to classify by occupations on the principles applied to the 1851 sample.

These results accord closely with the widespread contemporary conviction that 'the poorer classes usually marry and have families at an earlier age than the middle and upper classes', and the suggested discrepancy between 'the very early ages at which working men undertake marriage and how much later the prudent classes venture to do so'. The Registrar-General, basing himself on the marriages of 1884–5, was able to demonstrate that professional and independent males married latest (31.22) farmers next (29.23), followed by shopkeepers and shopmen (26.67) and clerks (26.25), with other workers all in the range 24–5.[22] As between their wives, the differences were also evident, but less marked.

Given the occupational structure of the York locality, the kind of results indicated in table 6.11 were to be anticipated, although very little comparable work has as yet been done. They attest to the exercise of prudence among all classes of bridegrooms, but especially those of the higher social strata. As Malthus remarked, 'the most cursory view of society in this country must convince us, that throughout all ranks the preventive check prevails in a considerable degree'; even the labourer 'who earns eighteen pence or two shillings a day, and lives at his ease as a single man, will hesitate a little before he divides that pittance among four or five which seems to be not more than sufficient for one'.[23] Whether or not still further gains would have accrued to the working man by deferring marriage a year or two longer still, is of course another question.

FERTILITY LEVELS IN THE 1840S

Once again a lack of correspondence between marriage rates and fertility, noted above for the early decades of the century, presents itself when the statistics of the 1840s are considered. Indeed, whereas marriage rates were from 8 to 34 per cent above the national norm (table 6.4), the crude birth rates indicated in table 6.12 were 4 to 12 per cent below it, according to the year chosen.

TABLE 6.12   *Crude birth rates, 1841–51**

	England and Wales	York Registration District	Percentage Inferiority of York rate
1841	32.2	28.8	11
1842	32.1	28.1	12
1843	32.3	30.8	5
1844	32.7	28.7	12
1845	32.5	29.2	10
1846	33.8	31.0	8
1847	31.5	28.8	9
1848	32.5	31.0	5
1849	32.9	31.7	4
1850	33.4	31.6	5
1851	34.3	31.4	8

* Registrar-General's Annual Reports with base populations calculated according to chapter 4, note 58; Mitchell and Deane (1962) 29.

These comparatively low levels of crude fertility were not attributable to peculiarities of the age-structure; on the contrary, if the births of 1841–2 and 1850–2 are related to either (a) the total number of persons aged 15–44, or (b) the number of females in this age category, the low fertility of the York District is shown to be still more marked than the crude rates appear to indicate (table 6.13).

In fact, the persistent peculiarities of the sex-composition go far to explain these results; table 6.9 indicates a heavy preponderance of females, and shows also that the excess of females in the marrying age groups (20–39) was becoming more marked, not less, over the decade. By 1851, the excess of females within the Municipal Borough was actually 13.8 per cent (for all age-groups), and 19.1 per cent in the age groups 20–39. The excess at all ages was above that of the counties remarked upon by the Census authorities – 11 per cent in Gloucestershire, 10 per cent in Somerset, 13 per cent in London. If the comparison is made within the 20–39 age groups only, the greatest female excesses recorded in the census were in Gloucester and Somerset (22 per cent), Devon (21 per cent) and Bedfordshire

TABLE 6.13 *General Fertility Rates, 1841 and 1851**

	1841
York Registration District	
No. of persons aged 15–44	22,836
No. of females aged 15–44	12,042
Average number of births, 1841–2	1,374
Births per 1,000 persons aged 15–44	60.2
Births per 1,000 females aged 15–44	114.1
England and Wales	
Births per 1,000 persons 15–44	70.0
Births per 1,000 females 15–44	135.2
	1851
York Registration District	
No. of persons aged 15–44	27,112
No. of females aged 15–44	14,374
Average number of births, 1850–2	1,806
Births per 1,000 persons aged 15–44	66.6
Births per 1,000 females aged 15–44	125.6
England and Wales	
Births per 1,000 persons aged 15–44 (1850–2)	74.3
Births per 1,000 females aged 15–44 (1850–2)	144.3

* 1851 Census. Population Table sii (2); Registrar-General's Annual Reports. Age data for 1841 by registration districts from Pt. iii of the Appendix to the 9th Annual Report.

(16 per cent).[24] The York (Municipal Borough) excess was 19 per cent, almost exactly the same as London. Reference was made by the census authorities in the case of London to 'the large number of female servants . . . and of women . . . preparing articles of dress', both being factors which would also have applied to York.

Given a sex-ratio so unfavourable to women, one would expect that many would remain spinsters, and this is precisely what tables 6.7 and 6.8 indicate. These observations are highly relevant to any discussion of fertility. Since a lower proportion of women of child-bearing age were actually married in the York District, then the use of the conventional ratio, births/ number of women aged 15–44 is not wholly appropriate. In effect, the true fertility position is likely to be understated, and *marital* fertility may have been as great or even greater than elsewhere.

Unhappily, the best data is not yet available to test this proposition, but a brief comparison may be usefully made between York and London. The sex-ratios, both at all ages and in the 20–39 group, were almost exactly the same for the two cities. Furthermore, the proportion of females over twenty who were actually married differed insignificantly (53.4 per cent in York, 53.3 per cent in London). Their average fertility over the years 1850–2, expressed in terms of the number of births per 1,000 females aged 15–44, was 125.6 (York), 120.9 (London). If a comparison is made with other towns, York with its female proportion married of 53.4 per cent and general fertility rate of 125.6 is seen to be comparable with such places as Plymouth (52.8 per cent and 123.2); Norwich (55.1 per cent and 123.6); and Nottingham (55.5 per cent and 124.8). The fertility rate is much below that encountered in cities where the proportion of married females was greater (Birmingham, 63.5 per cent married and 162.6; Bradford 62.9 per cent and 160.4); it is also considerably above that observed where the proportion of married adult females was still lower than in York (Exeter 48.9 per cent and 99.3; Cheltenham 44.9 per cent and 90.5; Bath 42.7 per cent and 95.1).[25] These figures and rates suggest that bearing in mind its peculiar sex-distribution and the relatively low proportion of females who were actually married, fertility in York was about average, that is, it stands up to the test of comparison with other towns.

We are often warned to beware of national means which conceal more than they illuminate. This is also true of averages of areas within a town, or averages of different social groups within it. Within the York Registration District, widely differing general fertility rates are observable for the various subdistricts, in 1850–2 (table 6.14).

Substantial fertility differences are thus concealed by the global figures. The least salubrious district of the city showed distinctly higher fertility than the others; in fact it stood at some 9 per cent higher than the national level, which was otherwise

TABLE 6.14   *Births per 1,000 females aged 15–44, by sub-district**

	No. females aged 15–44	Average births 1850–2	Births per 1,000 females aged 15–44
Bootham	4,101	389.3	94.9
Micklegate	3,492	381.6	109.3
Walmgate	4,794	754.6	157.4
Three urban sub-districts	12,387	1,525.6	123.2
Rural surround	1,987	280.0	140.9
York Registration District	14,374	1,805.6	125.6
England and Wales	4,234.8 (000)	611.0 (000)	144.3

* 1851 Census. Population Tables II (2); Registrar-General's Annual Reports.

not attained in any part of York Registration District. As table 6.15 shows Walmgate also had by far the highest local illegitimacy rate, approximately twice that pertaining to Bootham and Micklegate sub-districts, and once again, this was the only part of the registration district where this was above the national average.

TABLE 6.15   *Illegitimate birth rates per 1,000 females aged 15–44, by sub-district**

	Annual average illegitimate births 1850–2	Rate per 1,000 females aged 15–44
Bootham	29.7	7.2
Micklegate	18.7	5.4
Walmgate	58.7	12.2
Three urban sub-districts	107.0	8.6
Rural surround	18.3	9.2
York Registration District	125.3	8.7
England and Wales	41,596	9.8

* 1851 Census. Population Tables II (2); Registrar-General's Annual Reports.

Earlier in the decade, there is further evidence of comparatively high fertility in Walmgate; Dr Laycock's 'Sanatory Table' gives 'the number of inhabitants to one birth annually', over the years 1839–41. Knowing the actual number of inhabitants for the city and for each parish (from the 1841 census, also used by Laycock), we can calculate the actual number of births, and re-express his figures in modern conventional form, i.e. births per 1,000 population. Laycock gave ratios for each parish, except St George. These parish figures may be grouped by their respective sub-districts, and it should be noted that since Laycock was concerned only with the Municipal Borough, the results shown in table 6.16 are for those parts of the three sub-districts which lay within the borough.

TABLE 6.16   *Crude birth rates: averages of the years 1839–41**

	Total births	Population as stated by Laycock	Birth rate
Micklegate (6 parishes)	186	6,871	27.1
Bootham (16 parishes)	305	10,572	28.9
Walmgate (9 parishes, lacking St George)	337	10,465	32.2

* Calculated from Laycock (1844) 245. See figure 4.

Thus the evidence of tables 6.14 and 6.16 suggests that Walmgate maintained higher fertility rates throughout the 1840s. Such contrasts are partly explained by differences in the sex-ratios of these districts, as table 6.17 shows.

TABLE 6.17   *Sex-Ratios for the several sub-districts of York Registration District, 1851: females per 1,000 males*

	(a) At all ages	(b) 20–39 group	General fertility rate, births per 1,000 females 15–44 (table 6.14)
York R.D.	1,082	1,132	125.6
Bootham	1,179	1,336	94.9
Micklegate	1,134	1,150	109.3
Walmgate	1,060	1,100	157.4
Rural Surround	924	895	140.9
England and Wales	1,027	1,042	144.3

* 1851 Census. Population Tables II (2).

The fertility rates which differed most from the national for 1851 were Micklegate, and more especially Bootham. Bootham had an abnormally high excess of females, especially domestic servants, which is likely to have meant that proportionately fewer of them were married. To some extent this also applied to Micklegate, though in Walmgate, where the sex-ratio more closely resembled the national, fertility was slightly above the national level.

Class differences in fertility

In the nation as a whole, birth rates began the significant decline which has led to the modern small family in the later 1870s, with the upper classes in the vanguard.[26] This is not to say that fertility had previously been uncontrolled; on the contrary, Matras has shown that some 19.5 per cent of the generation of wives born in 1831–45 were already fertility controllers, in the sense that their reproductive performance fell below that of the 1911 female rural population of Ireland, age at marriage having been controlled for.[27]

By the later nineteenth century inter-class fertility differences had come to be very marked and were a matter of common observation, which raises the interesting question of how far back in time they can be traced. Stevenson found that earlier inter-class differences (on a marriage cohort basis) were very much less than for those of 1881–91. Thus for 1851–61 the fertility of social class I marriages was calculated to be some 10 per cent below that of the other classes, which among themselves had much the same fertility on a standardized basis, a conclusion endorsed by Innes, writing a few years later.[28] Stevenson added that 'if the comparison could have been carried twenty years further back, a period of substantial equality between all classes might possibly have been met with'.[29]

The necessary material to adequately test such hypotheses on the national or local level is not at present available to historians; perhaps if the restrictions placed on it by the Registrar-General come to be lifted in the future, it will be

possible to apply to civil registration material family recon-
stitution methods analogous to those currently being used on
eighteenth-century parish registers. In the meantime, as a
modest contribution to this debate, it is worth indicating that
there is some tentative suggestion of inter-class fertility differ-
entials in York in the 1840s, albeit inconclusive in character.
Our starting point is table 6.18.

TABLE 6.18 *Children aged 0–4 per 1,000 married women, aged 15–49, by
class, 1851**

Class I	Class II	Class III	Class IV	Class V
863	745	862	831	796
(22 wives)	(47 wives)	(232 wives)	(59 wives)	(54 wives)
783 (±219)		862 (±119)	814 (±167)	
(69 wives)			(113 wives)	

* 1851 Census sample.

As we have seen, higher class brides did not marry significantly later than their plebian counterparts; at least, not
to the extent which would make much difference to their
fertility.[30] Their fecundity (innate biological capacity to
reproduce) might if anything, be somewhat higher and certainly not lower, given that in general they would ordinarily have
enjoyed throughout their lives better standards of nutrition.
Regarding the children in the calculation, we can be certain
that child mortality bore more hardly on the lower classes than
the upper, although we cannot precisely measure the different
rates.[31] Thus, if the top two classes (taken together) could
only manage a ratio of 783 as against 862 and 814 for those
below them in the social scale, there is some suggestion that
their marital fertility may have been lower.

It is true, the numbers of cases are regrettably small, and
each of the means given has a substantial range of error; the
fertility ratio for classes I and II may have been as high as
1,002 and those of the other two grouped classes as low as
743 (class III) and 647 (classes IV–V), at the 95 per cent
confidence level. But much the same pattern of results emerges

with the 1841 data, given in table 6.19, which somewhat enhances the possibility of a real difference in procreation between the upper classes and the rest bearing in mind once again the differential child mortality factor.

TABLE 6.19   *Children aged 0–4 per 1,000 married women aged 15–49, by class, 1841**

Class I	Class II	Class III	Class IV	Class V
857	771	841	980	727
(14 wives)	(48 wives)	(189 wives)	(49 wives)	(44 wives)
790 (±265)		841 (±127)	860 (±190)	
(62 wives)			(93 wives)	

* 1841 Census sample.

Within what I have described as the upper class, class II fertility appears to be lowest in both years, which raises the interesting possibility that in this period it was what one might perhaps call the lower-middle class (II), struggling to keep up the distinction between themselves and the manual working classes, who practised birth control most widely. On the other hand, it has been shown that in the case of sixty-one Nottingham wives of indubitably high-class citizens the comparable ratio in 1851 was only 655 children aged 0–4 per 1,000 wives in the same age group.[32]

In regard to the results for classes III, IV and V, little can be said. Tables 6.18 and 6.19 do appear to hint that the census fertility ratio of class IV–V wives might have been lower, relative to class III, in 1851 than in 1841. If this is valid (the differences are not statistically significant), the explanation might well lie in a relative, though not necessarily absolute worsening in the incidence of child mortality amongst the lowest classes.[33]

The tables tell us little that is conclusive on the question of differential fertility, and the speculations I have based on them are highly tentative. But they may have more value when further work has been carried out, preferably using bigger samples enabling detailed age-specific comparisons to be made.

7 Household and Family Structure

Fletcher has observed that the family is and always has been, the most intimate and one of the most important human groups; being the smallest of the formal associations in society, it is the social unit within which the most fundamental appreciation of human qualities and values takes place.[1] With a few honourable exceptions,[2] historians have been strangely reluctant to admit that the evolution of the family merits serious study, and the consequence is that, in general, they content themselves with atempting to sift and evaluate contemporary impressions.[3] These sources, in turn, are apt to lay a great deal of emphasis on the disintegrative influences of industrialism on the quality of family life.[4]

Sociologists have been bolder; they have tended to assert that urban-industrial society reduced both the size and range of functions of the family or household. Thus, Le Play drew a contrast between the patriarchal type of family, marked by strong ties between the generations, living together or proximately in a state of stable self-sufficiency in an unchanging agrarian society, and the unstable family characterizing modern society – rootless and independent, created by the marriage tie, and transient in the sense that once the children leave and parents die, it passes out of existence. In the same vein, Linton differentiated the consanguine (i.e. extended) type of family of traditional, stable agricultural society from the conjugal, nuclear, or elementary type – head, wife and children, isolated from wider kinship contact and highly self-reliant. McIver stressed the multi-functional character of the family in traditional society, and the gradual curtailment of its roles which has occurred on account of the loss of its economic function (that is, the separation of 'work' and 'home'), as well as sundry health, nursing and educational functions as a result of the recent advance of community provision, etc.[5]

The critical factor deemed to have affected the traditional structure is generally taken to be industrialization. Against the background of these hypotheses, York forms an interesting case study, presenting a situation of comparatively rapid urban growth without the factory-based industrial development which was its frequent concomitant elsewhere. In some respects the material discussed in this chapter is complementary to what Anderson has written, with great sociological perception, on Preston. So far as the way in which I collected my data allows,[6] these findings on York will be presented in a comparable manner. Most are based on the 1851 census sample (the first to require 'relationship to head of family'), with some support from that of 1841.

FAMILY SIZE AND NUMBERS OF CHILDREN

On the basis of the families of household heads only, the mean size of families enumerated at the time of the census was 3.45 in 1851, 3.41 in 1841.[7] The mode value in each case was 2, and, as table 7.1 shows, at each census the vast majority of all families were below 6 in size.

No significant differences were observed in relation to the birthplace origin of household heads, but for both years, there

TABLE 7.1   *Percentage distribution of family sizes**

	1841	1851
$N =$	781	628
1 person	15.0	15.7
2	24.5	23.7
3	20.5	18.1
4	12.9	15.6
5	12.7	11.5
6	6.5	7.2
7	3.8	4.1
8	2.2	2.2
9	1.4	1.3
10	–	0.6
11 or more	0.3	0.1

* 1841 and 1851 census samples.

is some indication of systematic variation by social class in table 7.2.[8]

TABLE 7.2 *Mean family size by social class**

	Class I–II	Class III	Class IV–V
1841	2.88 ($N = 164$)	3.76 ($N = 271$)	3.65 ($N = 146$)
1851	3.13 ($N = 166$)	3.70 ($N = 386$)	3.43 ($N = 201$)

* 1841 and 1851 census samples.

For 1841 the differences between classes I–II and III, and I–II and IV–V are significant at the 95 per cent confidence level; whilst the same is also true of the difference between classes I–II and III in 1851. Otherwise, the general resemblance of the two distributions may be noted, although comparisons between absolute levels are out of the question on account of having to use somewhat different conventions for distinguishing 'class' and family, in the two census years.[9]

Of course, these static or instantaneous glimpses of family size are the outcome of the complex interplay of the demographic factors discussed in previous chapters. Short of the ultimate demographic explanations however, it is evident that they may be largely accounted for in simple mechanical terms, by reference to a series of independent characteristics of the sample sub-groups under study. To begin with, no fewer than 39.8 per cent of household heads in classes I–II were widowed or single, as against 18.4 per cent for class III, and 23.9 per cent for classes IV–V, in 1851. For 1841, somewhat arbitrary assumptions have to be used in deciding whether or not a household head was married or not, but the same contrast emerges, if anything in a heightened degree (single or widowed heads 50.6 per cent in classes I–II, 17 per cent in class III, 20.5 per cent in classes IV–V). Moreover, the proportion of class I–II household heads in the stage of life where family sizes were naturally likely to be at a maximum (aged up to 45), was only 42.7 per cent in 1851, as against 56.2 per cent for classes III–V combined. In 1841 the comparable proportions were 45.7 and 63.5 per cent respectively.

Naturally, these characteristics had a close bearing on the numbers of children likely to be enumerated; the findings are set out in table 7.3.[10]

TABLE 7.3   *Children per household head**

		Social class	
	I–II	III	IV–V
1841			
(i) Percentage of heads having no children	45.1	26.2	25.3
(ii) Mean number of children (all heads)	1.39	1.93	1.86
(iii) Mean number of children (married heads only)	1.88	2.11	2.09
$N =$	164	271	146
1851			
(i) Percentage of heads having no children	41.0	29.0	33.3
(ii) Mean number of children (all heads)	1.54	1.92	1.73
(iii) Mean number of children (married heads only)	2.00	2.10	1.90
$N =$	166	386	201

* 1841 and 1851 census samples.

The differences between classes I–II and the rest are significant in respect of characteristics (i) and (ii) both in 1841 and 1851.[11] But it must be emphasized that these differences virtually disappear when attention is paid to characteristic (iii). In other words, we may conclude that differences in marital fertility are unlikely to have been a major factor governing mean numbers of children and hence family size; on the contrary, the gross differences are to be accounted for largely in terms of the finding that fewer upper-class families were 'complete', in the sense that they were headed by a married and living couple; and in addition, the fact that their heads tended to be older.

It is noticeable that with both samples, the mean number of children per head recorded for class IV–V was lower than for class III. These differences are not statistically significant at the 95 per cent confidence level, but the fact that the same result appeared twice is interesting. If in fact there was a difference between the skilled worker/small shopkeeper class and the rest, it is likely to have arisen out of differential patterns of mortality, having the following effects:

(i) Fewer class IV–V household heads were actually living in the married state at the time of the census, and correspondingly, more were widowed or single.

(ii) Perhaps more potently, infant and child mortality would have borne more severely on classes IV–V, so removing more of their offspring from the census purview.[12]

DOMESTIC SERVANTS

I have already shown that these made up an abnormally large proportion of the total labour force in York. As might be anticipated, their maintenance was confined very largely to the upper two classes, I and II; but since this obvious characteristic has never been measured before, it is worth reproducing the overall results in table 7.4.[13]

TABLE 7.4   *Distribution of domestic servants by social class of household**

	Social class				
	I	II	III	IV	V
Percentage with 1 or more domestic servants	81.4	57.9	9.1	5.8	–
2 or more	52.5	13.1	2.6	1.0	–
3 or more	30.5	1.9	0.5	1.0	–
4 or more	15.3	1.9	–	1.0	–
$N =$	59	107	386	103	98

* 1851 census sample.

It is singularly interesting to note that for Nottingham, Smith has shown that class I–II household heads (defined on the same basis) averaged only 0.7 domestic servants each, as against 1.15 for York, whilst the overall proportion of households with servants was only 11.7 per cent as against 19.7

for York.[14] Such a contrast must be attributed to more wide-spread alternative sources of employment for females in the Midland city, especially in lace manufacture.

Domestic servants were generally fairly young. In 1851 87.8 per cent were aged below 35, the largest absolute number being in the 15–24 age group (53.3 per cent). For 1841 the figures were 87.4 and 63.8 per cent respectively. Despite the existence of small numbers who performed a lifetime of service, and whose loyalty was encouraged by the York Faithful Female Servants Society, it is clear that most servants must have left on marriage. Prospective suitors of female servants would undoubtedly have gravitated towards the west and central districts of the city, since, faithfully reflecting the 'class' com-position of the different areas, the urban parishes of Bootham sub-district (27.9 per cent of household heads in class I–II) averaged 0.53 servants per household, and the district contained 36.7 per cent of all the domestic servants in York. By contrast the Walmgate parishes contained only 0.19 domestic servants per household.

LODGERS

In this study, the category has been used as residual; that is to say it includes all those not identifiable as members of the household head's family, nor described as kin, domestic servants or visitors. It therefore includes lodgers in the sense of contractual boarders, together with their dependants (if any), and living-in assistants in the household head's business (journeymen, shop assistants, apprentices, etc.) It must be admitted that the scope of the category is too wide, and that some differentiation within it would have been desirable; also that this procedure has led to a slight overcount of lodgers, in the sense in which later researchers have come to use the expression (usually, to denote boarders only). In that sense, my estimate that, on the evidence of the 1851 sample, 21.3 per cent of households contained at least one lodger must be treated with caution, where comparisons are made with other communities.[15]

TABLE 7.5   *Incidence of lodgers by social class of household head**

	Social class				
	I	II	III	IV	V
Percentage of households with no lodger	94.9	70.1	80.3	77.7	78.6
Percentage with 1 or more	5.1	29.9	19.6	22.3	21.4
Percentage with 2 or more	3.4	12.1	9.8	10.3	17.3
Percentage with 3 or more	1.7	3.7	5.7	7.5	10.2
Mean lodgers per household	0.22	0.53	0.46	0.52	0.73
$N =$	59	107	386	103	98

* 1851 Census sample.

For what it is worth however, the distribution of lodgers between the various social classes is set out in table 7·5, which is capable of meaningful if limited interpretation. The table suggests, as expected, that the proportion of householders with lodgers in class I was low, whilst classes II–V were considerably more likely to take lodgers. A pooled estimate test indicates a significant difference between classes III and V in the tendency for the latter to accommodate larger groups of lodgers – note the value of 17.3 as against 9.8 per cent with two or more for class III, and the consequent effect on the mean figures.

But for the high incidence of lodgers in class II, the last characteristic (mean lodgers in all households) would have borne a symmetrical, inverse relationship to class, as indeed appears to have been the case, in this sample, with regard to proportions with three or more lodgers. The eccentric behaviour of class II is to some extent an artifact and in part explicable by the special characteristics of that class.

(i) it is an artifact in the sense that a number of class II household heads were so classified on the evidence that they were self-employed small business proprietors; it was the appearance of apprentices (etc.) in the household (here treated as lodgers) which served to register its status.

(ii) An unusually high proportion of class II household heads were single women or widows (27.1 per cent, against

23.7, 11.6, 17.5 and 15.3 per cent for classes I, III, IV, V, respectively). And it was generally the case that such householders were significantly more likely to accommodate lodgers than others as table 7.6 shows.

TABLE 7.6 *Distribution of lodgers by marital status of household head**

Head's status	$N =$	Percentage with one or more lodgers	Mean: lodgers per household where lodgers were found	Mean: lodgers in all households
Married male	548	19.2	2.39	0.51
Married female	22	18.2	4.00	0.73
Single male	27	25.9	3.57	0.93
Single female	38	28.9	1.27	0.37
Widowers	38	15.8	3.00	0.47
Widows	108	30.6	2.03	0.62
Widows/single females		30.1		
All other categories		19.2		

* 1851 Census sample.

Although I am dealing here with a category of such heterogeneity that future researchers will certainly wish to subdivide it, some further characteristics of lodgers, as defined here, are worth mention. The following breakdown is useful in the present context, and could possibly have some future comparative value.

(i) There were in all, 391 lodgers, of which 62.9 per cent were male, 37.1 per cent female.

(ii) In terms of age-composition, it is clear that young persons aged 15–29 were proportionately over-represented. In the Municipal Borough part of the sample, 42.1 per cent were found to be aged 15–29, as against 28.5 per cent in the population as a whole, stated in the printed census volume. The over-29s were present in much the same proportion (40.0 as against 39.5 per cent) whilst children aged 0–14 (17.9 per cent against 32.0 per cent) were definitely under-represented. Had my data been arranged in a different form, it would have been possible to go further; for Preston Anderson notes that 'half of all single male lodgers and three-fifths of single female lodgers were aged 15–24', whilst a sizeable minority of married couples in life cycle stages 1 and 2 (wife under 45, and either no children or one small baby only) were likely to be lodgers as against occupying houses on their own account.[16]

(iii) 161 lodgers (41.2 per cent) were members of 'sharing family units' defined as a married couple or a male or female lodger with at least one child. These were distributed in the manner anticipated, i.e. inversely in relation to social class of the head of the household in which they were to be found, although the differences are very slight, and are only statistically substantiable at the 95 per cent confidence level where classes I–II and IV–V (combined) are compared (table 7.7).

TABLE 7.7   *Sharing of dwellings in relation to social class of household head**

	Social class				
	I	II	III	IV	V
Percentage not sharing	98.3	98.1	94.0	92.2	88.8
Percentage sharing with one further family unit, or more	1.7	1.9	6.0	7.8	11.2
$N =$	59	107	386	103	98

* 1851 Census sample.

(iv) The mean size of 'sharing family units', so defined, was well below average family size for household heads in the city as a whole, at 2.82, including 1.82 dependants. This again suggests that Anderson's point mentioned under (ii) above, applied to York.

(v) 169 (43.2 per cent) lodgers were males without co-residing dependants, and 40 (10.2 per cent) were females in the same situation.

(vi) 74 (18.9 per cent) lodgers shared the same occupation as the household head. But some of these were cases where both head and lodger were obviously employed by a third party (e.g. the railway), or where both were described as 'agricultural labourer', etc.; only 35 (9.0 per cent of all lodgers) could be confidently stated to have been employed by the household head.

VISITORS

It is difficult to know what to make of this category, but for the record, it may be noted that the proportion of households with one or more visitors varied only within the narrow limits of 3.9 and 8.5 per cent for classes I, III, IV, and V. But 18.7 per cent of class II households contained visitors, and in view of the high propensity of this class to have lodgers, we may perhaps conclude that the term was, in some cases at least, a genteel alternative for lodger, or paying guest.

KIN

Earlier generations of sociologists devoutly believed that industrialization had a marked tendency to reduce both the size and range of functions of the family. The consanguine or extended family (including kin) was taken to be the essential characteristic of social organization in 'patriarchal', 'agrarian', 'stable', or 'traditional' societies, whilst the ('rootless', 'unstable', 'transient') nuclear or conjugal family of head, wife and children only, was the contrasting form in modern societies. Recent publications have shown beyond doubt that preindustrial England, at any rate, was not characterized by a high degree of kinship *co-residence*, nor by the existence of multi-generational family or household units; and that, contrary to expectation, the industrial towns of Preston and Nottingham actually had a higher incidence of kinship coresidence than did the old society.[17]

A fairly extended treatment of the situation in a traditional town at the mid-nineteenth-century mark may serve to throw further light on this question, from a comparative point of view. I have taken here, as kin or relatives, all persons in a given household with a stated relationship to the household head in the fourth column of the 1851 enumerators' books (mother-in-law, niece, sister, aunt, etc.), together with the spouses of the married children of household heads.[18]

The first finding is that as in industrial Preston and Nottingham, the proportion of households containing kin, and the incidence of three-generational households was considerably higher than for the selection of pre-industrial villages and townships studied by Laslett (table 7.8). This suggests that the factors working to produce such a result could include extended urbanization as well as modern industrialization *per se*. On the other hand, the proportion of York households containing only one generation was higher than either, for reasons which will be touched on below.

TABLE 7.8   *Incidence of kin co-residence**

	York	Preston	61 Pre-industrial communities
(a) Proportion of households containing kin	21.6	23	10.1
(b) Proportion of one-generation households	32.9	15	23.7
Proportion of two-generation households	58.5	75	70.4
Proportion of three-generation households	8.6	9	5.8

* 1851 sample for York – 781 households: Anderson (1972d) 220–2; Laslett (1969) 219.

What types of household were the more likely to contain kin? There was very little substantive difference where the incidence of kinship co-residence was related to heads' birthplaces. Irrespective of whether the head had been born in York, in the East and North or West Ridings, the rest of England, Scotland or Ireland, the proportion of households containing kin varied between the narrow limits of 20.4 and 24.0; only in the case of the northern counties heads was the proportion out of line, at 10.7 per cent. In general these findings suggest that immigration was by no means associated with a breakdown in communications and affective contacts with the relatives left behind. I have already shown that the vast majority of immigrants came to York as teenagers or young persons, and these statistics strongly suggest that contacts were maintained with some perseverance over the years. Very probably, as Anderson has suggested, the ties of kinship had much to do with obtaining jobs and a suitable base for young newcomers;[19] 50.6 per cent of all kin were aged below 20, as against 42.0 per cent in the city at large, as noted below.

Married female heads had co-residing kin in only two cases out of twenty-two in the sample; but otherwise it is clear that households headed by a married couple were significantly less likely to contain kin than those headed by single and widowed persons, especially where the household head was male (table 7.9).

TABLE 7.9   *Proportion of households with co-residing kin: by marital status of household head**

Married male	Married female (absent husband)	Widower	Single male	Widow	Single female
19.2	9.0	26.3	55.5	23.1	31.6
$N = 548$	22	38	27	108	38

* 1851 Census sample.

As a general rule, the oldest household heads (60 plus) were significantly more likely to have co-resident kin and we may assume that they stood to gain most from arrangements of this kind: otherwise the householder's age was not a critical variable, except that in absolute terms, the burden seems to have been shouldered to a greater extent by the younger age groups (up to 39) than by the middle-aged (41–59). Or perhaps, where the wife was working and/or where their own families were large, they too, stood to gain much from the arrangement. The details are set out in table 7.10.

TABLE 7.10 *Age of head, in households containing resident kin**

Age of head	Number of households containing kin	Percentage of all heads in each age group	$N =$
−24	5 ⎫	19.2	26
25−	13 ⎬ 64	14.4	90
30−	19 ⎭	19.8	96
35−	27	23.9	113
40−	15 ⎫	17.4	81
45−	16 ⎬ 50	18.0	89
50−	19 ⎭	16.1	118
60−	34 ⎫ 55	32.7	104
70−	21 ⎭	32.8	64

* 1851 Census sample.

Finally, there is some suggestion in table 7.11 below that upper-class (I–II) households were marginally more likely to contain kin, which, if the finding is valid,[20] could be ascribed to three factors:

(a) Such householders were better placed to support dependants.

(b) Their kinsfolk may have enjoyed greater longevity.

(c) Many such householders were business proprietors, requiring the services of their married offspring and probably kinsfolk on a wider basis – very often, given the nature of the local economy,[21] on a residential footing.

TABLE 7.11 *Proportion of households with co-residing kin: by social class**

	Class I–II	Class III	Class IV–V
Percentage with no kin	72.9	79.0	80.6
Percentage with 1 relative or more	27.1	21.0	19.4
Percentage with 2 or more	8.4	5.2	5.0
$N =$	166	386	201

* 1851 Census sample.

Who were the kin? Table 7.12 sets out the details, and it will be apparent that, although the basis of classification is different in some respects, these findings support Anderson's conclusion that most of them were either nephews or nieces, grandchildren or brothers and sisters (siblings) of the household head or his wife. No doubt, as in Preston, these included many adopted orphans.[22] The fact that there were comparatively few household heads' parents may be ascribed principally to the higher levels of mortality (hence lower life expectation) of the period.

TABLE 7.12 *Relationship of co-residing kin to household head* *

	Number		Percentage of all kin
Grandfather, grandmother	1		
Father, father-in-law	3		
Mother	14	27	
Mother-in-law	9		
Son-in-law	13		
Daughter-in-law	6	19	
Grandchild	65		26.5
Great grandchild	1		
Niece	40		22.4
Nephew	15	55	
Head's brother	18		
Head's sister	42	69	28.2
Head's sister-in-law, brother-in-law	9		
Aunt, uncle	2		
Cousin, second cousin	5		
Unspecified	2		
	245		

* 1851 Census sample.

Reflecting this distribution, it may be noted that in 1851 50.6 per cent of all kin were aged below 20 and 19.6 per cent 50 and over; the relevant proportions of the population in the Municipal Borough were 42.0 per cent and 14.4 per cent. The co-residing relatives in the sample were thus both younger and older than the norm.

A SUMMARY VIEW OF HOUSEHOLD AND FAMILY STRUCTURE

Mean household size in 1851 was 4.70 ($\pm$ 0.18), with class differences set out in table 7.13.

TABLE 7.13   *Variation of household size in 1851**
(i) *By individual classes*

	Social class				
	I	II	III	IV	V
$N =$	59	107	386	103	98
Mean; no. of household heads	1.00	1.00	1.00	1.00	1.00
Mean; wives per household	0.54	0.61	0.78	0.70	0.71
Mean; children	1.85	1.37	1.93	1.52	1.94
Mean; size of family	3.39	2.98	3.71	3.22	3.65
Mean; Domestics	1.88	0.75	0.12	0.10	–
Mean; Lodgers	0.22	0.53	0.46	0.52	0.73
Mean; Relatives	0.41	0.41	0.29	0.24	0.34
Mean; Visitors	0.12	0.26	0.08	0.07	0.08
Mean household size	6.02	4.93	4.66	4.15	4.80

(ii) *By combined classes*

	Class I–II	Class III	Class IV–V
$N =$	166	386	201
Mean; household heads	1.00	1.00	1.00
Mean; wives per family	0.58	0.78	0.71
Mean; children per family	1.54	1.93	1.73
Mean; size of family	3.12	3.71	3.44
Mean; domestics	1.15	0.12	0.05
Mean; lodgers	0.42	0.46	0.63
Mean; relatives	0.41	0.29	0.29
Mean; visitors	0.21	0.08	0.07
Mean household size	5.31 ($\pm$0.46)	4.66 ($\pm$0.22)	4.48 ($\pm$0.33)

* 1851 Census sample.

There was a clear difference between class I–II and both classes III and IV–V; on the other hand the difference between classes III and IV–V is not to be relied upon, i.e. 5.31 is significantly greater than either 4.66 or 4.48, but the latter two cannot be shown to have differed at the 95 per cent confidence level.

Average household size in 1841 was 4.56 ($\pm$ 0.19), with class differences indicated in table 7.14.

TABLE 7.14 *Variation of household size in 1841**
(i) *By individual classes*

	Social class				
	I	II	III	IV	V
$N =$	45	119	271	80	66
Mean; no. of household heads	1.00	1.00	1.00	1.00	1.00
Mean; wives per household	0.38	0.54	0.83	0.75	0.85
Mean; children	1.29	1.43	1.93	1.80	1.93
Mean; size of family	2.67	2.97	3.76	3.55	3.78
Mean; domestics	2.07	0.91	–	0.06	0.03
Mean; relatives (identifiable)	0.13	0.20	0.07	0.05	0.09
Mean; all other	0.49	1.05	0.64	0.58	0.52
Mean household size	5.36	5.13	4.46	4.24	4.41

(ii) *By combined classes*

	Class I–II	Class III	Class IV–V
$N =$	164	271	146
Mean; household heads	1.00	1.00	1.00
Mean; wives of heads	0.49	0.83	0.79
Mean; children	1.39	1.93	1.86
Mean; family size	2.88	3.76	3.65
Mean; domestics	1.23	–	0.05
Mean; relatives	0.18	0.07	0.07
Mean; all other	0.90	0.64	0.55
Mean household size	5.19 ($\pm$0.44)	4.46 ($\pm$0.27)	4.32 ($\pm$0.35)

* 1841 Census sample.

The pattern of results is much the same in both census years, and it is again clear that the combined average household size of classes I–II was significantly higher than those of the other classes, which cannot be shown to have differed. Above all, it was the presence of relatively large numbers of domestic servants which made the higher-class households rather larger, despite the fact that in respect of average number of children, and mean family size, they tended to be smaller. The attachment of domestic servants to upper-class families was not fully offset by the tendency for lower-class families to have more lodgers, and the balance in respect of relatives living in, as we have seen, favoured the upper classes. Not surprisingly, class I households, in both samples, tended to be the largest of all, since they had most domestic servants.

From time to time in the course of this analysis, I have pointed to variations in the age-composition of the various 'components' summed into the above tables, and it is possible to pursue the matter a little further. Table 7.15 gives the proportions, by age-group, enumerated as 'head', 'wife',

TABLE 7.15   *Percentages of each age-group in six enumeration categories**

				Enumerated as:			
Age group	Household head	Head's wife	Head's child	Visitor	Lodger	Domestic servant	Kin
0–	–	–	81.6	2.6	7.1	–	8.6
5–	–	–	87.9	0.3	5.8	–	6.0
10–	–	–	82.8	0.3	4.1	5.7	7.0
15–	1.1	–	50.1	3.6	12.7	21.6	10.8
20–	6.6	11.4	31.3	3.0	20.5	17.5	9.6
25–	26.4	24.6	15.0	2.3	14.1	12.9	4.7
30–	34.3	28.2	11.4	3.6	9.3	8.9	4.3
35–	45.6	28.2	5.6	3.2	11.3	4.4	1.6
40–	37.2	35.3	3.2	3.2	14.2	4.1	2.8
45–	48.4	35.9	4.3	1.1	7.6	1.1	1.6
50–	49.4	28.5	0.8	2.1	10.9	2.5	5.9
60–	57.5	20.4	–	1.1	11.0	1.7	8.3
70–	52.5	18.0	–	1.6	12.3	–	15.6
N =	781	541	1,372	85	391	255	245

* 1851 Census sample.

'lodger', etc., in the 1851 sample, and permits the introduction of a dynamic element into the analysis.

Points of interest emerging from the table are:

(i) That the proportions encountered as 'head' or as 'wife' only surpass those enumerated as 'child' of household head with the 25–9 age-group. This is some confirmation of the probable age at marriage, which appears to have been generally in the later rather than earlier twenties.[23]

(ii) It is also at that critical juncture (25–9) where the proportion enumerated as domestic servants (at its peak in the 15–19 age group) first falls below the number of 'wives'.

(iii) The proportion classed as 'head' or 'wife', does not absolutely predominate over all other designations until 25–9 (even then, 51 per cent will not be statistically significant); but by 35–9 about three-quarters of all persons in the sample are so classified, and the proportion remains surprisingly high even at the most advanced ages. On the other hand, the mounting proportion of heads without wives after 50 tells the tale of increasing mortality as a factor in the separation of husband and wife.

(iv) The lodger category is somewhat blurred in this study, but many journeymen, etc., would be lodgers prior to marriage, so tending to raise the proportions in the age-groups 15–29 as I have already noted.

(v) As indicated above, kin were likely to be aged under 24 and over 50. In the case of the young, I should be inclined to account for this in the terms of Anderson's explanation, which lays stress on the kinship network as a means of obtaining urban jobs and basis of easing assimilation into what would in many cases be a novel environment.[24] In the case of old persons, there were good reasons why, in the context of a textile town with many married women workers, a bargain with old persons (whether related or not), should be struck on a 'calculative-instrumental basis'; they were ideal child-minders. Accordingly, 'of those aged 65 and over, no fewer than 66 per cent of non-institutionalized widowers and 64 per cent of widows had one or more kinsmen in the same household', which, in effect, was virtually all of them once allowance had been made for the chances that they had surviving offspring.[25] Unfortunately my data has not been assembled or analysed in that form, but table 7.16 enables some tentative conclusions to be drawn.

TABLE 7.16 *Residential patterns of elderly persons aged 60 and over**

Enumerated as	60 and over	70 and over
Householder with wife	59	22
Householder's wife	59	22
Householder, without wife	109	42
[including solitary householder	23	10]
Visitor	4	2
Child of householder	–	–
Domestic servant	3	–
Lodger	35	15
Relative	35	19
	304	122

* 1851 Census sample, absolute numbers of cases.

Apparently a high proportion of the non-institutionalized aged population continued to enjoy the status of householder, or householder's wife. Only a minority, on this evidence, were dependent for accommodation as kin, or as lodgers. But such an interpretation would undoubtedly tend to overstate the independence of the aged from reliance on kin; presumably there were some aged householders who could not have maintained themselves without assistance or income from younger co-residing kinsfolk, featuring in the census simply as relatives. Indeed, in some cases, census headship would have been titular only.

Thus it is desirable to rework the data to throw some further light on the question of old-age living arrangements in general. In the 1851 sample, 77 elderly (60-plus) householders lived with their wives (of various ages), and 59 elderly wives with their husbands (predominantly the same age or older). Another 26 household heads without wives (these could be of either sex), accommodated relatives, and a further 35 persons, aged 60 and over, were themselves designated as relatives.

Summing these figures (197), we can tentatively conclude that 65 per cent of the non-institutionalized elderly age-group (304) were co-residing with relatives using the term to include kin through the marital tie. The remainder of the 60-plus age-group were either visitors (4), domestic servants (3), lodgers (35), or old persons without either spouse or co-residing kin (65); these included 23 solitary householders. A rough idea of the absolute numbers involved in York as a whole can be had by multiplying the numbers throughout by 10, since this is a 10 per cent sample. If the same steps are carried out for the 70-plus age group, it is found that 77 out of 122 (63.1 per cent), were living with spouses, or kin. Among the remainder, 15 were classed as lodgers, and 10 were solitaries.

These findings cannot be strictly compared with those of Anderson, but they do afford further evidence of the functional importance of kinship in an age before the advent of old age pensions; in England and Wales in 1966, approximately one-tenth of all households contained no person related to the head, and in Swansea (1960) the proportion was at least 10 per cent, two-thirds of this group being aged over 65.[26] Better chances of survival, reduced fertility and the provision of old age pensions, coupled with a range of economic and social pressures that can only as yet be guessed at, appear to have raised the problem of old-age isolation to much higher levels with the passage of time. In 1851 the pattern was different and reliance on kinship ties much greater; although it may be suspected that the pattern was marginally less highly developed in York than in industrial Preston, where the economic incentives to 'calculative-instrumentality' were probably stronger. The basis for this statement is given by one statistic on which the methodology does not differ – in Preston only 1 per cent of all households were single-person, in York 5.1 per cent. In York, 57.5 per cent (23 out of 40 in the sample) of such solitary householders were aged 60 and over.[27] This is at least a part of the explanation of the comparatively high proportion of one-generation households in York noted in table 7.8 above.

8   Conclusions

During the first half of the nineteenth century economic change in York was determined largely by the prosperity of the farming classes in the extensive region which the city served as a marketing and distributive centre. The coming of the railways did not lead to the development of York as an industrial town, though the city re-asserted its ancient importance as a centre of communications. The structure of occupations reflected this situation faithfully, notable features being a high concentration of professional people and shopkeepers, counter-balanced to some extent by large numbers of female domestics and an above-average proportion of labouring men. What was missing was modern industry, and factory employment, on any significant scale.

The population of York was comparatively well educated, which almost certainly owed a great deal to the absence of extensive opportunities for the employment of children; possibly the fact that much of this education was instilled in denominational schools helps to explain why the population was more formally 'religious' than in most other large towns. These features may be taken as evidence of social stability and imply widespread acquiescence in the *status quo*. It is true, poverty was deeper and more widespread than when Rowntree came to survey the situation two generations later, and quite probably discrepancies of income and wealth were more acute in York than within the growing industrial towns. Status differences must have been keenly felt, but the nature of the local economy and society was such that these were unlikely to result in a situation of class confrontation; certainly any indications of the articulation of a distinctive working-class point of view, as it might have found expression in a labour 'movement', are slight indeed. As Foster has acutely observed, class-consciousness was only likely to manifest itself where there appeared to be any chance of changing the existing social system, which in the mid-nineteenth century was infrequent.[1]

Against this background I have tried to interpret the socio-demographic data in chapters 4–7. Although the increase of population during the first half of the century was slow by comparison with the burgeoning industrial towns it was, nevertheless, probably faster than in any corresponding fifty year period in the city's history. Immigration waxed and waned in accordance with the level of economic prosperity and expansion and certainly played a major role in population growth during the 'railway decade' upon which much of my attention has been focused. Most of it (with the notable exception of the Irish) was local, as might be anticipated, and weighted towards females. Much of my discussion of immigration has necessarily been framed in terms of net balances, although it is clear from the scrutiny of birthplaces that there must also have been a significant outflow, which is an aspect of population mobility that historians have yet to attend to.

On the basis of somewhat insecure statistics drawn from the *Parish Register Abstracts*, I have suggested that mortality fell between *c.* 1750 and the 1820s. This appears to have been possible in the context of a population increase of some 75 per cent over seventy years, but further growth of 67 per cent in just thirty years between 1821 and 1851 (on constant Municipal Borough boundaries) implies greatly increased density and appears to have put an end to the favourable trend. It would appear that York mortality rates of the 1840s, though clearly not among the worst in the country, were comparatively high at 22–4 per 1,000, and signify that where urban growth occurred in that period (with or without industrialization) it brought various apparently inescapable public health problems.

Present evidence on marriage and fertility (chapter 6) gives little support to the idea of rising fertility as a motor of population growth through the late eighteenth and early nineteenth centuries. An interesting feature, maintained into the 1840s, when more satisfactory evidence becomes available, was the co-existence of high marriage rates and low crude fertility rates. This I have attributed primarily to an imbalance in the sex-composition and to a lesser extent to slightly later marriage[2] (tending to lower the proportion of females 'ever-married'), and the evidence is that when these factors are taken into account, marital fertility in York was much the same as in other English towns in a corresponding demographic situation. This is not, of course, to say that it was uncontrolled. It is possible to point to the existence of fertility differences (at the crude level) in different parts of the city corresponding with what is known of their socio-economic characteristics; and there is some suggestion that marital fertility among the higher social classes may have been slightly below the average, which, if it is true, accords with the suspicions of a number of demographic historians commenting on the national scene.

In chapter 7, the size and structure of households and families was discussed. This is not the place to make wide-ranging comparisons,[3] but in regard to household size (4.7 for York in 1851) and mean family size (3.5) there is a close correspondence with the findings of scholars working on Ashford (a small market town, similar to York in almost every respect save absolute size) and Nottingham (another county town, with however, a much more substantial manufacturing sector). These results also accord closely with those arrived at by Laslett in a study of one hundred pre-industrial communities with the critical difference that, while all the 1851 communities (including York) had a higher proportion of households containing related kin and lodgers than did pre-industrial communities in general, a smaller proportion, even in York, contained servants. Thus the superficial correspondence of mean household size between pre-industrial and mid-nineteenth-century communities conceals some very interesting and significant social structural changes, even where, as in York and Ashford, changes in the mode of production were slight. In other words the underlying currents of social change touched even such communities as these. There were however, more notable changes elsewhere; it has been shown that in Radford (adjacent to Nottingham) and Preston, both highly dependent on textile manufacture, family sizes appear to have been larger (Radford 4.1; Preston 4.2) owing to the higher number of children enumerated. In Preston mean household size (at 5.4) was higher than in any other community mentioned here, not because there were more households with servants (which was a primary determinant with Laslett's pre-industrial communities), but because many more had co-residing kin and lodgers.

Summarizing these chapters naturally inclines me to wonder how far the various characteristics I have described were peculiar to York, and to what extent, following Kohl's suggestion, it is representative of an English urban sociological type. Indeed, it may turn out to be an international type, as recent work on the ancient French city of Dijon in 1851 appears to suggest. Viennot, summarizing the results of his researches, writes

The occupational structure of Dijon in 1851 is that of a town which has not known the industrial revolution . . . domestic services represent an important part of the active female population. Through its landed proprietors, workpeople and indirectly its shopkeepers, Dijon lives to a great extent on the surrounding countryside . . . the importance of [the bourgeoisie] has as a consequence the immigration of a large number of young female domestics, which explains the high percentage of females aged 20–39, the low ratio of males, low proportion of married females which in turn lowers the percentage of children . . . if Dijon had been an industrial town, the sex and age structure, distribution of marital status and composition of families would have been very different.[4]

Like York, Dijon was just beginning to feel the effects of railway development in reviving its economic life.

Of course, there existed also impressive differences, and the one city was by no means a mere replication of the other, in respect of its socio-demographic structure. Although Dijon was approximately the same size as York in total population (32,000 inhabitants), earlier population figures suggest that it had stagnated over a longer period. The age-pyramid for intra-mural East Dijon, shows a marked deficiency of young children, so that (for females) every quinquennial age-group up to 50–4 was actually larger than the 0–4 – an extraordinary state of affairs not paralleled in York. With this is associated census fertility ratios (children aged 0–4 per 1,000 females aged 20–44) of 241 for Dijon and 183 for Dijon East;[5] with which compare 559 for York. One is reminded of Wrigley's finding, in discussing demographic trends on the north European coalfield, that while comparing like regions reveals marked resemblances, residual national differences of a mysterious, cultural nature remain to be accounted for.[6]

Looking back over what this study has achieved, and forward to promising lines of enquiry in the future is a salutary exercise. I have already drawn attention to a few methodological imperfections,[7] which might, perhaps, be expected in a work that is exploratory and not intended to do more than sketch out some of the opportunities which historians have hitherto mostly overlooked. More generally, it would have been possible to extend this study to span the censuses of 1861 and 1871, for which the enumeration books are now available. I have deliberately chosen not to do this in order to leave the way open for a subsequent study of York which would cover 1861–1914, and which must necessarily be written with Rowntree's survey of poverty in mind. Perhaps the chief weakness of his classic enquiry was a failure to set its findings in an adequate historical and comparative context, and in that respect they still await the reassessment of social historians.

I have also come to see that future researchers should pay more attention to what historians can learn from social geographers, especially in the matter of elucidating patterns of spatial arrangement within cities, or, in Robson's words, spatial patterns as a reflection of social processes.[8] More advanced statistical techniques, especially multivariate analysis, clearly have a large part to play in this kind of work. So far as the present study is concerned, the decision to sample the city on a 10 per cent household basis precluded linking the 1841 and 1851 data, and as a general rule, house by house analysis of specific streets or neighbourhoods.[9] There is also scope for directly integrating census data to a very much greater extent with information drawn from other universes, especially perhaps, rate-books, which as yet have received very little attention in this country.[10]

Despite its limitations, I believe that this study will come to be counted with a number of others, mostly recently published or still under research, as marking the early stages of what Briggs has described as an international boom in social history.[11] It has been remarked, 'History is subject to generational changes; our perspectives and our understanding of the past tend to shift as successive generations come to maturity.'[12] The characteristic of the present shift is towards a greater readiness to employ quantitative techniques and social science concepts in historical analysis, a feature which my work shares with, for example, that of Laslett, Anderson, Drake and Pearce, Williams and Vincent in England; Goheen, Katz, Knights, Thernstrom, Greven, Lockridge, Lees, Gutman and Glasco in North America, and a number of European and Japanese studies.[13]

It is true that their ultimate aims, considered individually, vary widely from social scientists interested in establishing uniformities and furthering theoretical understanding, to historians concerned with the uniqueness and particularity of community and social structures. Of course, we can never know what is unique without reference to what is ascertained to be general, and in practice social scientists and historians can travel far down the road in each other's company. On the whole this tends to be more freely conceded by social scientists. For example, the geographer Lawton, whilst hoping to develop general models of value, not only in understanding the past, but of relevance to the study of areas of more recent urbanization, agrees that we should not disregard the individuality born of differences in time, place and personality which the historian Briggs had in mind when he wrote that the study of Victorian cities 'must necessarily be concerned with individual cases'.[14]

In the final analysis, as might be expected from an historian, this study of York leans towards the descriptive rather than the theoretical pole, though it emphasizes those features capable of measurement. Of course, I do not believe that all aspects of social history can be quantified, and obviously, many matters which are the legitimate and proper concern of social historians will never be amenable to this kind of analysis.[15] At the present time however, the invocation of theory in general, and quantitative methods in particular, still has to make its way against a great deal of scepticism and entrenched hostility amongst historians. I have heard an American historian say, quite seriously, that what his country lacked, in the historical field, was not so much people who could count, but people with ideas, as though the two were mutually exclusive categories! A respectable British social historian once advanced the opinion, in a review of an earlier resumé of the studies described in this book, that it appeared merely to attach figures to what was already well known.[16] And even Louis Chevalier, doyen of French social history, has argued that those who use statistical methods and concepts springing from the social sciences lack common sense, are devoid of sensitivity, and do not understand the mystique of traditional historical scholarship.[17]

At bottom, such hostility appears to spring from a false antithesis between the quantitative and the 'qualitative' (traditional, literary) approach. No one would deny that excessive utilization of historical statistics without reference to possible errors or to the circumstances in which they were collected, has its dangers; but to ignore the prospect of fruitful co-operation with the social sciences brings still graver ones – that history, as traditionally practised, will ossify and increasingly come to be viewed as irrelevant to modern thought. Economic historians have long been most ready to employ such tools and perspectives, and the consequence has been that this has been widely accepted as the most dynamic branch of historical studies.

In practice, as I hope this study has shown, it is usually impossible to treat quantitative data in isolation from other types of evidence. The very effort to interpret necessarily leads us back to already well-known 'literary' sources. As this kind of work proceeds, well-known evidence will frequently take on a new meaning, and it will be necessary at other points to assemble scattered and fragmentary sources of information which no previous historian, however literate, has ever dreamed of considering.[18] Quantitative and qualitative research naturally go hand in hand,[19] and if historians will consent to add numeracy to their acknowledged literacy, one can envisage a bright future for social history. An increasing volume of careful analysis in this field will enable historians to measure the intensity of the so-called 'obvious' relationships as they varied by time and place, and in time to come they will be able to discover new ones. It should certainly be possible to analyse Victorian social structure, urban history and social history generally with increasing sensitivity in the years ahead.

Statistical Appendices

I. ANALYSIS OF SAMPLE DATA

Testing the samples

The representativeness of the 1841 and 1851 census samples was examined by comparing the age, sex, and birthplace characteristics of the Municipal Borough element of the two sample populations with the distributions given for York in the printed census volumes at each date. The most appropriate test for this purpose is chi-square (χ^2), which in this context is used to show whether or not the sample distributions of observed frequencies were within the ranges in which nineteen out of twenty repeated samples would have fallen. For example,

1851 Sample

(a) Age distribution

TABLE S.A. 1 *Age data for the Municipal Borough in 1851*

(a) Age group	(b) Census (printed volume)	(c) Expected frequency on 3,301 cases (proportional to b)	(d) Observed sample frequencies
0–	4,254	387	413
5–	3,728	339	339
10–	3,639	331	280
15–	3,625	330	324
20–	3,526	321	297
25–	3,210	292	308
30–	2,783	253	256
35–	2,391	218	225
40–	2,175	198	199
45–	1,745	159	165
50–	2,481	225	217
60–	1,683	153	163
70–	1,063	97	115
	36,303	3,303	3,301

From this data, the calculation of the χ^2 statistic is as follows: for age-group 0–4 calculate $(d-c)^2/c$, and add to this the 'omission frequency' $(h-j)^2/h$, where h = expected frequency among individuals omitted from the sample (4,254 minus 387 in the case of the 0–4s), and j = frequency which would have been encountered if all other cases had been examined (that is, in this case, $b-d$, or 4,254 − 413).

The same steps are carried out with each age-group and the χ^2 statistic for the distribution is the sum of the terms

$$\frac{(d-c)^2}{c} + \frac{(h-j)^2}{h}$$

In this distribution $\chi^2 = 18.88$. With 12 degrees of freedom (there being 13 cells in the table), the 5 per cent critical limit for $\chi^2 = 21.0$ (read off from published tables: see for example Spiegel (1961) 345).

In the same manner

(b) *Sex distribution*
$\chi^2 = 0.47$: 5 per cent level with one degree of freedom = 3.84.

(c) *Birthplace distribution*
$\chi^2 = 22.97$: 5 per cent level with 5 degrees of freedom = 11.1.

1841 Sample

(a) *Age distribution*
$\chi^2 = 23.46$: 5 per cent level with 12 degrees of freedom = 21.0.

(b) *Sex distribution*
$\chi^2 = 0.61$: 5 per cent level with one degree of freedom = 3.84.

(c) *Birthplace distribution*
$\chi^2 = 9.26$: 5 per cent confidence level with 4 degrees of freedom = 9.49.

Conclusions

The 1851 sample was a good representation with respect to age and sex-structure. On birthplaces it failed the test applied, mainly on account of a deficiency of Irish-born (observed frequency 133, expected 174). The other values were York/Yorkshire 2,751 (2,708); northern counties 205 (174); rest of England and Wales 136 (160); Scotland 37 (43); elsewhere 12 (15). This deficiency of Irish was clearly caused by the omission of institutions and large lodging houses (see p. 11) and has been met to some extent by studying a small separate sample of Irish from a selected quarter of the city in a sub-sample (see p. 125).

The 1841 sample was a satisfactory fit on sex and birthplace distributions. On ages the main deficiency came in the older age-groups (60–, observed frequency 103, expected 131; 70–, 55 (78) and was probably attributable to the omission of institutions), but elsewhere the fit was reasonably good, as follows:

0–, observed frequency 326, expected 310; 5–, 283 (269); 10–, 233 (253); 15–, 253 (257); 20–, 278 (276); 25–, 257 (239); 30–, 206 (223); 35–, 169 (158); 40–, 168 (156); 45–, 110 (104); 50–, 192 (179).

Where there is any opportunity of examining the representative-ness of samples from historical data, tests of this or a similar nature should be carried out. They will certainly expose any glaring sample bias. But interpreting the results is to some extent a matter of judge-ment. We do not know whether the yardstick of comparison (the published abstracts) is in all cases exactly correct, and the overall pattern of results here is such as to suggest that the sample data may be used with fair confidence in its representativeness.

The estimation of population proportions and means from sample evidence

Throughout the text, except where there is specific mention to the contrary, readers may assume that appropriate tests have been carried out where assertions of significance of difference based on sample data have been made. The chosen level is ordinarily the 95 per cent confidence limit.

Ranges of error for sample proportions at this level of confidence are given by the formula

$$p \pm 1.96 \sqrt{\left\{ \frac{p\,(1-p)}{n} \right\}}$$

where p is the sample proportion and n the number of cases. Where two ranges of error, so calculated, overlap, an assertion of significance of difference can still sometimes be made, using a pooled estimate test. Assume that two sample populations indicate proportions of p_1 and p_2 for a given characteristic. The hypothesis is then made that both samples could have come from a population with the same characteristic, π. This pooled estimate (π) is given by the formula

$$\frac{n_1\,p_1 + n_2\,p_2}{n_1 + n_2}$$

H*

where n_1 and n_2 are the numbers of cases involved. Now, the standard error of the difference between the two original proportions is given by

$$\sqrt{\left\{ \pi\,(\mathrm{I}-\pi)\left(\frac{\mathrm{I}}{n_1}+\frac{\mathrm{I}}{n_2}\right)\right\}}$$

and where the actual difference between p_1 and p_2 is greater than 1.96 times the standard error, a significant difference between p_1 and p_2 can be asserted at the 95 per cent confidence level.

In dealing with sample *means*, it is first necessary to compute the standard deviation of the sample variable (σ), given by the formula

$$\sqrt{\left\{\frac{\mathrm{I}}{n}\sum (x-\bar{x})^2\right\}}$$

where n is the number of cases, $\bar{x}$ the sample mean and x represents each value for the characteristic in the sample. In effect, what is measured is the dispersion around the mean. The population mean for the characteristic at the 95 per cent confidence level will lie in the range $\bar{x} \pm 1.96\,(\sigma/\sqrt{n})$. Again, where two means are compared and an overlap of ranges of error is found, it is sometimes possible to assert significance of difference by calculating the standard deviation of the difference between the two means, which would be given by

$$\sqrt{\left\{\frac{(\sigma_1)^2}{n_1}+\frac{(\sigma_2)^2}{n_2}\right\}}$$

If the actual difference between the two means is greater than 1.96 times the standard deviation of the difference, so calculated, assertion of a significant difference at the 95 per cent confidence level can still be made.

Such methods are applicable to 'large' sample sizes, where the cell values are thirty or over in size. These brief notes are intended to clarify the procedures used in this study, and readers may be safely referred for fuller details to Moroney (1951), Allen (1949), Spiegel (1961), Blalock (1960), or to two recent volumes written with the historian's problems in mind, Dollar and Jensen (1971), and Floud (1973).

II. FLOUR PRICES IN YORK, 1841–51

The source of the data given below is the Minute Books of the Board of Guardians for the period. Reference is usually made to prices in shillings 'per sack', but there are occasional fuller statements which show that the customary sack contained 36 stones. Occasionally the quarterly reference was given as so much 'per stone', and where this was so, the relevant price has been multiplied by 36.

These are wholesale contract prices, no doubt well below what the purchaser of small quantities would have to pay: on the other hand the trends facing the small consumer were probably much the same. On an annual average basis, they closely reflect the Gazette price of wheat (itself an average of various markets) set out in Mitchell and Deane (1962) 488. This close conformity is not unexpected. Granger and Elliott (1967) 262 have shown that the autonomy of local markets in wheat can be seriously overstated even for the pre-1750 period, and there is general agreement that as transport improvements proceeded, local divergencies were still less likely to obtain (see, *inter alia*, Ashton (1955) 86; Mantoux (1961) 129).

TABLE S.A. 2 *Contract prices paid for flour by York Poor Law Union, 1841–51 (in shillings and pence per 36-stone sack, 'seconds' quality)*

Year	March	June	September	December
1841	47/– (129)	43/4 (119)	44/– (121)	45/6 (125)
1842	41/– (113)	40/– (126)	38/– (104)	31/11 (88)
1843	31/6 (87)	33/9 (93)	34/10 (96)	36/8 (101)
1844	38/– (104)	37/– (102)	31/9 (87)	31/8 (87)
1845	32/6 (89)	32/3 (89)	38/– (104)	41/– (113)
1846	38/6 (106)	37/6 (103)	36/8 (101)	47/11 (132)
1847	53/– (146)	63/– (173)	41/8 (115)	37/6 (103)
1848	37/6 (103)	37/6 (103)	37/6 (103)	34/2 (94)
1849	29/2 (80)	31/– (85)	29/2 (80)	27/6 (76)
1850	26/– (71)	28/– (77)	30/– (82)	29/– (80)
1851	25/5 (70)	32/6 (89)	29/3 (80)	26/– (71)

N.B. The table is read as follows: the price paid in March 1841 was 47/- and the relevant index number 129, on the base 36/5, the average for the whole period = 100. Two values (for June 1848 and September 1851) were not given in the source and were interpolated on the averages of preceding and subsequent quarters.

III. MISCELLANEOUS DATA FOR INDIVIDUAL YORK PARISHES, 1841–51

Key and notes to Table S.A. 3

Columns (a) and (b) Population size in 1841 and 1851 respectively. *N.B.* the 1841 Enumeration Abstract does not state separate population totals for the Parliamentary Borough sections of the townships of Clifton, Heworth and Fulford.

Columns (c) and (d) Numbers of houses inhabited or uninhabited in 1841 and 1851 respectively, according to the census enumeration abstracts. Houses under construction are excluded.

Column (e) indicates the registration sub-district of each parish (Bootham, Micklegate or Walmgate), also, whether each parish was intra-mural (IM), an older suburb (OS; extra-mural but within the Municipal Borough boundaries), or newer suburb (NS; outside the Municipal Borough but within the parliamentary boundary). *N.B.*, these are simply convenient labels in connection with table 3.8; in fact the city wall is not and never has been complete, and the abbreviations OS and NS only denote (roughly) distance from the city centre. It is not intended to imply that the older suburbs were full and had stopped growing, nor that new suburbs had necessarily begun to take on a specifically dormitory character. Heworth for example, was still very much an agricultural village in this period.

Column (f) denotes ward attributions as follows: W (Walmgate), B (Bootham), G (Guildhall), C (Castlegate), MK (Monk), M (Micklegate).

Column (g) sets out drainage groupings according to Laycock (1844). See p. 133. W = worst-drained parishes, B = best drained and I = intermediately drained. *N.B.* Laycock gave separate drainage altitudes for Minster Yard and the Bedern, which are usually linked together in most other works, e.g. the censuses. He gave no data for St Nicholas parish, or for York Castle, New St and Davygate (extra-parochial areas).

Column (h) Annual value of houses assessed to property and income tax 1842–3, from *PP* 1845 xxxviii 239 (£). There is no separate data for St George, but this parish was often linked with St Dennis in civil matters.

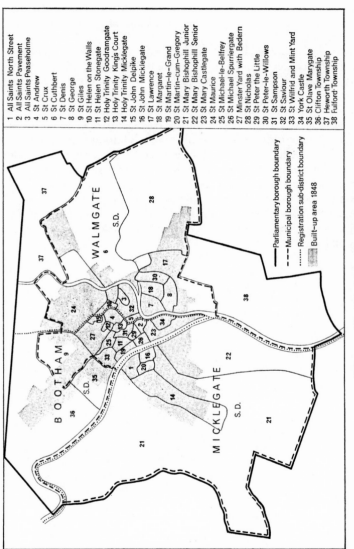

Map 2. Parish identification map

Columns (i) and (j) Details of the total number of rate assessments, and the number rated at £10 and upwards in 1850–1 from *PP* 1852 XLV 57. Once again there is no separate return for St George, and St Cuthbert also takes in St Helen-on-the-Walls and All Saints Peaseholme.

Column (k) Number of Irish-born inhabitants by parish, counted from the census enumerators' books of 1851, including those in institutions. *N.B.* this count came to 1,836 for the Municipal Borough, somewhat fewer than the 1,928 given in the census printed abstracts, which are presumably in error. Perhaps the census clerks erroneously included Irish soldiers in Fulford barracks (just outside the city boundary), who numbered about 100.

Column (l) Drink purveyors in each parish according to a count from the census enumerators' books. Only household heads were included and I counted those described as innkeeper, hotel keeper, beer seller, licensed victualler, publican, and wine and spirit merchant, whether or not this was in combination with some other trade. Brewers, or those described as retired, were excluded.

TABLE S.A. 3 *Miscellaneous data for individual parishes*

	(a)	(b)	(c)	(d)	(e)	(f)	(g)	(h)	(i)	(j)	(k)	(l)
	Parishes partly or wholly within the Municipal Borough											
All Saints, North St	1,199	1,308	294	268	M (IM)	C	W	2,690	296	51	2	5
All Saints, Pavement	417	423	67	72	B (IM)	C	B	3,874	81	66	3	9
All Saints, Peaseholme	373	426	85	96	W (IM)	MK	W	621	See notes		1	4
St Andrew	318	365	59	65	B (IM)	MK	W	1,002	82	24	5	1
St Crux	910	920	191	201	W (IM)	W	W	3,817	164	102	6	11
St Cuthbert (part of)	1,178	1,666	306	433	W (OS)	MK	W	2,410	711	78	11	5
St Dennis	1,314	1,479	281	318	W (IM)	W	W	4,059	373	75	223	11
St George	1,024	2,095	218	449	W (IM)	W	W		See notes		412	3
St Giles (part of)	1,258	2,059	238	394	B (OS)	B	B	4,609	427	120	13	1
St Helen-on-the-walls	444	398	121	89	W (OS)	MK	W	859	See notes		8	2
St Helen, Stonegate	607	551	109	110	B (IM)	G	B	3,359	118	92	4	3
Holy Trinity, Goodramgate	551	526	89	91	B (IM)	MK	B	1,188	115	40	19	4
Holy Trinity, King's Court	685	720	134	140	B (IM)	G	B	2,783	164	97	7	9
Holy Trinity, Micklegate	1,212	1,505	212	280	M (OS)	M	B	5,085	311	148	37	8
St John Delpike	351	386	66	78	B (IM)	MK	B	1,190	83	40	2	8
St John Micklegate	1,026	915	258	186	M (IM)	C	W	2,682	96	82	8	6
St Lawrence (part of)	981	1,380	209	361	W (OS)	W	W	3,376	375	44	28	11
St Margaret	1,207	1,595	297	369	W (IM)	G	W	2,075	468	20	159	5
St Martin-le-Grand	513	523	92	89	B (IM)	M	I	4,758	111	94	2	2
St Martin-cum-Gregory	554	619	130	122	M (IM)	M	B	2,596	141	67	9	7
St Mary, Bishophill, Jnr (part of)	1,757	3,526	381	759	M (OS)	M	B	6,016	786	248	121	7
St Mary, Bishophill, Snr	1,123	1,227	250	254	M (OS)	M	I	2,783	305	95	39	3
St Mary, Castlegate	952	1,043	162	150	B (IM)	C	W	2,722	197	64	108	5
St Maurice	1,477	2,928	327	664	W (OS)	MK	W	4,878	655	96	27	7

TABLE S.A. 3 *Miscellaneous data for individual parishes (cont.)*

	(a)	(b)	(c)	(d)	(e)	(f)	(g)	(h)	(i)	(j)	(k)	(l)
St Michael-le-Belfry	1,238	1,115	201	194	B (IM)	B	B	6,188	203	128	8	4
St Michael, Spurriergate	499	585	113	123	B (IM)	C	I	4,086	95	84	38	8
Minster Yard with Bedern	910	1,108	135	120	B (IM)	B	See notes	3,041	135	81	333	3
St Nicholas	182	217	36	41	W (OS)	W	,,	616	90	43		1
New St and Davygate (extra-parochial)	40	24	6	6	B (IM)	G	,,					
St Peter-the-Little	573	294	104	66	B (IM)	G	B	1,774	98	53	5	2
St Peter-le-Willows	497	588	109	126	W (IM)	W	W	812	137	13	144	
St Sampson	761	758	141	139	B (IM)	G	B	3,770	157	89	7	13
St Saviour (part of)	2,100	2,538	469	582	W (OS)	MK	W	4,602	634	109	31	10
St Wilfred (inc. Mint Yd)	356	319	67	56	B (IM)	B	B	2,388	73	65	13	3
York Castle (extra-parochial)	255	174	1	1	W (IM)	B					3	

Further areas within the Parliamentary Borough

	(a)	(b)	(c)	(d)	(e)	(f)	(g)	(h)	(i)	(j)	(k)	(l)
Township of St Olave, Marygate	661	677	112	125	B (NS)							2
Township of Clifton (part of)		2,009			B (NS)							4
Township of Heworth (part of)	649	295		633	W (NS)							1
Township of Fulford (part of)		1,075			W (NS)							3

Works cited in the text

(i) Dates of first editions or of writing in the case of originally unpublished works are given in second brackets following those of modern editions. In the notes on pp. 228–49, references are to the edition actually used.

(ii) In instances where no publisher is given, items may be assumed to have been privately printed, usually at the author's instruction.

(iii) Individual contributions to composite works (e.g. *Victoria County History*) are mentioned separately, with cross-reference.

(iv) Official reports, etc., are arranged in order of date of publication, with Parliamentary Paper references where appropriate.

(v) Items mentioned in sections IV and V are located in York Public Library, unless stated to be in the Public Record Office, Borthwick institute, or British Transport Commission Archives (these materials have recently been removed to the B.T.C.A.'s national archive in London).

I. *Books, Articles, Theses, etc.*

Alexander, D. (1970). *Retailing in England during the Industrial Revolution*. Athlone, London.

Allen, O. (1845). *History of the York Dispensary, containing an account of its origin and progress to the present time*. York.

Allen, R. G. D. (1960) (1949). *Statistics for Economists*. Hutchinson University Library, London.

Allison, K. J. and Tillott, P. M. 'York in the Eighteenth Century', in *Victoria County History* (1961), q.v.

Anderson, M. (1972a). *Family Structure in Nineteenth Century Lancashire*. Cambridge University Press.

(1972b). 'The study of family structure', in E. A. Wrigley (ed.) *Nineteenth Century Society* (1972), q.v.

(1972c). 'Standard tabulation procedures for the census enumerators' books, 1841–1891', in E. A. Wrigley (ed.) *Nineteenth Century Society* (1972), q.v.

(1972d). 'Household structure and the Industrial Revolution; mid-nineteenth century Preston in comparative perspective', in P. Laslett (ed.) *Household and Family in Past Time* (1972), q.v.

Armstrong, W. A. (1965). 'La population de l'Angleterre et du Pays de Galles, 1789–1815', *Annales de démographie historique*, **2,** 135–89.

(1966). 'Social structure from the early census returns', in E. A. Wrigley (ed.) *Introduction to English Historical Demography*. Weidenfeld and Nicolson, London.

(1967). 'The Social Structure of York, 1841–51'. Ph.D. thesis, University of Birmingham.

(1968a). 'The interpretation of the census enumerators' books for Victorian towns', in H. J. Dyos (ed.) *The Study of Urban History* (1968), q.v.

(1968b). 'Social structure from the early census returns – a rejoinder'. *Ec.H.R.*, 2nd series, **21,** 609–13.

(1972a). 'The use of information about occupation', in E. A. Wrigley (ed.) *Nineteenth century Society* (1972), q.v.

(1972b). 'A note on the household structure of mid-nineteenth century York in comparative perspective', in P. Laslett (ed.) *Household and Family in Past Time* (1972), q.v.

Ashley, P. (1906). *Local and Central Government*. John Murray, London.

Ashton, T. S. (1954). 'The treatment of capitalism by historians', in F. A. Hayek (ed.) *Capitalism and the Historians*. Routledge and Kegan Paul, London.

(1955). *An Economic History of England: the eighteenth century*. Methuen, London.

Bagwell, P. (1963). *The Railwaymen: a history of the National Union of Railwaymen*. Allen and Unwin, London.

Baines, E. (1969) (1822–3). *History, directory and gazetteer of the county of York*, 2 vols. David and Charles, Newton Abbot.

Baines, T. (c. 1875). *Yorkshire, Past and Present*. 4 vols. Mackenzie, London.

Baker, W. P. (1961). *Parish Registers and Illiteracy in East Yorkshire*. East Yorkshire Local History Society, York: series 13.

Banks, J. A. (1954). *Prosperity and Parenthood*. Routledge and Kegan Paul, London.

Barker, T. C. and Harris, J. R. (1959). *A Merseyside town in the Industrial Revolution: St. Helens, 1750–1900*. Cass, London.

Beckwith, F. (1948). 'The population of Leeds during the Industrial Revolution', *Thoresby Society*, **41,** 118–96 and 401.

Benson, G. (1932). 'History of Education in York, 1789–1902'. Ph.D. thesis, London University.

(1968) (1911–25). *An Account of the City and County of York, from the Reformation to the Year* 1925, 3 vols. S.R. publishers, Wakefield.

Blalock, H. M. (1960). *Social Statistics*. McGraw-Hill, New York.

Blaug, M. (1963). 'The myth of the Old Poor Law and the making of the New', *Journal of Economic History*, **23**, 151–84.

Booth, C. (1886). 'Occupations of the people of the United Kingdom, 1801–1881', *JSS*, **49**, 314–444.

Briggs, A. (1961). *Social Work and Social Action: a study of the work of Seebohm Rowntree, 1871–1954.* Longmans, London.

(1963). *Victorian Cities*. Odhams, London.

(1968). 'The Victorian City: quantity and quality', *Victorian Studies*, **11** (Supplement), 711–30.

(1973). 'Booming social History', *Guardian*, 31 May 1973.

Briggs, G. (1909). *York Equitable Industrial Society Limited: a jubilee history.* C.W.S., Manchester.

Brown, R. (1799). *General View of the Agriculture of the West Riding of Yorkshire.* Board of Agriculture, Edinburgh.

Brownlee, J. (1916). 'The history of the birth and death rates in England and Wales, taken as a whole from 1570 to the present time', *Public Health*, **29** (June, 211–22; July, 228–38).

Buer, M. C. (1968) (1926). *Health, Wealth and Population in the Early Days of the Industrial Revolution.* Routledge and Kegan Paul, London.

Caird, J. (1968) (1852). *English Agriculture in 1850–51.* Cass, London.

Chadwick, E. (1965) (1842). *Report on the Sanitary Condition of the Labouring Population of Great Britain*, edited with introduction by M. W. Flinn. Edinburgh University Press.

Chaloner, W. H. (1950). *Social and Economic Development of Crewe.* Manchester University Press.

(1959). 'Manchester in the latter half of the eighteenth century', *Bulletin of the John Rylands Library*, **42**, 40–60.

Chambers, J. D. (1957). *The Vale of Trent, 1670–1800: a regional study of economic change.* Supplement No. 3 to *Ec.H.R.*

(1960). 'Population change in a provincial town: Nottingham 1700–1800', in L. S. Pressnell (ed.) *Studies in the Industrial Revolution.* Athlone, London.

(1972). *Population, Economy and Society in Pre-Industrial England.* Oxford University Press.

Chambers, J. D. and Mingay, G. E. (1966). *The Agricultural Revolution, 1750–1880.* Batsford, London.

Chandrasekhar, S. (ed.) (1967). *Asia's population problems.* Allen and Unwin, London.

Works Cited in the Text

Chapman, S. J. (1904). *The Lancashire Cotton Industry*. Manchester University Press.

Checkland, S. G. (1964). *The Rise of Industrial Society in England, 1815–1885*. Longmans, London.

— (1968). 'Toward a definition of urban history', in H. J. Dyos (ed.) *The Study of Urban History* (1968), q.v.

Cherry, S. (1972). 'The role of a provincial hospital; the Norfolk and Norwich Hospital, 1771–1880', *Pop. Stud.*, **26**, 291–306.

Chevalier, L. (1966). 'A reactionary view of urban history'. *Times Literary Supplement*, 8 September 1966.

Church, R. A. (1966). *Economic and Social Change in a Midland Town: Victorian Nottingham, 1815–1900*. Cass, London.

Clapham, J. H. (1932). *An Economic History of Modern Britain*, II, *Free Trade and Steel, 1850–1886*. Cambridge University Press.

Collier, F. (1965) (1921). *The Family Economy of the Working Classes in the Cotton Industry, 1784–1833*. Chetham Society, Manchester.

Cowgill, U. (1967). 'Life and death in the sixteenth century in the City of York', *Pop. Stud.*, **21**, 53–62.

— (1970). 'The people of York, 1538–1812', *Scientific American*, January, 104–12.

Creighton, C. (1965) (1894). *A History of Epidemics in Britain*, 2 vols. Cass, London.

Crozier, D. (1965). 'Kinship and occupational succession', *Sociological Review*, new series, **13**, 15–43.

Deane, P. and Cole, W. A. (1962). *British Economic Growth, 1688–1959*. Cambridge University Press.

Dollar, C. and Jenson, R. (1971). *Historian's Guide to Statistics: quantitative analysis and historical research*. Holt, Rinehart and Winston, New York.

Drake, F. (1736). *Eboracum*. York and London.

Duckham, B. F. (1956). 'Economic Development of York, 1830–1914'. M.A. thesis, Manchester University.

Dyos, H. J. (1968). 'Agenda for urban historians', in idem, *The Study of Urban History* (1968), q.v.

Dyos, H. J. and Baker, A. B. M. (1968). 'The possibilities of computerizing census data', in idem, *The Study of Urban History* (1968), q.v.

Dyos, H. J. (ed.) (1968). *The Study of Urban History*. Arnold, London.

Engels, F. (1958) (1845). *The Condition of the Working Class in England*. Translated and edited by W. O. Henderson, and W. H. Chaloner. Blackwell, Oxford.

Eversley, D. E. C. (1958). 'Le Cholera en Angleterre', in L.

Chevalier (ed.) *Le Cholera: la première épidemie du XIXe siècle*. Imprimerie centrale de l'Ouest, La Roche sur Yon.

(1965). 'Population, economy and Society', in D. V. Glass and D. E. C. Eversley (eds.) *Population in History* (1965), q.v.

Fletcher, R. (1966). *The Family and Marriage in Britain*. Penguin, Harmondsworth.

Floud, R. (1973). *An introduction to quantitative methods for Historians*. Methuen, London.

Floud, R. C. and Schofield, R. S. (1968). 'Social structure from the early census returns', *Ec.H.R.* 2nd series, **21,** 607–9.

Foster, J. (1968). 'Nineteenth century towns – a class dimension', in H. J. Dyos (ed.) *The Study of Urban History* (1968), q.v.

Foster, L. (1902). *The Chicory Duty*. York.

Gale, A. H. (1959). *Epidemic Diseases*. Penguin, Harmondsworth.

Gaskell, P. (1968) (1836). *Artisans and Machinery*. Cass, London.

Gayer, A. D., Rostow, W. W. and Schwarz, A. J. (1953). *Growth and Fluctuation of the British Economy*, 1790–1850. 2 vols. Oxford University Press.

George, M. D. (1966) (1925). *London Life in the Eighteenth Century*. Penguin, Harmondsworth.

Gill, C. and Briggs, A. (1952). *History of Birmingham*. Oxford University Press.

Glaisby, J. (1838). *Guide to the City of York*. York.

Glass, D. V. (1938). 'Marriage frequency and economic fluctuations in England and Wales, 1851–1934', in L. Hogben (ed.) *Political Arithmetic*. Allen and Unwin, London.

(1951). 'A note on the under-registration of births, in the nineteenth century', *Pop. Stud.*, **5,** 70–88.

Glass, D. V. and Eversley, D. E. C. (1965). *Population in History*. Arnold, London.

Goheen, P. G. (1970). *Victorian Toronto*, 1850–1900. Chicago University Press.

Gosden, P. H. J. H. (1961). *The Friendly Societies in England*, 1815–75. Manchester University Press.

Gould, D. (1966). 'Cold the killer', *New Statesman*, 11 November 1966.

Granger, C. W. J. and Elliott, C. M. (1967). 'A fresh look at wheat prices and markets in the eighteenth century', *Ec.H.R.*, 2nd series, **20,** 257–65.

Greven, P. (1970). *Four Generations: population land and family in Colonial Andover, Massachusetts*. Cornell University Press.

Griffith, G. T. (1967) (1926). *Population Problems of the Age of Malthus*. Cass, London.

Guy, W. A. (1843). 'The influence of the seasons on sickness and mortality', *JSS*, **6**, 113–49.

Habakkuk, H. J. (1958). 'The economic history of modern Britain', *Journal of Economic History*, **18**, 486–501.

(1971). *Population Growth and Economic Development since 1750*. Leicester University Press.

Hardwick, C. (1857). *History of the Borough of Preston*. Simpkin, Marshall, London.

Hargrove, A. E. (1847). *The Baneful Custom of Interment in towns, and the York Graveyards*. Herald Office, York.

Hargrove, W. (1818). *History and Description of the Ancient City of York*, 3 vols. Alexander, York.

Harrison, B. (1968). 'City Lights', *New Society*, 12 September 1968.

Heaton, H. (1965) (1920). *The Yorkshire Woollen and Worsted Industries*. Oxford University Press.

Hewitt, M. (1958). *Wives and Mothers in Victorian Industry*. Rockliff, London.

Holderness, B. A. (1971). 'Personal mobility in some rural parishes of Yorkshire, 1777–1822', *Yorkshire Archaeological Journal*, **42**, 444–54.

Hollingsworth, T. H. (1968). 'The importance of the quality of the data in historical demography', *Daedalus*, **97**, 415–32.

(1969). *Historical Demography*. Sources of History Ltd, with Hodder and Stoughton, London.

Hopkin, N. D. (1968). 'The Old and New Poor Law in East Yorkshire'. M.Phil. thesis, Leeds University.

Hoskins, W. G. (1968) (1935). *Industry, Trade and People in Exeter, 1688–1800*. Exeter, The University.

Humphreys, W. G. (1903). *York Waterworks, 1677–1903: a short historical and Descriptive Account*. York.

Hutton, B. (1969). *Clifton and its People in the Nineteenth Century*. Yorkshire Philosophical Society, York.

Inglis, K. S. (1960). 'Patterns of religious worship in 1851', *Journal of Ecclesiastical History*, **11**, 74–86.

Innes, J. W. (1938). *Class Fertility Trends in England and Wales, 1876–1934*. Princeton University Press.

Jones, E. L. (1964a). 'The agricultural labour market in England, 1793–1872', *Ec.H.R.*, 2nd series, **17**, 322–38.

(1964b). *Seasons and Prices: the role of the weather in English agricultural history*. Allen and Unwin, London.

Katz, M. (1969). 'Social structure in Hamilton, Ontario', in S. Thernstrom and R. Sennett (eds.) *Nineteenth Century Cities: essays in the new urban history* (1969), q.v.

Kay, J. P. (1969) (1832). *Moral and Physical Condition of the Working Classes Employed in the Cotton Industry in Manchester*. E. J. Morten, Manchester.

Knight, C. B. (1944). *History of the City of York*. Yorkshire Herald, York.

Knights, P. R. (1971). *The Plain People of Boston, 1830–60*. Oxford University Press, New York.

Kohl, J. G. (1844). *England, Wales and Scotland*. Chapman and Hall, London.

Krause, J. T. (1958). 'Changes in English Fertility and Mortality, 1781–1850', *Ec.H.R.*, 2nd series, **11**, 52–70.

   (1965), 'The changing adequacy of English registration, 1690–1837', in D. V. Glass and D. E. C. Eversley (eds.) *Population in History* (1965), q.v.

Lambert, R. S. (1934). *The Railway King, 1800–1871*. Allen and Unwin, London.

Langford, J. A. (1871). *A Century of Birmingham Life*, 2 vols. Simpkin, Marshall, London.

   (1873). *Modern Birmingham and its Institutions*, 2 vols. Simpkin, Marshall, London.

Laslett, P. (1969). 'Size and structure of the household in England over three centuries', *Pop. Stud.*, **23**, 199–223.

   (ed.) (1972). *Household and Family in Past Time*. Cambridge University Press.

Lawton, R. A. (1955). 'The population of Liverpool in the mid-nineteenth century'. *Transactions of the Historic Society of Lancashire and Cheshire*, **107**, 89–120.

   (1972). 'An age of great cities', *Town Planning Review*, **43**, 199–224.

Laycock, T. (1844). Report on the state of the City of York. See Official Publications below.

   (1847). 'Lecture on epidemic catarrh, or influenza', *London Medical Gazette*, **5**, 1,050–5.

Lees, L. H. (1969). 'Patterns of lower-class life: Irish slum communities in nineteenth-century London', in S. Thernstrom and R. Sennett, *Nineteenth Century Cities: essays in the new urban history* (1969), q.v.

Lewis, S. (1842). *An Atlas comprising maps of the several counties . . . divided into unions*. London.

Lockridge, K. A. (1966). 'The Population of Dedham, Massachusetts, 1636–1736', *Ec.H.R.*, 2nd series, **19**, 318–44.

Malthus, T. (1958) (1803). *An Essay on Population.* Dent, London.

Manchester Statistical Society (1837). *Report of a Committee on the State of Education in York in 1836–7.* Ridgway, London.

Mantoux, P. (1961) (1928). *The Industrial Revolution in the Eighteenth Century.* Methuen, London.

Matras, J. (1965). 'Social strategies of family formation: data for British female cohorts born 1831–1906', *Pop. Stud.*, **19**, 167–82.

Matthews, R. C. O. (1954). *A Study in Trade-Cycle History; economic fluctuations in Great Britain, 1833–1842.* Cambridge University Press.

McCulloch, J. R. (1847). *Statistical Account of the British Empire.* 2 vols. Longman, Brown, Green, Longmans, London.

　(1852). *A Dictionary, Geographical, Statistical and Historical, of the Various Countries, Places . . . in the World.* Longman, Brown, Green, Longmans, London.

McKeown, T. and Brown, R. G. (1955). 'Medical Evidence Related to English Population Changes in the Eighteenth Century', *Pop. Stud.*, **9**, 119–41.

Melville and Co. (1855). *Directory and Gazetteer of the City of York, Kingston-upon-Hull, etc.* York.

Mitchell, B. R. and Deane, P. (1962). *Abstract of British Historical Statistics.* Cambridge University Press.

Moroney, M. J. (1951). *Facts from Figures.* Penguin, Harmondsworth.

Morrell, J. B. and Watson, A. G. (1928). *How York Governs Itself.* Allen and Unwin, London.

Needham, J. P. (1833). *Facts and Observations Relative to the Disease called Cholera, as it has recently prevailed in the City of York.* Longman, Rees, Orme, Brown, Green, London.

Parson, W. and White, W. (1830). *Directory of the Borough of Leeds, the City of York, and the Clothing Districts of Yorkshire.* Leeds.

Pelling, H. (1963). *A History of British Trade Unionism.* Penguin, Harmondsworth.

Perkin, H. (1962). 'Social History', in H. P. R. Finberg (ed.) *Approaches to History.* Routledge and Kegan Paul, London.

　(1969). *The Origins of Modern English Society, 1780–1880.* Routledge and Kegan Paul, London.

Pickard, R. (1947). *Population and Epidemics of Exeter in pre-census times.* Townsend, Exeter.

Pickering, W. S. F. (1967). 'The 1851 religious census – a useless experiment?', *British Journal of Sociology*, **18**, 382–407.

Pickwell, W. (1886). *The Temperance movement in the City of York: its origin, basis and progress*. York.

Picton, J. A. (1873). *Memorials of Liverpool*, 2 vols. Longmans, Green, London.

Pigot and Co. (1829). *Directory of Yorkshire*. Leeds.

Pinchbeck, I. (1969) (1930). *Women Workers and the Industrial Revolution*, 1750–1850. Cass, London.

Pollard, S. (1959). *A History of Labour in Sheffield*. Liverpool University Press.

Potter, B. (1895) (1891). *The Co-operative Movement in Great Britain*. Swan Sonnenschein, London.

Prest, J. (1960). *The Industrial Revolution in Coventry*. Oxford University Press.

Ravenstein, E. C. (1885). 'The laws of migration'. *JSS*, **48**, 162–235.

Razzell, P. (1965). 'Population change in eighteenth-century England: a reinterpretation'. *Ec.H.R.*, 2nd series, **18**, 312–32.

(1972). 'The evaluation of baptism as a form of birth registration through cross-matching census and parish register data: a study in methodology', *Pop. Stud.*, **26**, 121–46.

Redford, A. (1964) (1926). *Labour Migration in England*, 1800–1850. Manchester University Press.

Redford, A. and Russell, I. S. (1939–40). *The History of Local Government in Manchester*, 3 vols. Longmans, London.

Robson, B. T. (1969). *Urban analysis; a study of city structure with special reference to Sunderland*. Cambridge University Press.

Robson, R. (1957). *The Cotton Industry in Britain*. Macmillan, London.

Rosser, C. and Harris, C. (1965). *The Family and Social Change: a study of family and kinship in a South Wales town*. Routledge and Kegan Paul, London.

Rowntree, B. S. (1902) (1901). *Poverty: a study of town life*. Macmillan, London.

Rowntree, J. and Sherwell, A. (1900) (1899). *The Temperance Problem and Social Reform*. Hodder and Stoughton, London.

Schofield, R. S. (1971). 'Historical Demography: some possibilities and some limitations', *Transactions of the Royal Historical Society*, 5th series, **21**, 119–32.

Sennett, R. and Thernstrom, S. (1969). *Nineteenth Century Cities: essays on the new urban history*. Yale University Press.

Shannon, H. A. and Grebenik, E. (1943). *The Population of Bristol*. National Institute of Economic and Social Research: Occasional paper No. 2. Cambridge University Press.

Works Cited in the Text

Shapter, T. (1971) (1849). *The History of the Cholera in Exeter in 1832.* S.R. Publishers, Wakefield and London.

Sheahan, J. J. and Whellan, T. (1855). *History and Topography of the City of York, the Ainstry Wapentake, and the East Riding of Yorkshire,* 2 vols. Beverley.

Sheppard, J. A. (1961). 'East Yorkshire's agricultural labour force in the mid-nineteenth century', *Agricultural History Review,* **11,** 43–54.

Sigsworth, E. M. (1961). 'Modern York', in *V.C.H.* (1961), q.v.

(1966). 'A provincial hospital in the eighteenth and early nineteenth centuries', *The College of General Practitioners' Yorkshire Faculty Journal,* June, 1–8.

Sjoberg, G. (1965) (1960). *The pre-industrial city.* Free Press, New York.

Smelser, N. (1959). *Social Change in the Industrial Revolution: an application of theory to the Lancashire cotton industry,* 1770–1840. Routledge and Kegan Paul, London.

Smith, R. J. (1968). 'The Social Structure of Nottingham and Adjacent Districts in the mid-nineteenth century'. Ph.D. thesis, Nottingham University.

(1970). 'Early Victorian household structure', *International Review of Social History,* **15,** 69–84.

Spackman, W. F. (1847). *Analysis of the Occupations of the People . . . of the United Kingdom.* London.

Spiegel, M. R. (1961). *Theory and Problems of Statistics.* Schaum Publishing Co., New York.

Stevenson, T. H. C. (1920). 'The fertility of various social classes in England and Wales from the middle of the nineteenth century to 1911', *JRSS,* **83,** 401–44.

Storey, T. (1836). *Report on the Great North of England Railway connecting York and Leeds with Newcastle-Upon-Tyne.* Darlington.

Strickland, H. R. (1812). *General View of the Agriculture of the East Riding of Yorkshire.* Board of Agriculture, York.

Thernstrom, S. (1964). *Poverty and Progress.* Harvard University Press.

Thompson, D. M. (1967). 'The 1851 Religious census: problems and possibilities', *Victorian Studies,* **11,** 87–97.

Tillott, P. M. (1972). 'Sources of inaccuracy in the 1851 and 1861 censuses', in E. A. Wrigley (ed.) *Nineteenth Century Society* (1972), q.v.

Tomlinson, W. W. (1914). *History of the North-Eastern Railway.* Reid, Newcastle upon Tyne.

222

Tooke, T. and Newmarch, W. (1928) (1838–57). *History of Prices, 1793–1857*, 6 vols. King, London.

Tuke, J. (1800). *General View of the Agriculture of the North Riding of Yorkshire*. Board of Agriculture, London.

United Nations (1962). *Demographic Year Book*. U.N.O., New York.

Vernon, A. (1958). *A Quaker Business Man: the life of Joseph Rowntree, 1836–1925*. Allen and Unwin, London.

Victoria History of the Counties of England. A history of Yorkshire: City of York (1961). Ed. P. M. Tillott. Oxford University Press.

Viennot, J.-P. (1969). 'La population de Dijon d'après le recensement de 1851', *Annales de démographie historique*, **6**, 241–60.

Vincent, J. R. (1967). *Pollbooks: how Victorians voted*. Cambridge University Press.

Webb, S. and B. (1963a) (1908). *English Local Government*, II and III: *the manor and the borough*. Cass, London.

(1963b) (1929). *English Local Government*, VIII and IX: *English Poor Law History: the last hundred years*. Cass, London.

Whishaw, F. (1970) (1842). *The Railways of Great Britain and Ireland*. David and Charles, Newton Abbot.

White, F. & Co. (1851). *General Directory and Topography of Kingston-upon-Hull and the City of York*. Sheffield.

White, W. (1782). 'Observations on the Bills of Mortality at York', *Philosophical Transactions of the Royal Society of London*, **72**, 35–43.

White, W (1838). *History Gazetteer and Directory of the West Riding of Yorkshire, with the City of York and the Port of Hull*, 2 vols. Leeds.

(1840). *History, Gazetteer and Directory of the East and North Ridings of Yorkshire*. Leeds.

White, W. (1845). *The Economy of Health [and]* . . . *Sanitary condition of the City of York*. York.

Williams, W. M. (1963). *A West Country Village, Ashworthy: family, kinship and land*. Routledge and Kegan Paul, London.

Williams and Co. (1843). *City of York Directory*. Hull.

Wilson, C. (1959). 'The other face of mercantilism', *Transactions of the Royal Historical Society*, 5th series, **9**, 81–101.

Wiseman, L. H. (1872). *Memoir of Mrs. Benjamin Agar, of York*. Wesleyan Conference Office, London.

Wood, G. H. (1962) (1909). 'Real wages and the standard of comfort since 1850', in E. M. Carus-Wilson (ed.) *Essays in Economic History*, III. Arnold, London.

Wrigley, E. A. (1961). *Industrial Growth and Population Change*. Cambridge University Press.

(1968). 'Mortality in pre-industrial England: the example of Colyton, Devon, over three centuries', *Daedalus*, **97**, 546–80.

Wrigley, E. A. (ed.) (1972). *Nineteenth Century Society: essays in the use of quantitative methods for the study of social data.* Cambridge University Press.

York Health of Towns Association (1852). *Report of the Committee on the Smoke nuisance.* York.

Young, G. M. (1960) (1936). *Victorian England: portrait of an age.* Oxford University Press.

II. *Official Publications*

Abstract of answers and returns . . . for taking an account of the population of Great Britain in 1801.

Enumeration abstract (England) *PP* 1801 vi.

Parish Register abstract.

Abstract of answers and returns . . . for taking an account of the population of Great Britain in 1811.

Preliminary observations, Enumeration abstract, Parish Register abstract. *PP* 1812 xi.

Abstract of answers and returns . . . for taking an account of the population of Great Britain in 1821.

Preliminary observations, Enumeration abstract, Parish Register abstract. *PP* 1822 xv.

Comparative account of the population of Great Britain, 1801–31. *PP* 1831 xviii.

Abstract of the population returns of Great Britain.

Enumeration abstract. *PP* 1833 xxxvi–xxxviii.

Parish Register abstract.

Select Committee appointed to enquire into the state of agriculture, and into the causes and extent of the distress. *PP* 1836 viii.

Report of Commissioners appointed to report and advise on the boundaries and wards of certain boroughs and corporate towns, Pt. iii. *PP* 1837 xxviii.

Abstract of answers and returns (Enumeration abstract, 1841). *PP* 1843 XXII.

Abstract of answers and returns (Age abstract 1841). *PP* 1843 XXIII.

Report on the state of the City of York . . . by T. Laycock, Physician to York Dispensary. First Report of the Royal Commission for enquiring into the state of large towns and populous districts. *PP* 1844 XVII.

Abstract of answers and returns (Occupation abstract, 1841), pt. 1. *PP* 1844 XXVII.

Abstract of answers and returns (Parish Register abstract, 1841). *PP* 1845 XXV.

Total annual value of real property in each parish . . . assessed to the Property and Income Tax, in 1843. *PP* 1845 XXXVIII.

Return of total amount of assessed taxes for each of the years . . . (1845–7) . . . for places sending members to Parliament. *PP* 1847–8 XXXIX.

Tables of the rates of increase . . . and rates of mortality . . . (and) ages of the male and female population in 1841. Appendix to Registrar-General's Ninth Annual Report. *PP* 1849 XXI.

Report to the General Board of Health on a preliminary inquiry into . . . the sanitary condition . . . of York. By James Smith. H.M.S.O., 1850.

Minutes of Committee of Council on Education, Correspondence (etc.) . . . and Reports of H.M. Inspectors of Schools, 1848–50. *PP* 1850 XLIII.

Registrar-General. Report on the mortality of cholera in England, 1848–9. By W. Farr. H.M.S.O., 1852.

Returns from the several parishes and townships . . . of the number of separate assessments in the rate for the relief of the poor, etc. *PP* 1852 (2) XLV.

Works Cited in the Text

Census of Great Britain, 1851. Population tables, Pt. I. Numbers of inhabitants, etc. *PP* 1852–3 LXXXV–LXXXVI.

Census of Great Britain, 1851. Population tables, Pt. II. Ages, civil conditions, occupations, birthplaces. *PP* 1852–3 LXXXVIII, Pts. I and II.

Census of Great Britain, 1851. Religious worship (England and Wales). *PP* 1852–3 LXXXIX.

Census of Great Britain, 1851. Education report (England and Wales). *PP* 1852–3 XC.

Census of England and Wales, 1861. Population tables vol. II. Ages, civil condition, occupations and birthplaces. *PP* 1863 LIII Pts. I, II.

1891 Census, England and Wales. Ages, marital condition, occupations, birthplaces. *PP* 1893–4 Cd. 7058 CVI.

Board of Agriculture. Report on the cultivation and drying of chicory in Great Britain and Belgium. *PP* 1904 Cd. 2169 XVI.

Census 1951. Classification of occupations. H.M.S.O. 1951, reprinted 1956.

Census 1961, England and Wales. County Report, Yorkshire West Riding. H.M.S.O., 1963.

Registrar-General. Statistical Review of England and Wales for the year 1970. Pt. I. (Tables, Medical). H.M.S.O., 1972.

(*Series*) Registrar-General of Births, Deaths and Marriages in England: Annual Reports.
First (*PP* 1839 XVI), Second (1840 XVII), Third (1841 (2) VI), Fourth (1842 XIX), Fifth (1843 XXI), Sixth (1844 XIX), Seventh (1846 XIX), Eighth (1847–8 XXV), Ninth (1847–8 XXV), Tenth (1849 XXI), Eleventh (1850 XX), Twelfth (1851 XXII), Thirteenth (1852 XVIII).

III. *Newspapers and Periodicals*

Railway Times.

York Chronicle.
York Courant.
York Herald.
York Temperance Visitor.
Yorkshire Gazette.

IV. *Miscellaneous Local Printed Sources*

York Amicable Friendly Society: Rules, etc. (1851).
YNMR *Prospectus* (1836). BTCA YNM 1/13.
YNMR *Half-yearly annual reports of the directors.* BTCA YNM 1/13.

V. *Manuscript Sources*

Borthwick Institute of Historical Research; Marriage registers for Holy Trinity Micklegate, St John Ousebridge, Holy Trinity Goodramgate, St Maurice, St Helen Stonegate.

PRO H.O. 107/1353, 1354, 1355. Enumerators' Schedules for York Registration District (1841).

PRO H.O. 107/2353, 2354, 2355. Enumerators' Schedules for York Registration District (1851).

PRO H.O. 129/515. Original returns for the 1851 Religious Census (York Registration District).

PRO M.H. 32/41. Correspondence between the Poor Law Board and W. H. Hawley, Assistant Commissioner.

York Board of Guardians. Minute Books, 1840–52; General Lodgers 1840–52; Letter Books 1837–54.

York Corporation Records: House Books.

YNMR File of names, grades and wages of staff at York and Newcastle General Stations. BTCA YNM 15/5.

YNMR Minute Books. BTCA YNM 1/1–1/15.

Notes

For brevity, references to Parliamentary Papers are made by the usual notation (*PP* . . .). They are ordered according to date of publication in the list of works cited in the text. In the exceptional case of the Registrar-General's Annual Reports I have preferred to refer to the 8th, 10th, etc., to assist the reader, since these are listed in the bibliography as a separate consolidated series, on p. 226.

CHAPTER 1. INTRODUCTION

1. Professor H. J. Perkin and Dr W. H. Chaloner attribute this dictum to the late Professor Redford, although the latter suggests that it may have originated with C. R. Fay. It is quoted here as representative of a common point of view.

2. Perkin (1962) 51.

3. Eversley (1965) 24.

4. Perkin (1962) 59, 62–71.

5. Ashton (1955) 17.

6. Wilson (1959) 100–1.

7. Perkin (1962) 59–60.

8. Dyos (1968) 22.

9. Dyos (1968) 9.

10. Checkland (1968) 361.

11. Mr A. Peacock of York University promises a detailed study of the city's political history covering a comparable period.

12. Habakkuk (1958) 487–8.

13. Perkin (1962) 58; Checkland (1968) 366.

14. Briggs (1968) 713.

15. See, for example, pp. 70, 136.

16. *V.C.H.* (1961) 279–81.

17. *PP* 1852–3 LXXXVIII Pt. 1 (1) cxix.

18. *YG* 5 April 1851. The Irish at first refused to give information, and 'it was not until the influence of the Roman Catholic priest had been brought to bear on them that they would heed the applications of the enumerator'.

19. Glass (1951) 80.

20. I.e. 635 household heads and 484 wives. The technique is described in United Nations (1962) 16–17, and is designed to measure digital preference (concentration on round numbers).

21. Tillott (1972) 107. 88 per cent gave ages 9, 10 or 11 years older than in the previous census, and 12 per cent yielded a higher discrepancy.

22. Anderson (1972b) 75.

23. *PP* 1893–4. c 7058 cvi 36.

24. Dyos (1968) 92.

25. Lawton (1955) 89–120.

26. Ashton (1954) 35, notes that the frequently cited blue books naturally refer to the 'social grievances' of the time.

27. Clapham (1932) 24–5.

28. Armstrong (1966) 209–35. In passing it may be noted that sampling individuals rather than households would be preferable in some fields of enquiry, as in the work of Gutman and Glasco on social mobility in mid-nineteenth-century Buffalo (N.Y.).

29. Floud and Schofield (1968) 607–9.

30. Armstrong (1968b) 609–13.

31. *PP* 1852–3 LXXXV, cxlv.

32. Anderson (1972c).

33. Armstrong (1972a), using Booth (1886) as a basis.

34. Armstrong (1972a) 209–14.

35. Thernstrom (1964) 84.

36. Cf. Rosser and Harris (1965) 93.

CHAPTER 2. THE ECONOMIC CHARACTERISTICS OF YORK IN THE FIRST HALF OF THE NINETEENTH CENTURY

1. McCulloch (1852) 938.

2. *Railway Times* 15 June 1839.

3. Caird (1968). Letters XXXIV–XXVII, esp. 310, 315.

4. *YH* 26 May 1827.

5. Baines (1822–3) II, 61.

6. Hargrove (1818) II, 310–2, 530–1; White (1840) 86; White (1838) II, 553, 748; Pigot (1829) 1132.

7. Ashton (1955) 16, 94, appears to lend support to this view.

8. Drake (1736) 239–40.

9. *York Chronicle* 27 August 1790.

10. Benson (1925) III, 124.

11. Town Clerk's evidence before the Municipal Commissioners, *YH* 26 November 1833; Parson and White (1830) 410–26.

12. Sigsworth (*V.C.H.* 262) states that the Corporation's income from this source averaged £800 per annum, 1820–33; at £25 per head this yields the annual average mentioned.

13. *YCR*, House Book 21 January 1814; 15 November 1841; 9 November 1844 for example.

14. *YH* 26 November 1833.

15. Knight (1944) 436, 630, 636, 623.

16. *YC* 31 December 1833; 7 October 1835.

17. *V.C.H.* (1961) 262. In the course of his work he collected evidence to show that at Horsehay, Shropshire, coal made up 32–6 per cent of the cost of making pig-iron in 1810. On the other hand only 4.2 per cent of the cost of refining the pigs, 5.48 per cent of the cost of making up blooms and 2.26 per cent of the cost of making iron bars was made up of coal. Moreover, coal formed only 2.8 per cent of the cost of making tin-plate in South Wales in 1893 and 1.8 per cent of the cost of making rubber in 1853; and only 0.8 to 1.3 per cent of the cost of spinning linen yarn in Leeds (1808 and 1811) or 3.1 per cent of such spinning in Shrewsbury in 1819.

18. *V.C.H.* (1961) 262ff.

19. Hargrove (1818) 1, 308; Knight (1944) 617.

20. Duckham (1956) 66; Knight 536, 573.

21. *YC* 3 December 1833; *YG* 30 November 1833.

22. *V.C.H.* (1961) 263–4.

23. Glaisby (1838) 152–3; *V.C.H.* (1961) 208–9, 512, 517–18.

24. Quoted in Ashley (1906) 218.

25. Webb (1963a) 466, 470, 476–8, 565

26. Webb (1963a) 406ff, 721. On the other hand, of course there, were places where reasonably efficient municipal government and rapid growth did co-exist, e.g. Leeds, Liverpool.

27. The classic example is Manchester, which during the period of its most prodigious growth rates was 'governed' by a parish vestry and a body of Paving Commissioners with very limited powers.

28. Walker, producer of wrought-iron goods, built the railings of the British Museum, exported some of his wares (gates for the Governor's house at Mauritius), and was 'purveyor of iron and smithy work' to the Queen.

29. See Heaton (1965) 259.

30. Chapman (1904) 153, stresses the proximity of Liverpool, availability of cheap coal, and 'an atmosphere suited to the production of cotton goods' as key factors in the explanation of Lancashire's growth. Robson (1957) 33, notes that once inter-related specialisms developed, 'it became very difficult for a mill established outside this concentration to compete with the mills inside'.

31. Armstrong (1972a) 226–310. Using the abbreviations contained in that analysis, the composition of the eight groups distinguished here is:

(1) M1: MF 1–5, MF 18–22   (2) AG 1–4   (3) B 1–3
(4) T 1–5   (5) IS 2   (6) DS 1–3
(7) PP 1–14; IS 1   (8) M 2–3; MF 6–17, 23–31; D 1–13.

32. That is, MF 23 with D 5 and D 7.

33. Alexander (1970) 92–3, 95.

34. McCulloch (1852) 941.

35. Pigot (1829) 1, 132; Baines (1822–3) 1, 643–52; 11, 595–604.

36. This case is argued in *V.C.H.* (1961) 259, 266–8.

37. *YH* 21 September 1833.

38. Spackman (1847) Appendix, 42–3. See chapter 4, note 14 for the Ainsty.

39. The price trends quoted here and on the next few pages are based on national data in Mitchell and Deane (1962) 471–2, 488–9. Obviously local series would be preferable, but would require lengthy research. In any case, with the creation of a national market prices moved in close sympathy all over the country; note that the York flour prices of the 1840s mirrored national wheat price trends perfectly. See Statistical Appendix, 11.

40. These indicators are drawn from the relevant census volumes and parish register abstracts of the years 1801–41.

41. Rousseau index, in Mitchell and Deane (1962) 471–2.

42. *YH* 19 November 1825; 26 November 1825; 5 February 1825.

43. Based on Alexander (1970) 253–4.

44. List drawn from *V.C.H.* (1961) 260.

45. Matthews (1954) 29.

46. *PP* 1836 viii Pt. 1; see answers to questions 5318–5613.

47. The following account is based on Hutton (1969) 3, 9–10.

48. *Railway Times* 15 June 1839.

49. The following account is based on Tomlinson (1914); Lambert (1934); and material from local newspapers, especially *YC* 31 December 1833, and *YH* 10 October 1835, 17 October 1835.

50. YNMR Prospectus and YNMR Minute Book, 13 October 1835. How far the capital was local is not known precisely, although Hudson remarked in 1845 that York citizens held a quarter of a million in the York and North Midland alone. My demonstration of the large numbers of 'independents' and persons of 'independent means' suggests that the prospects of raising capital locally would have been good.

51. Lambert (1934) 45–9.

52. Benson (1925) III, 137; *V.C.H.* (1961) 270; Whishaw (1842) 442.
53. Williams (1843) 130–2; Melville (1855) 41–2.
54. Duckham (1956) 80.
55. *YH* 15 February 1851; and YCR House Book 10 February 1851.
56. *YH* 23 October 1841.
57. McCulloch (1852) 941.
58. Baines (*c.* 1875) III, 76–7.
59. Based on data in Alexander (1970) 253–4.
60. Importations of wheat meal and flour rose from 4,723 (000) cwt in 1845 to 9,398 (1846) and 17,840 (1847); Mitchell and Deane (1962) 98.
61. Laycock (1844) 10.
62. *V.C.H.* (1961) 275.
63. Ibid. 480–1.
64. Lambert (1934) 121; Hutton (1969) 26. The North Eastern Railway (1854) was the climax of a series of amalgamations of local lines.
65. YNMR 20th Half-yearly report of the Directors, 7 July 1846.
66. 73 per cent of all railway workers among household heads and lodgers in the 1851 sample were immigrants. This accords closely with the results of Sigsworth's complete count, 76 per cent, *V.C.H.* (1961) 269.
67. Again, according to the 1851 sample.
68. Based on data in Alexander (1970), 253–4.
69. White (1851) 375; Sheahan and Whellan (1855) 581.
70. *YG* 1 February 1851.

CHAPTER 3. SOME SOCIAL CHARACTERISTICS OF EARLY
VICTORIAN YORK

1. Kohl (1844) 91.
2. Cf. Briggs (1961) 26.
3. Rowntree (1902) chapter 4.
4. In general, good wage material tends to be available only for industries which excited the special attention and interest of parliamentary or other observers. Thus, there is comparatively full information on textile manufactures, which Anderson (1972a) 30, and Foster (1968) 284, are able to exploit for Preston and Oldham, for example.
5. See, for example, Chandrasekhar (1967) 25.
6. Mainly because great capitalists and men of wealth derived from manufacturing activity often tended to live outside the towns in

which their riches were made. See for example Engels (1958) 55 or McCulloch (1852) 678, contrasting the dingy appearance of Sheffield with the surrounding countryside, 'embellished as it is . . . by the numerous villas of the opulent bankers, merchants and manufacturers of Sheffield'.

7. Rowntree (1902) 120, 137.

8. Ibid. 110.

9. Wood (1962) 132–43.

10. Wholesale coal prices did not differ by more than about a shilling a ton in London when 1847–51 and 1896–1900 are compared. See Mitchell and Deane (1962) 483. In addition, the prices of boots (5–5s. 6d.), an adequate suit of clothes (15s.) or soap (3d. or 4d. per lb.) were much the same in 1899 as in 1850. (Compare Rowntree (1902) 393–4, with details in York Board of Guardians Minute Book, 21 March 1850.)

11. Anderson (1972a) 31 approaches the problem of setting an appropriate consumption standard for 1851 in broadly the same manner, comes to the same conclusion and accepts the 1899 costings without adjustment.

12. Railwaymen's wages from Bagwell (1963) 262; by this time there was little regional variation. Labourers' wages from Rowntree (1902) 132, while the wages for building workers (ibid. 162) are arrived at by multiplying up average rates by fifty-four (a 54-hour week being usual at this period).

13. See sources mentioned in chapter 4, note 39.

14. Bagwell (1963) 162 implies that railway employees were losing ground relatively in the later nineteenth century.

15. Rowntree (1902) 128.

16. These estimates exclude lodging families and their children.

17. Rowntree (1902) 205 and chapter VII generally.

18. Data on collective days of inmaintenance from York Poor Law Union, General Ledgers for appropriate dates.

19. See pp. 104–5.

20. *YG* 23 January 1847.

21. I am indebted to Professor Eversley for this suggestion. One of his students, Mr F. Mendels, encountered similar complex relationships between agrarian and industrial employment opportunities, wage levels, relief and migration, in the context of eighteenth-century Flanders, which could only be accounted for in these terms.

22. Webb (1929) 422–4. The second of these acts appeared to confer irremovability on all persons who had resided for five years in a parish, and to those who had become chargeable as a result of temporary sickness or accident. Lawyers of the period failed to agree on its exact meaning. Hopkin (1968) 390, notes that Pocklington and other East Riding Unions paid out a good deal less for 'non-resident' paupers after this legislation.

23. Rowntree (1902) 136–7.

24. Whether or not other things were equal would demand the scrutiny of relative wage and price levels, availability of women's and children's work, etc. The approach taken here is analogous to the 'life-cycle stage' analysis developed and refined by Anderson (1972a) 202, to which the reader is referred.

25. Rowntree (1902) 308.

26. Rowntree and Sherwell (1899) 3–4.

27. Pickwell (1886) 8.

28. Rowntree (1902) 308.

29. Ibid.

30. *York Temperance Visitor*, January 1857; Pickwell, 16, 25, 40.

31. *YH* 6 July 1839; 26 June 1841.

32. *YH* 30 October 1847; 6 November 1847; 27 May 1848.

33. O'Connor's election owed something to Tory support and a depression of trade afflicting the town more severely than York. Mass support for Chartism in Nottingham was also related to the plight of the framework knitters. See Church (1966) 144–5, 157.

34. Bagwell (1963) 52.

35. *YH* 3 April 1841; 7 February 1846; 21 February 1846; *YG* 31 January 1846; 4 July 1846.

36. YNMR Minute Book 5 March 1850, 15 March 1850. Maximum daily rates for long-service drivers now stood at seven shillings.

37. Potter (1895) 77.

38. Briggs (1909) 12, 28, 32.

39. E.g. Pelling (1963) Pt. I.

40. Laycock (1844) 236–7.

41. Armstrong (1967) 315–16, utilizing Gosden (1961).

42. York Amicable Society. Rules, etc. (1861).

43. Manchester Statistical Society (1837) 5, 6, 16.

44. Ibid. 16.

45. *PP* 1852–3 xc.

46. Baker (1961) 9.

47. Sanderson (1967) 266 and Stone (1969) 125–6, who cites evidence of a calamitous decline in literacy in Halifax, 104–5.

48. *PP* 1850 xliii cclxii.

49. Benson (1933) 191.

50. Manchester Statistical Society (1837) xv gives the details.

51. That is, the rate of increase for the comparable age-group in the Municipal Borough as a whole.

52. White (1851). I have excluded from his list of 'academies' all schools not obviously private, e.g. National, British, charity, etc., as well as institutions not strictly for young children, e.g. the teachers training colleges, Yorkshire School for the Blind, etc.

53. See, inter alia, Thompson (1967) and Pickering (1967).

54. Inglis (1960) 78.

55. *PP* 1852–3 LXXXIX clii; Inglis (1960) 79.

56. *PP* 1852–3 LXXXIX cxxix.

57. Inglis (1960) 79–82.

58. Ibid. 82–3.

59. PRO H.O. 129/515.

60. The details are discussed more fully in Armstrong (1967) 233–8.

61. *PP* 1852–3 LXXXIX clviii–clxi.

62. See pp. 29–30 and note 6 above.

63. Checkland (1964) 263.

64. Foster (1968) 284–90.

65. Chadwick (1965) 397.

66. Thernstrom (1964) 37. Note that the prospering grocer, Joseph Rowntree, remained at the original Pavement shop until 1845, despite being 'hemmed in by a mass of little houses and close courts', a 'horror' of a kitchen infested with rats and mice and other inconveniences. Only when he had acquired five children did he move, and then only to Blossom Street, within easy walking distance. See Vernon (1958) 18–25.

67. See p. 136.

68. Sjoberg (1960) 95–103.

69. Briggs (1963) 32.

CHAPTER 4. THE GROWTH OF POPULATION: MIGRATION AND NATURAL INCREASE

1. Krause (1958) 52–70; ibid. (1965) 379–93. But see p. 111 below and chapter 6, note 2.

2. Griffith (1967) 16. Note that, although the last published parish register abstract covered 1831–40, the published data was aggregated by the new registration district (as against the Municipal Borough to 1830), so that a continuation of the calculation beyond 1831 is impracticable.

3. *V.C.H.* (1961) 255; and Church (1966) 10.

4. See p. 110 and p. 154.

5. *V.C.H.* (1961) 255–6; and Shannon and Grebenik (1943) 9–10.

6. Glass (1951) 83, suggests that the deficiency for births in the 1840s was 6 to 8 per cent. Omissions of deaths are not generally believed to have been as great.

7. The difference between the urban and rural rates of natural increase is entirely attributable to the lower death rates prevailing outside the city. The rural death rate for the decade averaged 19.9 per 1,000, the urban 24.9 (see p. 130). If the rural death rate had actually applied in the urban area, the total number of deaths during the decade would have been 8,570 instead of the 10,945 which actually occurred. Relating this figure to that of births (13,273), yields growth by natural increase of 12.2 per cent for the urban area.

8. *V.C.H.* (1961) 256.

9. The *English Life Table No.* 3 was published in R.G. 28th Ann. Rept lxvii–xci. Comparative age-specific mortality rates for York and England and Wales are set out on p. 127 below; none of the age groups in the range 0–4 to 65–74 presents a difference of more than 5 points per 1,000 when the two series are compared. In so far as age-specific death rates for York Borough were higher than those of the Registration District as a whole, then naturally my calculation of the extent of immigration will tend to be somewhat conservative, and the gains indicated should be viewed as minimum estimates.

10. See p. 168.

11. In the event, this conclusion is strikingly similar to that arrived at using the Shannon–Grebenik method. See p. 80.

12. Ravenstein (1885) 196–9.

13. Redford (1964), 183ff.

14. The area and population of the City and Ainsty were 49,720 acres and 38,321 persons respectively. The Ainsty was a wapentake lying to the south and west of the city which had lain under the jurisdiction of the city from medieval times. The Municipal Corporations (Boundaries) Act of 1836 established the Ainsty as part of the West Riding for all purposes, and we may assume that it remained linked with York City in 1841 in order to preserve comparability with earlier censuses.

15. There was substantial redistribution of population within the York Union itself. The three sub-districts of Bootham, Micklegate and Walmgate rose by 9,242 between 1841 and 1851. The balance between births and deaths was 2,328, so that the migration increase was 6,914. The four wholly rural sub-districts of Skelton, Dunnington, Escrick and Flaxton had a balance of births over deaths of 943, but the population of this area only rose by ninety-six (from 9,372 to 9,468). Hence the rural fringe had lost 847 by migration – presumably to the urban core.

16. This was probably not the case with West Riding immigrants, some of whom would have come from towns. Anderson (1972a) 157 notes that only 11 per cent of town-born immigrants into Preston were in labouring or similar occupations, as against 38 per cent of those born in agricultural villages.

17. E.g. George Hudson and James Agar, born at Howsham and in the Hambleton Hills (both North Riding). See Lambert (1934) 30; Wiseman (1872) 42.

18. See p. 98.

19. The Bedern Irish are not represented in table 4.9, but were chosen for special intensive study. See p. 125.

20. See p. 76.

21. Laycock (1844) 224.

22. *YH* 17 September 1842.

23. Redford (1964) 156.

24. Rowntree (1902) 10; Benson (1925) III, 134–5.

25. Foster (1902).

26. *PP* 1904 Cd. 2169 XVI 377.

27. Ibid. 90–5.

28. Foster (1902) 4, 11.

29. E.g. *YH* 15 February 1851. 'John and James Kilmartin were charged with having assaulted Patrick Weir at Dunnington the 6th instant. The two defendants and other Irishmen on that day were in the act of selling some bags of chicory to a person named Creaser, when the complainant said they had stolen it . . .' For similar incidents see *YH* 22 April 1848; *YG* 11 January 1851, 25 January 1851.

30. In 1847 the Medical Officer noticed that some convalescent Irishmen in the typhus fever hospital had left to go to help with the harvest, 'perhaps sooner than prudence would indicate'. (York Board of Guardians, Minute Book, 26 August 1847).

31. See pp. 176–8.

32. See pp. 64–5.

33. Tuke (1800) 56.

34. Chambers (1972) 45.

35. Holderness (1971) 446–8, 453–4.

36. Ibid. 448–9; Sheppard (1961) 53–4.

37. Tuke (1800) 320.

38. Chambers and Mingay (1966) 102–3. Hopkin (1968) 31–3 discerns some signs of population pressure on jobs by the 1820s and 1830s in the East Riding.

39. PRO M.H. 32/41, correspondence of W. H. Hawley (Poor Law Assistant Commissioner), letter dated 24 January 1850; YNMR. File of names, grades and wages of staff at York and Newcastle Central; York Poor Law Union Letter Book no. 2, item dated 20 January 1843.

40. Jones (1964a) 326.

41. Brown (1799) 13–15; Tuke (1800) 41.

42. Strickland (1812) 41–2.

43. Shepherd (1961) 53–4.

44. Tooke and Newmarch (1928) IV, 9, 13, 16. The Gazette price of wheat fell from 64s. in 1841 to 57s. and 50s. in the two subsequent years, according to Mitchell and Deane (1962) 488; and local flour prices (see Statistical Appendix II) closely reflected these national trends.

45. York Board of Guardians, Letter book, item dated 20 January 1843.

46. *YH* 26 November 1843.

47. *YH* 30 September 1843.

48. *YH* 30 November 1844.

49. *YH* 27 April 1844.

50. Except that the York–Leeds line was never completed, leaving only a monumental bridge at Tadcaster, and the schemes for a direct connection with London perished temporarily.

51. See p. 64.

52. *YH* 28 November 1846.

53. *YH* 22 January 1848.

54. Tooke and Newmarch (1928) IV, 22, 27, 33, and V, 8; Mitchell and Deane (1962) gives details of corn imports on p. 291, and the Gazette price of wheat on pp. 488–9.

55. *YH* 29 November 1845; 28 November 1846: 25 November 1848.

56. Jones (1964a) 327.

57. For details of one of several protest meetings in the locality, this one at Thirsk, see *YG* 19 May 1849.

58. Tooke and Newmarch (1928) V, 12–21, characterize the harvest of 1849 as good, that of 1850 as somewhat deficient and 1851 as reasonably good. Mitchell and Deane (1962), gives the Gazette price of wheat as 44s. in 1849, 40s. in 1850, 39s. in 1851; and as before, local prices shared in this trend.

59. *YG* 19 January 1850.

60. *G.* 12 January 1850.

61. PRO M.H. 32/41: Letters dated 13 July 1849 and 24 January 1850.

62. In effect, an infinite variety of curves is possible where the initial number of immigrants (at the beginning of the first year), is 0, and the total at the end of the last year is 6,914. I am advised that four elements are involved in plotting even the simplest curve, which is the 'compound interest', or constant rate of growth model. One must know the rate of immigration in year 1, the same in year 10, the total volume of immigration, and the number of years involved (or given any three of these, it is possible to calculate the fourth). Here, we have only two ascertained facts, the total net immigration and the number of years.

CHAPTER 5. MORTALITY

1. Cowgill (1967) 56. Elsewhere (1970) 109, she has drawn an even more startling survivorship curve for the seventeenth century, implying that only 20 per cent survived to the age of 10, and not more than 5 per cent to 40.

2. Wrigley (1968) 578.

3. Ibid. 571. Note however that the Colyton rate has been criticized as a considerable under-estimate on the suspicion that under-registration of infant deaths occurred on a large scale. See Hollingsworth (1968) 424–5.

4. Brownlee (1916) 232; Registrar-General (1971) 5.

5. Deane and Cole (1962) 127; White (1782) 37–8, 40.

6. Drake (1736) 242–3; White (1782) 37–8.

7. *V.C.H.* (1961) 212.

8. Deane and Cole (1962) 118; Chambers (1960) 122; Chaloner (1959) 43; Pickard (1947) 46–52; Beckwith (1948) 145.

9. Griffith (1967) 16.

10. Krause (1965) 385–93.

11. *PP* 1833 xxxviii 388.

12. Deane and Cole (1962) 108. For further comment see chapter 6, note 2.

13. White (1782) 43.

14. *V.C.H.* (1961) 207–11, 464.

15. George (1966) 108.

16. White (1782) 43.

17. Ibid. 42.

18. McKeown and Brown (1955) 125.

19. Sigsworth (1966) 4–6. For a similar argument in relation to the major hospital at Norwich, see Cherry (1972).

20. Allen (1845) 2; Laycock (1844) 239.

21. *V.C.H.* (1961) 214; White (1782) 42.

22. Razzell (1965), 312–31.

23. Chambers (1958) 32–3.

24. Eversley (1965) 57.

25. Chambers (1972) 12, 90–6.

26. *V.C.H.* (1961) 212.

27. Griffith (1967) 36.

28. McCulloch (1847) I, 421.

29. Buer (1926) 224–33.

30. Armstrong (1965) 177–8.

31. E.g. Flinn, introduction to Chadwick (1965) 12.

32. Krause (1958) 67–70.

33. Hollingsworth (1969) 346–7.

34. Schofield (1971) 130–1, rightly observes that such approaches stand historical method on its head, 'for they first assume the existence of universal laws of human behaviour and then reject all historical evidence which might cast doubt on them'.

35. Smith (1850) 4.

36. Laycock (1844) 220–1; Smith (1850) 37.

37. Smith (1850) 45.

38. Laycock (1844) 223.

39. Ibid. 221.

40. Ibid. 222.

41. Ibid.

42. Humphreys (1903) 29.

43. See Smith (1850) 36.

44. Laycock (1844) 227–8.

45. White (1845) 18–19.

46. Humphreys (1903) 18, 29.

47. Smith (1850) 26–7.

48. Laycock (1844) 226.

49. Hargrove (1847) 11–22.

50. Smith (1850) 28–9; *V.C.H.* (1961) 466.

51. Laycock (1844) 225.

52. The Health of Towns Association was established in York in September 1846. At the initial meeting, while the room was 'not crowded', it is clear that those present included some of the most socially concerned citizens – Messrs Laycock, Wm Gray, Vernon Harcourt, Tuke, Rowntree and White among others. (*TG* 12 September 1846). The Association continued to meet regularly and act as a pressure group for public health reform.

53. White (1845) 10.

54. Smith (1850) 16.

55. Ibid. 9–11. Thomas was one of the surgeons of York Poor Law Union.

56. Overall city means are drawn from chapters 6 and 7. See pp. 173, 176, 188.

57. Smith (1850) 10.

58. Base populations for inter-censal years were arrived at by adding the natural increase in each year (given by subtracting deaths from births in the Registrar-General's annual reports), and adding in one-tenth of the inter-censal net immigration (as calculated by the Shannon–Grebenik method described in chapter 4), annually.

59. Estimates derived from Laycock (1844) 245; i.e. the 'Sanatory table' illustrated in figure 4.

60. Utilizing the Registrar-General's Annual Reports covering 1842 and 1845–51; the national infant death rate figures are from Mitchell and Deane (1962) 36.

61. Morrell and Watson (1928) 108–9; *V.C.H.* (1961) 282.

62. Base populations arrived at according to the procedure outlined in footnote 58.

63. See figure 4; this calculation involves manipulating the data in columns 1, 6, 7 and 8 of the 'Sanatory table.' All parishes are listed by sub-district and by ward in Statistical Appendix, III.

64. Laycock (1844) 224.

65. Particularly to the registration data. See p. 5.

66. Laycock (1844) 230.

67. Laycock did not actually list the parishes comprised in each of the drainage groupings in table 5.7. But when the parishes are arranged in rank order (working from his 'Sanatory Table') one can, by a process of trial and error, determine the combinations of parishes which will yield (approximately) the average drainage heights (50, 43, 33) mentioned in table 5.7. In Statistical Appendix III the parishes are labelled according to their presumed position in Laycock's three drainage categories.

68. Class composition is derived from the 1851 sample; the annual value of house property assessed to tax (by parish) is given in *PP* 1845 XXXVIII 239. For data on rate assessments by parish, see *PP* 1852 (2) XLV 57.

69. Minster-Yard with Bedern is omitted from table 5.10, since one part was well-drained and one part intermediately drained. See the 'Sanatory table', figure 4.

70. Note that we cannot positively assert on social class difference between Bootham and Micklegate in 1851, though this is demonstrable for 1841.

71. See p. 76; also compare Goheen (1970) 84, 126, who notes that Toronto was a 'jumble of confusion in 1860 . . . commerce, industry and high-class residential properties were tightly intermixed'. Indeed the business classes of Toronto occupied the centre of the city whilst the lowest economic strata were encountered on the outer periphery.

72. Measured here rather crudely by the contract prices paid by the York Guardians for flour, which however, closely reflect the national grain prices and cost of living indexes for the period. See Statistical Appendix, II.

73. Guy (1843) 148. Note that Greenwich weather statistics are available throughout the period from the Registrar-General's Reports, but the variability of English weather precludes their use. Weather records for York start in 1848, but it is found that there were marked differences between places as close as York and Durham, especially in the matter of rainfall.

74. White (1782) 39.

75. Guy (1843) 149–50.

76. Gould (1966). It is pointed out that the cold winter of 1962–3 brought about 30,000 deaths more than usual; and that although hypothermia is still only rarely recorded as a cause of death, the British Medical Association believes its incidence to be 'much higher than is commonly supposed'.

77. See pp. 115–7.

78. Creighton (1894) II, 388–9, quoting a contemporary report contributed by Dr Laycock to the *Dublin Medical Press*.

79. R.G. 9th Ann. Rept 26. Note that table 5.11 indicates an above-average infant death rate for 1846.

80. Ibid. 31.

81. See p. 57.

82. Gale (1959) 74–5.

83. Laycock (1847) 1,054.

84. See note 73 above.

85. Creighton (1894) II, 614; Gale (1959) 102.

86. R.G. 14th Ann. Rept 38, 70.

87. Chambers (1957) 28–9.

88. Eversley (1958) 158ff.

89. Needham (1833) 63–4.
90. Ibid. 64–6.
91. Laycock (1844) 261.
92. Needham (1833) 75. For a similar account respecting Exeter, see Shapter (1971).
93. Laycock (1844) 261.
94. Creighton (1894) II, 821–2.
95. Using the totals given in the 1831 census; since Creighton did not give precise indications of the areas from which his statistics of cholera deaths were drawn, we cannot assume that these results are exact. Note also that the list covers only the nineteen provincial towns with the highest absolute number of deaths. It is possible that smaller places where absolute losses were small in total, had higher cholera death *rates* than some of these towns.
96. Gale (1959) 72–5.
97. York Board of Guardians, Minute Book, 25 March 1847.
98. Ibid. dates as stated.
99. Leeds appears to be an exception, the highest above-average rate occurring during the first quarter of the year, although this was not necessarily caused by typhus.
100. Gale (1959) 68.
101. Registrar-General, *Report on the Mortality of Cholera in England 1848–9* (1852) 288–9. In addition to the cholera deaths mentioned above, three deaths were attributed to diarrhoea in Dunnington sub-district, one in Flaxton, twelve in Bootham, thirteen in Micklegate and thirty-one in Walmgate.
102. York Board of Guardians, Minute Book; dates as stated.
103. Registrar-General (1852) 288–9.
104. Ibid. cxxxvii ff.
105. Gale (1959) 66. Modern epidemiology accepts the then revolutionary view of John Snow (*On the Communication of Cholera,* 1849) that the disease was spread by water contaminated with the excrement of cholera sufferers.

CHAPTER 6. MARRIAGE AND FERTILITY

1. See pp. 109–10
2. The only evidence relates to a late period, the years when parish registration and the new civil registration overlapped. (*PP* 1845 xxv – the Parish Register Abstract of 1841). As we have already seen (p. 111) this comparison shows East and North Riding in rather a favourable light. However, Hollingsworth has questioned

the plausibility of the register abstracts with a different argument. In 1837 baptismal rates soared, caused by 'a certain alarm at the prospects of civil registration', and among the counties showing the highest baptism peaks, 'certainly not caused by fertility fluctuations', was the East Riding with York City, where the 1837 peak was 40 per cent above the level of the surrounding years. (Hollingsworth (1969) 155). This does affect confidence in the quality of registration within the county *as a whole*, but it may be noted that in York Registration District, the 1837 baptism return was by no means abnormal. (1,242, against an average of 1,237 for 1835–6 and 1838–9, according to *PP* 1845 xxv 118.)

3. Cowgill (1970) 112.

4. *PP* 1822 xv 390–1, compared with Krause (1958) 68. Such calculations are, of course, affected by differential child mortality.

5. At that date, persons aged 15–44 made up 47.5 per cent of the population, against 45.9 per cent nationally; and 20–9, 18.0 per cent, against 17.5 per cent nationally. If all York marriages of 1851 (575) are related to these age-groups, the resultant rates are 21.2 and 56.0 per 1,000, against 18.7 and 49.2 nationally.

6. In 1841 49.6 per cent of the population in the borough was aged 15–44; in 1851, 48.8 per cent.

7. Cowgill (1970) 107.

8. Jones (1964b) 66–7.

9. Eversley (1965) 39.

10. Armstrong (1965) 170.

11. See Statistical Appendix, II.

12. Gayer Rostow and Schwarz (1953) II, 969–70.

13. Glass (1938) 251–82.

14. R.G., 8th Ann. Rept 26–7. At a later date the importance of low wheat prices in these years was said to be a factor. R.G. 17th Ann. Rept iii.

15. See pp. 105–6.

16. The 1847–8 fall was attributed by the Registrar-General in his 17th Ann. Rept iii–iv, to high food prices, but it was also a period of cyclical contraction in the British economy.

17. See p. 105.

18. Hewitt (1958) chapter 4.

19. Ordinarily, incumbents were inclined to use the phrase 'of full age' to describe those aged 21 and over. The collection of marriage data used here is based on the years and parishes for which precise information at age of marriage is usually given, and it is not, there-fore, a sample. The registers used were St Helen Stonegate (1841–

51); Holy Trinity Goodramgate (1843–51); St Maurice (1843–51); St John Ousebridge (1852–65) and especially, Holy Trinity Micklegate (1837–65). All marriages were surveyed for analysis, although it will be seen that the numbers of cases upon which various means are founded, varies (owing, for example, to the fact that one partner was given a specific age, but the other described as 'of full age', etc.). The amount of useful information thus naturally frequently falls below 724 cases.

20. Based on 641 and 551 first marriages for males; 641 and 601 first marriages for females. The national means are stated in R.G. 4th Ann. Rept 9, on the basis of 20,437 marriages; and 34th Ann. Rept xii.

21. It might be argued that this would to some extent be offset by York men marrying girls in the country and taking up residence in York; but the sex-composition of the population (a female surplus in York, male in the surrounding countryside) makes it more likely that rural males would need to seek out brides in York, and on balance, a net loss of newly married seems the more likely.

22. Hewitt (1958) 42–3, 45, quoting the Registrar-General, and Southwood Smith's evidence to the *Health of Towns Commission*, 1842.

23. Malthus (1958) I, 236–7.

24. *PP* 1852–3 LXXXVII (I) xxvi–xxvii, clxiii.

25. Calculations based on *PP* 1852–3 LXXXVIII (I and II), and R.G. 11th–13th Ann. Repts.

26. Mitchell and Deane (1962) 29; Banks (1954) 5, 6; Innes (1938) 3, 10–11.

27. Matras (1965) 169–72.

28. Stevenson (1920) 1–44; Innes (1938) 42. These authors, along with Matras, necessarily rely on the 1911 Fertility census. Naturally, comparatively few wives married as early as 1851 or before survived to come under the purview of this enquiry into total fertility, so there are obvious limitations to what it is possible to learn from backward extrapolation.

29. Stevenson (1920) 417.

30. McKeown and Brown (1955) 131–2 suggest on the basis of Irish data collected in 1911, that 'an advance in the mean age of wives at marriage of about 5 years would be needed to reduce the mean number of live births by 1'. Habakkuk (1971) 38 has suggested, using comparable Scottish data, that 'if the age at marriage of women fell by a year, one might expect them to add one-third of a child to their family'. Even if the second, more generous estimate is correct, and also applicable to an English county town in the

1840s, the respective ages at marriage for different socio-economic categories given in table 6.11 do not suggest that much impact on fertility could be anticipated from this factor.

31. See p. 135. This assumes of course, that all other factors (e.g. drainage, see pp. 137–8) are equal.

32. This calculation comprises the wives of all surgeons, bankers, solicitors, barristers, fundholders, landed proprietors, clergymen, physicians, attorneys, accountants, architects, army officers, lawyers and stock-brokers – all with domestic servants as a further check. Dr Smith subsequently reworked the data to cover the 15–44 age-group only. See Smith (1968) 237–8.

33. Note that in the case of two pooled occupational sub-groups (agricultural labourers, 18 wives aged 15–49, and general labourers, 23) the census fertility ratio in 1851 works out to only 707. This may be compared with ratios of 900 for 30 railway workers' wives and 841 for 63 building workers' wives at the same date. Such differences presumably reflect differential rates of child mortality within the working class, rather than marital fertility.

CHAPTER 7.   HOUSEHOLD AND FAMILY STRUCTURE

1. Fletcher (1966) 19, 26–7.
2. E.g. Pinchbeck (1930), Collier (1965), Hewitt (1958) and Smelser (1959); the latter two authors are in any case primarily sociologists rather than historians.
3. E.g. Perkin (1969) 149–160.
4. Particularly Engels (1958) (1844) and Gaskell (1968) (1836).
5. These classic views, and modern interpretations based on them, are ably summarized in Fletcher (1966) chapter 2.
6. See pp. 11–12.
7. Cf. for Nottingham 3.54, Radford 4.08 and Bingham 3.72 (Smith (1970) 72); Preston 4.2 (Anderson (1972d) 235); 100 pre-industrial communities 3.8 (ibid. based on Laslett's work); and Ashford 3.6 (ex. inf. M. Drake and C. Pearce). These results, except those for the pre-industrial communities, all relate to 1851. For York in 1841, certain assumptions had to be made, since relationships were not stated. The first listed female within fifteen years of the head's age was assumed to be his wife; other females, and all males bearing the same surname were regarded as children, provided that (from a consideration of their ages) they were born when the head (and wife where applicable) were aged not below 15 and not over 50. Where persons did not qualify to be so treated, they were included with

relatives. See Armstrong (1966) 229. No comparative results are at present available.

8. A similar pattern, whereby class III families were largest and those of classes I–II and IV–V smaller, occurs in Smith's work on Nottingham and Radford. See Armstrong (1968a) 71. However, Smith (1970) 73, does not stress these differences, preferring to amalgamate classes I–II and III–V as 'upper' and 'working' classes. Further research should establish whether this pattern is a regular and meaningful characteristic of mid-nineteenth-century social structure.

9. The modification of the 1851 classification scheme for 1841 was to raise those listed under classes II and III where domestic servants were employed. This was necessary in the absence of statements of numbers employed. See Armstrong (1966) 272–3; ibid. (1972a) 224, and p. 14 above.

10. The mean number of children in all classes for York in 1851 was 1.76, which may be compared with 1.82, 2.30 and 2.01 for Nottingham, Radford and Bingham respectively (Smith (1970) 82); Ashford 1.9 (ex. inf. Drake and Pearce); 2.1 for sixty-six pre-industrial communities and 2.5 for Preston (Anderson (1972d) 235).

11. Except for characteristic (ii) in 1851; in this sample, 1.54 is not significantly different from 1.73 at the 95 per cent confidence level.

12. See p. 135.

13. For 1841, since maintenance of domestic servants was one of the criteria of class allocation, such a table would be useless.

14. Armstrong (1968a) 71; Smith (1968) 336.

15. For Nottingham and Radford, where the methodology is directly comparable, these proportions are 21.8 and 13.7 per cent respectively. For Ashford the proportion communicated by Drake and Pearce is 17.5, and for Preston, despite a more conservative interpretation of the word lodger, it is 23.0 (Anderson (1972a) 46). The latter value therefore suggests an unusually high incidence of lodging, but what is still more striking is the high level in *all* communities compared with the pre-industrial past. Laslett (1969) 207, has shown that in most communities outside London, there were virtually no lodgers in the seventeenth century. Ibid. (1972) 134, contains a modification of his original view, without affecting the point at issue here.

16. Anderson (1972a) 47–9.

17. Ibid. (1972a) 44, puts the proportion of households with co-residing kin at 23 per cent. For Nottingham, Radford and Bingham (rural), Smith (1970) 81, calculates 17.3, 15.1 and 23.1 per cent respectively; while for Ashford, Drake and Pearce have communicated a figure of 21.0 per cent. Again, all these contrast sharply with the situation described by Laslett (1969) 218, who puts the proportion of households with kin in his pre-industrial communities at only 10.1 per cent.

18. Anderson (1972a) 45 treats married sons and daughters as kin. However, where proportions of households with kin are concerned (as distinct from the overall numbers described as kin), the York and Preston results obviously remain comparable.

19. Anderson (1972a) 118–20.

20. Not a statistically significant difference at the 95 per cent confidence level; but the pattern appears also in York (1841), Bingham and Radford (Smith (1970) Appendix E. Sect. 13), and perhaps also in Preston (Anderson (1972a) 123).

21. Crozier (1965) 17, indicates a high level of kinship co-residence (some 30 per cent) for an upper middle-class sample in Highgate, London.

22. Anderson (1972a) 45, 148–9.

23. See p. 163.

24. Anderson (1972a) 118–20, 152–60.

25. Ibid. 55.

26. Anderson (1972d) 220.

27. 1851 Census sample; Anderson (1972d) 219.

CHAPTER 8. CONCLUSIONS

1. Foster (1968) 263.

2. Also to the fact that some persons married in York who were not ordinarily resident there. See p. 163.

3. I have attempted to do so in Armstrong (1972b).

4. Viennot (1969) 258.

5. Ibid. 244, 246.

6. Wrigley (1961) 170.

7. The principal points are dealt with on pp. 11–12.

8. Robson (1969) 33. Lawton (1972) 199, 219 also makes a strong case, and we may expect a good deal of social area analysis in the large-scale study of Merseyside which he set in train in 1972 with the support of the Social Science Research Council.

9. Anderson's tactic of supplementing a 10 per cent household analysis with an intensive study of one area (1972a 20) has much to commend it.

10. Robson (1969) makes use of rating valuations in relation to

Sunderland, while Mr R. S. Holmes, a post-graduate researcher at the University of Kent, has recently begun to analyse the rate-books of Ramsgate, Kent, in conjunction with the census books. More generally, Professor K. M. Drake and Mrs C. Pearce in their work on Ashford, Kent, intend to link and merge by computer nominatively ordered data from the census books with that from poll-books, poor law records, etc. This will undoubtedly mark a great step forward though it should be pointed out that such research is expensive, even for a small community.

11. Briggs (1973).

12. Greven (1970) vii.

13. For references see the list of published works in the bibliography, in addition to which I have seen a number of mimeographed papers on research in progress. Valuable inventories are to be found in Sennett and Thernstrom (1969) and Laslett (1972), whilst the *Historical Methods Newsletter*, published by Pittsburgh University, is a valuable forum for discussion.

14. Lawton (1972) 199, 220, citing Briggs (1963) 32, who also asserts that 'however much the historian talks of common urban problems, he will find that his most interesting task is to show in what respects cities differed from one another'.

15. Young (1953) vi, contends that 'the real central theme of History is not what happened, but what people felt about when it was happening': this viewpoint, though perhaps overstated, commands respect.

16. Harrison (1968) 379. This reviewer (of Dyos (1968)) believes that more space in that volume should have been reserved for such 'neglected aspects of urbanisation' as riots, police, electoral corruption and recreational change.

17. Chevalier (1966).

18. No better example could be found than Anderson (1972a).

19. The sentiments expressed in these closing paragraphs accord closely with those expressed with great elegance and perception in Briggs (1968), to which unconvinced readers may be referred.

Index

This index excludes local worthies (unless of national reputation), and references to particular streets and districts of York. It includes towns and villages referred to more than once, or frequently made the subject of comparison with York. Modern authors are included where their evidence or opinions are quoted as part of the argument in the text or footnotes.

agriculture
  West Riding, 17
  North Riding, 17
  East Riding, 17–18, 34
  Howdenshire, 18, 34
  Vale of York, 18
  as a source of demand, 31–2, 35, 36, 103–6, 158, 195
  relationship to growth of York, 32–4, 41
  condition of labourers, 100–3, 126
  labourers resident in York, 44, 96–7, 126
  see also chicory cultivation
Ainsty, 236n
Alexander, D., 29
Allison, K. J., 109, 111, 115
Anderson, M., 9, 12, 176, 182, 183, 186, 188, 192, 194, 200, 232n, 233n, 234n, 237n, 248n, 249n
Ashford (Kent), 197, 246n, 247n, 248n, 249n
Ashton, T. S., 1–2, 10, 229n
assessed taxes, 30, 136, 137, 138, 208

Barnsley, 162
Bath, 30, 31, 73, 169
Bingham (Notts.), 246n, 247n, 248n
Birmingham, 2, 30, 160, 169
Bolton, 29, 73
Booth, Charles, 13, 27
Bradford, 27, 30, 61, 68, 77, 162, 169
Briggs, A., 5, 200, 249n
Bristol, 25–6, 61, 79, 146
Brownlee, J., 108
Buer, M. C., 115
building industry
  size, 29, 43
  house building, 32, 33, 36, 41
  public building, 33–4, 36
  strikes in, 64, 105
  and railways, 42
Bury, 66, 68, 69

Caird, James, 17
census enumerators' books
  contents and quality, 6–9, 228n, 229n
  sampling method and tests, 11–12, 203–5, 229n
  classification of occupational data, 13–15, 231n, 247n
  estimating parameters from sample evidence, 205–6
Chadwick, Edwin, 75–6
Chaloner, W. H., 228n
Chambers, J. D., 99, 101, 114, 144
Chapman, S. J., 230n
Chartism, 64
Checkland, S. G., 3, 75
Cheltenham, 30, 31, 73, 169
Chester, 16, 77
Chevalier, L., 201
chicory cultivation, 97, 237n
children, distribution of, *see* family size
cholera, *see* disease
Church, R. A., 234n
Clapham, J. H., 10
class consciousness, 75–6, 195
Clifton, 35–6, 41, 77–8
coal
  charges on, 22–3
  cost of, 23, 41, 124, 230n, 233n
Colyton (Devon), 108, 239n
co-operative movement, 65
Cowgill, U., 108, 155, 157, 239n
Creighton, C., 115, 146, 243n

Deane, P., and Cole, W. A., 108
Derby, 37, 90
Dijon, 198–9
disease
  in eighteenth century, 114–15
  bubonic plague, 114
  measles, 128, 140, 141, 144
  typhus, 140, 143, 146–52, 243n
  cholera, 115, 140, 141, 142, 143, 145–7, 152–3, 243n

Index

Printed in the United Kingdom
by Lightning Source UK Ltd.
106029UKS00001B/19-24

9 780521 019873